Gerontology in the Era
of the Third Age
Implications and Next Steps

Dawn C. Carr, PhD, received a doctorate in Social Gerontology at Miami University in Oxford, Ohio, where she also worked at Scripps Gerontology Center as a doctoral associate and subsequently as a research associate. She is currently a postdoctoral fellow in the Carolina Program for Health and Aging Research (CPHAR) based at the Institute on Aging at The University of North Carolina at Chapel Hill. Her research focuses predominantly on issues related to healthy retirement and the Third Age such as social capital, volunteering, and productive aging. Other research and publication areas include emergence of gerontology as a discipline, gerontological theory, arts and aging, and policy implications of wandering among individuals with dementia.

Kathrin Komp, PhD, is a postdoctoral researcher at the Prentice Institute for Global Population and Economy, University of Lethbridge, Alberta, Canada. She holds a doctorate in sociology from VU University Amsterdam, The Netherlands, and Master's degrees in political science and in nutritional science from Justus-Liebig-University Giessen, Germany. During her studies, she was a visiting researcher at the European University Institute (Florence, Italy), GESIS-Leibniz Institute for the Social Sciences (Mannheim, Germany), and Scripps Gerontology Center, Miami University (Oxford, OH, USA).

Kathrin Komp's research interests are population aging, in particular with respect to the emergence of a young old population, welfare policies, international comparisons, and quantitative research methods. Currently, Kathrin Komp is a coordinator of the Research Network on Ageing in Europe (European Sociological Association) and an Officer at Large of the Research Committee on the Sociology of Aging (International Sociological Association).

Gerontology in the Era of the Third Age

Implications and Next Steps

Dawn C. Carr, PhD

Kathrin Komp, PhD

SPRINGER PUBLISHING COMPANY

NEW YORK

Springer Publishing Company, LLC
11 West 42nd Street
New York, NY 10036
www.springerpub.com

Acquisitions Editor: Sheri W. Sussman
Senior Editor: Rose Mary Piscitelli
Cover design: Steren Pisano
Composition: Nick Barber/Techset Composition Ltd.

ISBN: 978-0-8261-0596-7
E-book ISBN: 978-0-8261-0597-4

11 12 13/ 5 4 3 2 1

The author and the publisher of this Work have made every effort to use sources believed to be reliable to provide information that is accurate and compatible with the standards generally accepted at the time of publication. The author and publisher shall not be liable for any special, consequential, or exemplary damages resulting, in whole or in part, from the readers' use of, or reliance on, the information contained in this book. The publisher has no responsibility for the persistence or accuracy of URLs for external or third-party Internet Web sites referred to in this publication and does not guarantee that any content on such Web sites is, or will remain, accurate or appropriate.

CIP data is available from the Library of Congress

Special discounts on bulk quantities of our books are available to corporations, professional associations, pharmaceutical companies, health care organizations, and other qualifying groups.

If you are interested in a custom book, including chapters from more than one of our titles, we can provide that service as well.

For details, please contact:
Special Sales Department, Springer Publishing Company, LLC
11 West 42nd Street, 15th Floor, New York, NY 10036-8002
Phone: 877-687-7476 or 212-431-4370; Fax: 212-941-7842
Email: sales@springerpub.com

Printed in the United States of America by Bang Printing

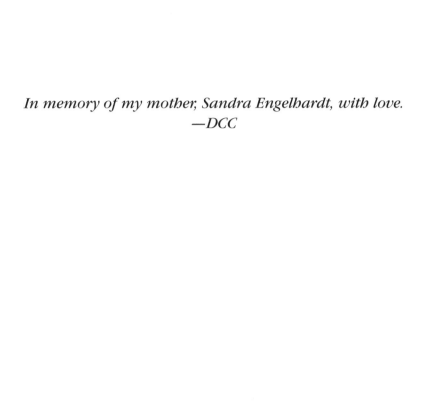

In memory of my mother, Sandra Engelhardt, with love.
—DCC

Contents

Contributors

Sara Arber, PhD, Professor, Centre for Research on Ageing and Gender, Department of Sociology, University of Surrey, Guildford, Surrey, UK

Scott Bass, PhD, Provost, American University, Washington, DC

Denise Brothers, MS, Doctoral Candidate, Department of Sociology and Gerontology, Miami University, Doctoral Associate, Scripps Gerontology Center, Oxford, OH

J. Scott Brown, PhD, Associate Professor, Department of Sociology and Gerontology, Research Fellow, Scripps Gerontology Center, Miami University, Oxford, OH

Toni Calasanti, PhD, Professor of Sociology; Affiliate Faculty, Women's and Gender Studies, and the Center for Gerontology, Virginia Tech, Blacksburg, VA

Stella Chatzitheochari, MPhil, PhD student/Marie Curie Research Fellow, University of Surrey, Guildford, UK, Researcher, National Centre for Social Research, London, UK

Linda K. George, PhD, Associate Director, Center for the Study of Aging and Human Development, Duke University, Durham, NC

Jenny de Jong Gierveld, PhD, Professor Emeritus, Social Sciences, VU University, Amsterdam, Honorary Fellow Netherlands Interdisciplinary Demographic Institute (Nidi), The Hague, The Netherlands

Chris Gilleard, PhD, Honorary Research Fellow, University College London, London, UK

Jon Hendricks, PhD, Dean and Professor Emeritus, Oregon State University, Corvallis, OR

Paul Higgs, PhD, Professor of the Sociology of Ageing, University College London, London, UK

Jürgen H. P. Hoffmeyer-Zlotnik, PhD, GESIS, Mannheim, Germany

Martha Holstein, PhD, Adjunct Instructor, Philosophy Department, Loyola University, Chicago, IL, Co-Director, Center for Long-Term Care Policy, Health and Medicine Policy Research Group, Chicago, IL

Neal King, PhD, Associate Professor, Department of Sociology, Women's & Gender Studies Program, Virginia Tech, Blacksburg, VA

Scott M. Lynch, PhD, Associate Professor, Department of Sociology and Office of Population Research, Princeton University, Princeton, NJ

Lydia K. Manning, MGS, Doctoral Candidate, Department of Sociology and Gerontology, Miami University, Doctoral Associate, Scripps Gerontology Center, Oxford, OH

Phyllis Moen, PhD, McKnight Presidential Endowed Chair, Department of Sociology, University of Minnesota, Minneapolis, MN

Graham D. Rowles, PhD, Professor, Graduate Center for Gerontology, University of Kentucky, Lexington, KY

Foreword

We come fresh to the different stages of life, and in each of them we are quite inexperienced, no matter how old we are.
Francois de la Rochefoucauld, 1613-1680

Focusing on the emergence of a new life stage (the Third Age), this book presents a compelling and novel approach to scholarship on aging and the life course—a new era for gerontology. The volume describes a major conceptual, methodological, and substantive expansion of the agendas for inquiry that define the field.

In the relatively few decades since it has emerged as a field of study, gerontology has been through other significant shifts in the view of our subject matter and appropriate methods, and in our guiding theoretical frameworks. From the time of Cowdry's 1939 book on the problems of aging, our substantive focus has shifted several times. We have sought to document physiological declines that were presumed inevitable; describe normal aging as a multidimensional process with social, psychological, physical, positive, and negative aspects; unlock the secrets to successful aging; and uncover patterns of diversity and heterogeneity with the aging population. This book offers further refinement, focusing on the causes and consequences of an evolving life-course structure. Whether or not these changes in fundamental subject matter qualify as paradigm shifts is open to debate. Either way, Thomas Kuhn's treatise on scientific revolutions is useful here. Kuhn (1962) eloquently describes the phases in development of a discipline, differentiating the phases according to the existence of a dominant paradigm which shapes theory and methods. In the stage of "normal science," shared assumptions about the appropriate questions to ask—a shared paradigm—constrain scholarly work, but also allow for the accumulation of knowledge about a particular set of questions. This stage is characterized by ever more sophisticated methods for solving a limited set of problems; for a time, novelties and anomalies are ignored because they are subversive to the fundamental paradigm. However, the accumulations of novelties, and the work of scholars seeking to make sense of those novelties, eventually move the field into a new phase, setting the stage for the possibility of a new view of the paradigm.

Carr, Komp, and the contributors to this book point us in the direction of a momentous novelty—the emergence of a new phase in the life course. They present the Third Age as a new life stage that was produced by a host of demographic, ideological, and social structural factors; as a stage with identifiable if controversial boundaries; as an opportunity that is not equally accessible to all, who, by virtue of chronological age, might enter it; and as a complex cultural construct. The authors accomplish several significant feats: they outline new research agendas related to the Third Age, articulate the unique theoretical constructs and methods that have been necessitated by questions about the Third Age, and describe novel applications of existing frameworks and research approaches to such questions. In addition, the book provides a critical perspective on the Third Age, and links Third Age scholarship to the life-course framework and to international comparative research; in doing so, these authors have placed Third Age scholarship squarely in the midst of three of the most important "paradigm-shifting" trends in the field.

As a whole, this volume directs our thinking back to the very biggest questions that have been shaping the field of gerontology since its beginnings: how and why does age matter, who says, and how can we know? Giving us an original perspective on these overarching questions, on the substantive questions that we ask in our scholarship, the frameworks that guide our research, and the methods that we employ, these authors are indeed signaling a new era for scholarship in gerontology.

Suzanne Kunkel, PhD
Director, Scripps Gerontology Center
Miami University, Oxford, Ohio

Preface

This book was born through the observation that, despite its visibility as a concept internationally, the meaning, purpose, and value of the Third Age had not been carefully examined. Furthermore, we noted that the extent to which the emergence of the Third Age is changing the field of gerontology as a whole had not been discussed, which is problematic given conversations, particularly at a policy level, about the costs and contributions of the growing healthy and retired population. These observations led us to invite leading scholars from across the globe who were exploring issues related to the Third Age to share their perspectives. They describe key issues related to this concept, explore ways that the Third Age is changing the conversations gerontologists are having about what it means to be an older adult in today's society, and describe ways to improve the lives of older adults.

The individuals invited to contribute to this edited volume consist of leading voices in the field of gerontology, and promising scholars who are, like us, committed to examining the ways in which the Third Age is defining a new set of questions, approaches, frameworks, and topics for gerontology. By bringing together the work of both junior and well-established gerontological scholars, we believe this book provides key scholarship that builds on existing ideas about aging as well as introduces new definitions for what it means to be an older adult in today's society.

This text highlights key research and discussions critical to advancing knowledge about the Third Age as a concept and explores how its emergence has brought greater attention to the potential of later life, rather than merely revisiting the detriments and/or losses associated with aging. The three major sections of the book provide powerful pedagogical tools for those learning about the construction of knowledge related to aging in the current era. Part I includes chapters that describe theoretical frameworks and concepts associated with the Third Age. Part II consists of chapters that describe current methodological tools and advances relevant to research on the Third Age, and Part III describes key emerging themes and controversies related to the Third Age.

With a burgeoning older population that is increasingly likely to have the capacity to engage actively in society, this book is timely. We believe that the discussions associated with the emergence of the Third Age are evidence that a paradigm shift is underway in gerontology. It is our hope that this book will provide a framework for emerging scholars to contextualize the changes associated with this new paradigm and inspire young and well-established scholars to consider how to better address the needs of older people in this new era.

Dawn C. Carr and Kathrin Komp

Acknowledgments

I would like to thank Drs. Jon Hendricks and Suzanne Kunkel for their stead-fast guidance, support, and feedback throughout the process of preparing this book.

—DCC

I would like to thank Alan Walker, Christof Wolf, Heike Schröder, Marije Boekkooi, Ralf Kaptijn, Susan McDaniel, and Theo van Tilburg for their useful comments on my chapters. Moreover, I would like to thank Sheri W. Sussman for her support and competent advice throughout the entire book project. Without her help, this book would not have been feasible.

—KK

Introduction

Dawn C. Carr and Kathrin Komp

*W*hen gerontology emerged as a field of study, older people were often depicted as needy and frail, scholars generally held an "age as decline" perspective, and the purpose for studying aging was to identify solutions to the many problems facing older adults (Binstock, 2005). Over the past several decades, however, public health improvements, increased standards of living, and the enactment of social policies targeting the needs of older adults have contributed to a change in the culture of aging, and gerontologists began advancing new agendas in which old age is also seen as a time of continued growth and development. With the vast majority of people in industrialized nations able to expect a substantial number of years during which they are retired but not yet facing serious health limitations, this new phenomenon, described as the "Third Age," has repositioned gerontology to pay greater attention to the many opportunities associated with later life.

In light of the emergence of the Third Age, gerontologists are taking a new approach to examining what it means to be an older adult in today's society and ways of improving the lives of older adults. Contributors to this volume contextualize implications of the emergence of the Third Age, and thus, propose new ways of thinking about how we: conceptualize the life course, think about the role of the welfare state in the lives of older people, negotiate social roles in later life, make meaning of our lives as we age, and cultivate relationships with others later in life. These discussions represent a global perspective, with chapters contributed by leading

1

researchers and educators from the following countries: United States of America, Netherlands, Germany, Canada, and the United Kingdom. This book brings together: (1) theoretical concepts and frameworks, (2) methodological advances, and (3) emerging themes and controversies that are redefining gerontology in the era of the Third Age. This book highlights important issues that warrant further exploration and discussion, advancing our understanding of the Third Age and focusing attention on critical issues that should be addressed in future Third Age research and scholarly development.

DEFINING THE THIRD AGE AND A NEW PARADIGM FOR GERONTOLOGY

Neugarten's path-breaking work provided an impetus for discussions about increasing complexity of later life and changes in transitions and roles associated with later life. In her classic 1974 article, "Age Groups in American Society and the Rise of the Young-Old," Neugarten described the extent to which gerontologists should be paying attention to an emerging group of older adults (she defined as being those approximately between ages 55 and 75), who were "relatively healthy, relatively affluent, relatively free from traditional responsibilities of work and family" and who were "increasingly well educated and politically active" (p. 187). She reflected on what the future might be like for that group of older adults and how they may impact society, encouraging scholars to consider the extent to which such a group was positioned to "become the social contributors, as well as the self-fulfilled." She also suggested that those older adults might "be the first to create on a large scale, new service roles and to offer their services to the community without regard to direct financial remuneration" (p. 198). In her thoughtful speculation about the potential for old age in light of the emergence of older adults she described as the "young-old," Neugarten sought to challenge ageist conceptions about what is possible in later life, and encourage gerontologists to work together to redefine what it means to be an older adult.

A little over a decade after Neugarten proposed new conceptual boundaries for examining the meaning and potential for old age, gerontologists were no longer imagining, but beginning to grapple with the reality that in many countries a growing proportion of the population could expect to spend a substantial number of years as healthy retirees. By the late 1980s and early 1990s, scholars and policy makers began exploring the individual and societal implications of a lengthy period of healthy retirement. Laslett's book, *A Fresh Map of Life: The Emergence of the Third Age*, popularized the concept of the "Third Age" as a way of describing this emerging group of older individuals who, because of their health and employment status, possessed the unique capacity for engaging in society in ways not accessible to previous generations of older adults (Laslett, 1989).

Subsequent to Laslett's writings about the Third Age, the concept has become a mass phenomenon. Not only in scholarly writings (e.g., Weiss & Bass, 2002), but also in popular literature, it has been depicted as a time for active engagement during later life. The popular media has marketed books describing ways third-agers can engage in more "purposeful" living (e.g., Sadler, 2000). A variety of websites, books, and companies have become dedicated to providing information (and marketing) to healthy individuals in the later stages of their careers and the early stage of retirement for whom the term "Third Age" resonates better than other language associated with later life such as "senior" or "older adult." Scholarly literature that describes issues related to the Third Age has highlighted the extent to which third-agers have opportunities for remaining productive in later life and engaging in valued social roles (e.g., Morrow-Howell, Hinterlong, & Sherraden, 2001; Weiss & Bass, 2002). With growing evidence that baby boomers especially are rejecting traditional images of old age that depict later life as a period of frailty, loneliness, and withdrawal, the language associated with the Third Age has come to represent a more positive, uplifting perception of later life, whereby aging is being reassigned qualities such as personal growth and meaningful engagement.

Growing relevance of aging issues associated with the Third Age (e.g., active aging, productive aging, healthy aging) suggest that a paradigm shift is underway with regard to the way old age is conceptualized and how older adults negotiate meaning, purpose, and value in their lives. It appears that the Third Age is defining, as Neugarten predicted, a new kind of old age. Although this new paradigm was initiated by the increasing amount of time between departure from the labor force and onset of major disabilities, the phenomenon of the Third Age is a complex concept that has been described in a variety of ways. For example, it has been depicted as a "social space delineated by opportunities for continuing participation in mass consumer society" (Gilleard, Higgs, Hyde, Wiggins, & Blane, 2005, p. S305), a social construct (Bass, 2006), an ideology (Leibing, 2005), a social category (Gilleard et al., 2005), a life phase (Weiss & Bass, 2002), an age period (James & Wink,

2007), and a "cultural sphere" (Katz & Marshall, 2003, p. 5). These characterizations demonstrate the multidimensionality of the Third Age, and the extent to which it cannot, and should not, be simplistically defined. In fact, a variety of working definitions are valuable to advancing our understanding of this phenomenon, all of which contextualize this new paradigm within the field of gerontology.

Rather than utilizing a particular definition, this book proposes the use of a broad distinction of the Third Age as the period of healthy retirement in later life. Contributors operationalize this definition in a variety of ways. For example, the Third Age concept is described by Moen in Chapter 1 as a "project" defined by individuals within the context of society, and in Chapter 2, by Gilleard and Higgs as the product of a variety of societal changes that have defined a new "cultural field." While in Chapter 6, Komp and Hoffmeyer-Zlotnik describe the Third Age as a concept that can be quantified based on life transitions and status positions, in Chapter 8, Rowles and Manning propose that we are still in the process of understanding the phenomenon of the Third Age and should be cautious about assumptions regarding what it means to be a third-ager. And in Chapter 5, Brown and Lynch propose that the Third Age may merely be an indicator of further demographic changes yet to come, and therefore, has not been fully delineated. While there is no clear consensus, contributors to this book move beyond definition of the Third Age, demonstrating its impact on the way we age and how we think about aging, and contextualizing the implications for individuals, society, and gerontology.

GERONTOLOGY IN THE ERA OF THE THIRD AGE

To advance our understanding of the phenomenon of the Third Age, this book highlights: the development of theoretical frameworks (Part I), research methods (Part II), and emerging themes and controversies associated with the Third Age (Part III). Together, these three sections describe perspectives, tools, and/or issues associated with aging that are uniquely relevant in the era of the Third Age. Component chapters in each section conclude with a description of how presented ideas set the stage for future research, including suggestions for other factors, questions, or issues that should be explored further. Below is a brief introduction to each of this book's three parts, including highlights of each chapter.

Part I: Theoretical Development and Frameworks in the Era of the Third Age

The four chapters within Part I describe frameworks useful for examining and understanding aging in the era of the Third Age. Among the four chapters within this section, three describe the existing gerontological frameworks that have application for examining and understanding the Third Age: the life-course perspective (Chapter 1), political economy theory (Chapter 3), and the feminist/critical perspective (Chapter 4). The fourth chapter (Chapter 2) proposes a new framework for thinking about the meaning and purpose of the Third Age as a generational field.

In Chapter 1, Moen introduces a life-course perspective on the Third Age, portraying it as a life phase. Owing to the de-institutionalization of the life course, she argues, persons have more and more leeway when shaping their lives. The Third Age, consequently, takes on the character of a project, instead of a predesigned and regulated part of life. When designing their Third Age project, however, persons are constricted by social structures.

In Chapter 2, Gilleard and Higgs describe the Third Age as a cultural field. Today's third-agers experienced the rise of a mass consumer society throughout their lives, which shaped their preferences, their way of thinking, and their lifestyle. A new subculture emerged around today's third-agers. When discussing the Third Age, they propose that we, therefore, need to keep the experiences and lifestyle of each generation of third-agers in mind.

In Chapter 3, Komp adopts a political economy-based perspective on the Third Age, explaining the role of third-agers in welfare states. She describes a third-ager as an ideal type of retiree, who can engage in productive activities and takes on the role of a resource to welfare states. Because of the role of third-agers, the effect of population aging on welfare states needs to be reevaluated. However, governments still seem hesitant to address third-agers in their role as a resource, due to, for example, stereotypes of old age.

In Chapter 4, Calasanti and King criticize the concept of the Third Age, using a feminist perspective as a starting point. They point out that the difference between second-, third-, and fourth-agers is not the only source of inequalities in later life, inequalities based on gender, race, and class, for example, are just as important. All those kinds of inequalities cannot be discussed independently from one another. Third Age research, therefore, needs to adopt a differentiated perspective and work against different kinds of stereotypes and forms of ageism.

Collectively, these chapters highlight ways gerontological theories are being redefined within a new context as well as the ways in which the Third Age mandates new frameworks for understanding and examining a new kind of later life.

Part II: Methodological Approaches for Third Age Research

Part II describes some of the methodological issues, tools, and approaches that are useful for examining the Third Age. Among the four chapters within this section, two describe methodological perspectives of important application for the era of the Third Age: demographic (Chapter 5) and qualitative (Chapter 8). The other two chapters describe methodological approaches to research seeking to measure the Third Age—one focusing on measurement issues at the societal level (Chapter 6) and the other on issues at the individual level (Chapter 7).

In Chapter 5, Brown and Lynch show how the Third Age can be approached from a demographic perspective. This perspective equates the Third Age to the time between the average retirement age in a population and the active life expectancy in the same population. In doing this, it links the Third Age to the development of morbidity and of retirement regulations. Moreover, it makes it possible to calculate the number of third-agers in a population from life tables.

In Chapter 6, Komp and Hoffmeyer-Zlotnik suggest treating the Third Age as a socio-demographic variable in quantitative country-comparative research. This kind of research helps us, among other things, to separate universal from country-specific characteristics of third-agers. This chapter demonstrates how third-agers can be identified with survey data and with data from national statistics. It provides examples for country-comparative Third Age research and discusses useful data sources.

In Chapter 7, Chatzitheochari and Arber explain how time-use studies can be utilized in order to gain an impression of third-agers' everyday activities. They demonstrate this kind of analysis with time-use data from the United Kingdom. In the analysis, third-agers are equated to persons aged 64 years and older who engage in active leisure activities, such as physical exercise and voluntary work. Their analysis indicates that every third British man and every fourth British woman aged 64 years and older can be considered a third-ager. Health status is a strong predictor for whether persons fall into this category or not.

In Chapter 8, Rowles and Manning describe how Third Age research can be approached with qualitative methods. These methods are useful for exploring new facets of the Third Age that have not been studied before. Phenomenological and ethnographic studies are only some of the qualitative methods that are of key importance to the development of Third Age research. They can help to reveal third-agers' individual experiences and the socially constructed phenomenon of the Third Age.

Taken as whole, these chapters provide evidence that the phenomenon of the Third Age is multifaceted and needs to be examined in a variety of different contexts from a variety of perspectives.

Part III: Emerging Themes and Controversies in the Era of the Third Age

The chapters that comprise Part III discuss one of the most salient areas of controversy among scholars of the Third Age: the tension between the rights and opportunities of individuals versus overall societal needs and expectations of remaining engaged during later life. Two chapters (Chapters 9 and 11) focus on the extent to which productive aging societies provide ample opportunities for some individuals to engage in both meaningful and productive ways, while needing yet to address barriers for certain other individuals and groups not afforded such opportunities. Similarly, another chapter (Chapter 10) explores how demographic factors associated with the emergence of the Third Age have changed the ways people cultivate relationships with others in later life and the extent to which these changes have positive and negative consequences. The final chapter (Chapter 12) raises concerns about societal expectations associated with the Third Age as ethically and morally problematic and suggests that individuals should be supported by policies that facilitate choices and opportunities about how to engage in later life.

In Chapter 9, Bass discusses recent changes in the meaning of productive aging, which refers to the engagement in activities such as paid work, volunteering, and informal caregiving. Third-agers are considered the ideal candidates for productive aging activities, thanks to their good health. However, an increasing number of older Americans are forced to work after retirement, due to insufficient pensions. Bass centers discussions about productive aging on the activity of paid work in later life.

In Chapter 10, Brothers and de Jong Gierveld explore personal relationships in the Third Age, rooting the topic's examination within the landscape of the demographic changes and accompanying socio-structural and cultural changes which have helped to not only bring about the opportunity for a Third Age, but have also altered the composition of family and households, including those in later life. In particular, changing gender relations, smaller family sizes, increasing levels of childlessness, living alone, remarriage, and cohabitation are all presenting opportunities and challenges to personal relationships. An examination of repartnering in general and living apart together specifically is provided as an example of a relationship opportunity for third-agers.

In Chapter 11, Carr and Hendricks discuss the relevance of social capital and life style for the Third Age. They call for a broader understanding of social capital. Instead of only stressing the benefits social capital brings to individuals, one also needs to underline the benefits social capital brings to society. Activities that generate social capital are, among other things, volunteering and civic engagement. They introduce a lifestyle framework for understanding the way third-agers' contributions vary.

In Chapter 12, Holstein adopts a critical perspective on the Third Age. She explains that the image and expectations toward third-agers are based on the kind of old age typical for a small privileged group. Discussions on productivity and consumerism in old age, consequently, tie in with the reality of only few third-agers, most of them affluent white males. She proposes that in order to gain a more accurate understanding of the Third Age, we need to challenge the prevalent norms concerning third-agers and embrace the diversity within the older population.

FINAL THOUGHTS AND A SHARED AGENDA

Predominantly in industrialized nations, welfare states in particular, what is expected and what is possible in later life have changed, largely due to the institutionalization of retirement and improved public health practices that not only increased the number of years people can expect to live, but also improved the quality of those years (Carr, 2009; Komp, van Tilburg, & Broese van Groenou, 2009). In this way, the Third Age not only suggests a new period in later life, but it also appears to have democratized a new social status. Although there have always been some privileged individuals who could afford to refrain from paid work and to enjoy a state similar to the Third Age for a considerable part of their lives (Applebaum, 1992), recent changes to the way people navigate later life are unique because today, most people within advanced societies can expect to depart from the labor force well before their health begins to decline (Carr, 2009). Thus, understanding the implications of the emergence of the Third Age is critical to society, individuals, and the field of gerontology.

The emergence of the Third Age as a new paradigm for gerontology requires scholars to consider the relevance of a substantial number of healthy years in which people have abundant discretionary time and resources in their later years. Following the footsteps of those who came before and seeking to build a foundation upon which to develop Third Age scholarship, contributors to this volume challenge readers to consider ways aging issues can and should be addressed and the roles older adults can fulfill in the era of the Third Age.

REFERENCES

Applebaum, H. (1992). *The concept of work: Ancient, medieval, and modern.* New York, NY: State University of New York Press.

Bass, S. A. (2006). Gerontological theory: In search for the holy grail. *The Gerontologist, 46*(1), 139-144.

Binstock, R. H. (2005). Old-age policies, politics, and ageism. *Generations, 26*(3), 73-78.

Carr, D. C. (2009). *Demography, ideology, and stratification: Exploring the emergence and consequences of the third age* [Doctoral Dissertation]. Networked Digital Library of Thesis and Dissertations.

Gilleard, C., Higgs, P., Hyde, M., Wiggins, R., & Blane, D. (2005). Class, cohort, and consumption: The British experience of the third age. *Journal of Gerontology: Social Sciences, 60B*(6), S305-S310.

James, J. B., & Wink, P. W. (Eds.). (2007). The crown of life: Dynamics of the early postretirement period. *Annual review of gerontology and geriatrics* (Vol. 26). New York, NY: Springer Publishing.

Katz, S., & Marshall, B. (2003). New sex for old: Lifestyle, consumerism and the ethics of aging well. *Journal of Aging Studies, 17*, 3-16.

Komp, K., van Tilburg, T., & Broese van Groenou, M. (2009). The influence of the welfare state on the number of young old persons. *Ageing and Society, 29*(4), 609-624.

Laslett, P. (1989). *A fresh map of life: The emergence of the third age.* London: Weidenfeld & Nicolson.

Leibing, A. (2005). The old lady from Ipanema: Changing notions of old age in Brazil. *Journal of Aging Studies, 19*, 15-31.

Morrow-Howell, N., Hinterlong, J., & Sherraden, M. (Eds.). (2001). *Productive ageing: Concepts and challenges.* Baltimore: The Johns Hopkins University Press.

Neugarten, B. (1974). Age groups in American society and the rise of the young-old. *The Annals of the American Academy of Political and Social Science, 415*(1), 187–198.

Sadler, A. W. (2000). *The third age: 6 principles of growth and renewal after forty.* Cambridge: Perseus Books.

Weiss, R. S., & Bass, S. A. (Eds.). (2002). *Challenges of the third age: Meaning and purpose in later life.* New York, NY: Oxford University Press.

Part I

Theoretical Development and Frameworks in the Era of the Third Age

Chapter 1

A Life-Course Approach to the Third Age

Phyllis Moen

THE LIFE COURSE IN THE ERA OF THE THIRD AGE

S ocieties, institutions, and groups develop expectations or cultural schema about behavior associated with particular positions and specific age groups. During the first decades of the 21st century we are seeing the development of a new phase of the life course—somewhere between the family- and career-building years and the frailer years of late adulthood (James & Wink, 2007; Moen & Peterson, 2009; Moen & Spencer, 2006). The Third Age life stage emerges from and is fostering macrolevel transformations in society, but also microlevel changes in the biographies of individuals and families, as well as shifts in how the two intersect. This is precisely the subject matter of life-course scholarship— the nature of large-scale social and historical forces; the biographies, life chances, and life quality of individuals, families, and households; and the dynamic interplay between them over time. Even the notion of a Third Age is enhanced by life-course scholars' investigations of prior standardization and institutionalization of (mostly men's) life course and its possible destandardization and deinstitutionalization (Brückner & Mayer, 2005; Kohli, 2007; Moen & Spencer, 2006). As existing age-graded policies, practices, and cultural beliefs unravel, there is the possibility of the institutionalization of this newly emerging life stage.

This chapter describes a gendered life-course approach (Moen, 2001; Moen & Spencer, 2006) to the Third Age. It offers an overview of key life-course concepts—including linked lives, transitions and trajectories, cohort and timing effects, turning points, cumulation of advantage and disadvantage, strategic selection, and biographical pacing. The gendered life course provides useful scaffolding for understanding this emerging life stage, recognizing that roles, resources, and relations are experienced differently by women and men at different life-course stages. The life-course approach (1) frames theoretical, empirical, and policy issues to focus on *time, context, process*, and *strategic selection* as key shapers of the Third Age, (2) provides *interdisciplinary* and *multilevel* lenses with which to view the Third Age, and (3) offers a *range of methodological approaches* to research addressing the dynamic links between society, organizations, and lives at this stage of the life course (Elder & Giele, 2009). A life-course framing can inform the gerontology of the Third Age across disciplinary boundaries, including anthropology, biology, demography, economics, epidemiology, history, law, medicine, political science, policy analysis, social psychology, and sociology.

The goal of this chapter is to provide a broad overview of the life-course paradigm (including orienting concepts and propositions) as well as challenges introduced by incorporating time, context, process, and strategic action—as well as gender—into analysis of the Third Age. The central thesis is that the Third Age is a *project*. Without taken-for-granted blueprints, people must strategically select their own pathways through this emerging life stage. The Third Age project involves strategic choices by individuals and couples to regain/retain a sense of control over their lives and life-course "fit" (Moen & Chesley, 2008; Moen & Huang, 2010; Moen, Kelly, & Magennis, 2009). The adaptive strategies they choose (or find themselves in) remain gendered, however. Women continue to be allocated (and often feel) responsibility for domestic chores, child and adult care, and family timetables, even in the Third Age years. Men are seen as—and continue to feel—responsible for the family economy, and are more apt than women in the Third Age to work for pay (see also Chapter 4, this book).

Women have had a history of making strategic selections around jobs, work hours, civic engagement, parenting, and adult-care provision. Accordingly, coming to a not-yet-institutionalized life stage such as the Third Age may be less problematic for them than for middle-class men who have traditionally followed full-time, full-year, continuous employment throughout adulthood (Moen & Roehling, 2005). On the other hand, men are at an advantage in terms of pensions and other economic resources. Clearly, women and men come to the Third Age with different experiences and expectations. What is not yet known is how women and men of different social classes, race/ethnicities, and biographies navigate this emerging stage.

THE THIRD AGE AS AGE IN TIME

Time and *age* are fundamental to a life-course approach to the gerontology of the Third Age. The literature on age and the life course (e.g., Elder, Johnson, & Crosnoe, 2003; Moen & Spencer, 2006; Settersten, 2003) has sensitized researchers to the multiple meanings and intersections of age and time. First, age is an indicator of *biological time*, meaning typical changes in physiological and cognitive functioning over the life course that limit social behavior. Advances in medicine, along with greater education and lifestyle changes, have produced unprecedented increases in longevity and unprecedented health and vitality among those in the Third Age years. In fact, it is precisely these shifts in longevity and the postponement of debilitating illnesses and the frailties associated with old age—the increases in *health* expectancy—that make the Third Age possible. However, healthy life expectancy differs by gender, race, and education (Crimmins & Saito, 2001). And health difficulties often do begin to surface in the Third Age and may reshape it markedly. The onset of disability or poor health can affect workers' decision-making regarding—and the timing of—retirement from their career jobs (Chirikos, 1993; Quinn & Burkhauser, 1990), a key Third Age transition. Women are more apt than men in this life phase to have chronic health difficulties or to be caring for someone (a parent, aunt, or spouse) who does. Much of people's apprehension about the later years of adulthood is related to concerns about health. The best-laid plans as to long-term employment, encore careers, civic engagement, or retirement timing can be destroyed by the onset of acute or chronic illness—of oneself, or relatives requiring care.

Second, age is a reflection of *biographical time*, as people move through various life stages. One's biography unfolds in tandem with the lives of significant others (what life-course scholars call *linked lives*; Moen & Hernandez, 2009). These connections, or "social convoys" (Kahn & Antonucci, 1980), affect both life quality and life chances in the Third Age. For example, the care-provider role in the Third Age falls disproportionately to women (Chesley & Moen, 2006), sometimes pushing them into retirement (Dentinger & Clarkberg, 2002) and limiting their possibilities in the Third Age years. The key is that the timing, duration, and sequencing of roles and relationships (Han & Moen, 1999) cannot be understood without integrating *all* the dimensions of age and time, along with the ages and circumstances of the people in one's life.

Third, age is a reflection of *social and institutional time*, the age-graded organization of roles, entrances, exits, and durations, independent of individuals' capacities and preferences, what Riley (1987) refers to as the *age stratification system*. Established governmental and organizational policies and practices shape the life course (Leisering, 2003; Mayer, 2004), including the Third Age, thereby constraining options around, for example, the timing of exiting from a career job as well as the opportunities for encore experiences following retirement (Moen, 2007). Also, culturally grounded norms and frames (or schema—see Sewell, 1992) shape both individual and societal expectations and beliefs about the "right" time to retire (Rook, Charles, & Heckhausen, 2006) even as the Great Recession that began in 2008 has placed new restraints on traditional retirement. The inertia built into existing rules, regulations, and practices limit the range of strategic selections of alternative pathways in the Third Age of life. This includes outdated age-graded policies and practices as to the timing, sequencing, and duration of schooling, paid work, and the leisure of traditional retirement. While mandatory retirement at a fixed age has disappeared, the myriad conventional time clocks and calendars organizing days, weeks, years, careers, and lives do *not* yet include the Third Age as an institutionalized life stage. Even though there is a trend in continued employment (but not necessarily career employment) and in expectations about delaying completed retirement (PEW Research Center, 2009), life in the Third Age remains constrained by outdated social and institutional clocks that promote retirement as a one-way, one-time, irreversible shift from full-time employment to the full-time leisure occurring around age 62 or 65. This is especially problematic for women; since their employment trajectories seldom follow career mystique expectations, women typically come to the Third Age years with small or no pensions and with little preparation (Moen & Altobelli, 2007; Munnell & Sass, 2008).

Fourth, life-course scholarship focuses on the unique experiences of each *cohort*, as individuals born around the same period move through history, institutions, and their own biographies. Age at any given point in time is an indicator of birth-cohort membership and life experiences shared with other members of that cohort (Ryder, 1965). The boomer cohort born in the post-World War II period between 1946 and 1964 is increasingly being called the "threshold generation" (PEW Research Center, 2009) as its members approach, think about, and move into retirement, perhaps *the* key transition occurring in the Third Age. They are also thresholders shaping the Third Age more broadly, redefining life before, during, and after the transition from full-time career jobs into encore careers, encore schooling, encore public and community service, and encore relationships and lifestyles (Freedman, 2007). *Historical time period* and the *timing* (age) when major social dislocations and turbulences occur in people's lives also shape how the Third Age is conceptualized within the life course. Thresholder boomers are experiencing the Third Age in the context of the Great Recession and the corresponding downward mobility of the traditional middle class, with rising debt, falling (or stagnant) income, and job insecurity frequently the backdrop upon which Third Age lives play out.

In sum, attention to the multiple dimensions of age and time is key for gerontologists to understand and investigate the *social forces* that shape the Third Age. This emphasis on social and temporal embeddedness locates the Third Age within the framework of an individual's prior biography, ongoing (and gendered) institutional constraints and opportunities, historical conditions and changes, and situational exigencies.

PROCESS: THIRD AGE DYNAMICS

The life course and ecology of human development perspectives (e.g., Bronfenbrenner, 2005; Elder & Giele, 2009; Elder et al., 2003; George, 1993; Moen, Elder, & Lüscher, 1995; Mortimer & Shanahan, 2003; Shanahan & Macmillan, 2007) point not only to the importance of *context* (such as the institutionalized time/age clocks and calendars described above), but also to the potential for shifts in perceptions and behavior accompanying major life *transitions*, both expected and unexpected, including those precipitated by political, economic, and labor market forces. Gerontologists of the Third Age can use a life-course lens to capture the *dynamic* nature of roles and relationships *(trajectories* and *transitions)* in conjunction with shifting opportunities, inclinations, and experiences *(timing* and *turning points)*. Two other life-course processes unfolding over time are *linked lives* (e.g., Moen & Hernandez, 2009) and the *cumulation of advantage or disadvantage* (e.g., Dannefer, 2003; O'Rand, 1996).

Transitions and Trajectories

A life-course perspective on the Third Age stresses the *social patterning* of events and roles over the lifespan of individuals, encouraging gerontologists to take a dynamic and long-range view of adult development, including the aging process. It calls attention to the manner in which decisions and behaviors earlier in life have long-term implications for health and well-being in the Third Age years. Certain patterns of health-related behaviors or service utilization over the life course may be particularly beneficial or detrimental to health in later life. Gerontologists interested in health changes in the Third Age need to consider the incidence, duration, and sequence of roles throughout the life course. For example, employment has been positively related to women's health, but knowing whether or not a woman is employed at any one point in time may be less useful than knowing the duration and patterning of her labor force participation throughout adulthood. The patterning of lives—employment trajectories, marriage trajectories, health trajectories—shape the *resources and options* available to subgroups of society in the Third Age, as does the historical, economic, social, and cultural milieu.

Timing and Turning Points

"Timing" suggests that *when* an event or major life change occurs in an individual's lifetime it can have important repercussions. Also, adult development is molded by specific historical conditions, such that being age 50, 60, or 70 in the early 21st century is far different from being age 50, 60, or 70 in the middle of the 20th century. "Turning points" can be both objective and subjective, occurring when life paths are seen as taking a sharp and decisive shift (Wethington, 2002).

Retirement is one such turning point. Individuals entering the Third Age through voluntarily exiting their career jobs (or being laid off or encouraged by buyouts to retire) may find themselves without the structure of goals and routines established by their jobs or by raising a family. From one perspective third-agers experience *maximum autonomy* in structuring their days, their social networks, and their identities. But in the absence of institutionalized organizational options and cultural expectations for this emerging life phase, one can regard third-agers as limited in opportunity, constrained by the lack of legitimate positions or status in society. Autonomy can shade for some into anomie, a sense of purposeless-ness, isolation, and foreboding. The fact is that the Third Age is embedded in social and organizational policy and practices designed for the second and fourth ages, policies and practices that are themselves eroding. Existing societal and institutional arrangements are obsolete in the face of the Third Age years of adulthood, providing few relevant guidelines for social behavior during these years and often cultivating, instead, a sense of uncertainty and ambivalence.

Linked Lives

Individual lives are always *linked lives* (Moen & Hernandez, 2009); one person's resources, resource deficits, successes, failures, chronic strains, and (expected or unexpected) transitions can become focal conditions, even turning points, in the lives of others, especially other family members. The life-course concept of linked lives highlights the ways in which individuals' choices are always embedded in and shaped by the people in their lives. Third Age relationships with children, siblings, parents, spouses, and close friends may be supportive, but they can be sources of conflict and strain as well. Lives are also linked with those of coworkers, neighbors, and other social network members. A person's social convoy of relationships can shift in size, supportiveness, and strain during the Third Age as various relationships emerge, end, change, or persist.

Cumulation of Advantage and Disadvantage

The notion of *cumulation of advantage or disadvantage* underscores continuity rather than discontinuity over the life course, with people who are already advantaged in terms of health, education, and material resources most apt to continue being so. There is growing recognition of enduring inequality across the life course based on race, class, and gender (Link, 2008; Phelan & Link, 2005). One key resource for health and life quality is ongoing connectedness or social integration (Pillemer, Moen, Wethington, & Glasgow, 2000). Since social integration is most common among those advantaged in other ways in society, we would anticipate that Third Age adults with high levels of education and with few health limitations would be involved in more roles (including paid work and community service) and would feel more socially connected than those with fewer such resources. Future research is needed to assess how health and educational resources influence the ability of third-agers to participate in paid or volunteer work.

THIRD AGE DYNAMICS IN CONTEXT

An important proposition of life-course analysis is that an understanding of one life phase, such as the Third Age, requires it to be placed in the larger context of life pathways. Past experiences matter: prior biographical experiences shape perceived options in the Third Age, and they also serve to define the resources and conditions men and women bring with them to this life stage. Because of its emphasis on timing, process, and context, the life-course perspective directs attention to *variability* in the Third Age, such as differences by gender, race/ethnicity, social class, community, and residential location. Moen and Spencer (2006) propose that the emerging Third Age is a time of narrowing of gender differences (convergence) while simultaneously widening within-gender and within-age group differences (divergence). In other words, the Third Age is a time of *converging divergence* in roles and routines between men and women, and to some degree across age groups.

Organizational and public policies and practices, together with cultural schema about age, work, retirement, and the lock-step life course, constrain options in the Third Age. The social organization of education, paid work, unpaid household and care work, and retirement serve to structure virtually all aspects of both men's and women's lives in the years leading up to and through the Third Age. Such consequences include the differential power, status, and earnings men and women accrue as a result of a life-course defined by the occupational career. Health insurance, pensions, unemployment insurance, disability insurance, and social security—all rest on the edifice of the male lock-step career mystique (Moen & Roehling, 2005). Given the gendered character of the contemporary life course, American men and women moving toward the Third Age have experienced both enduring gender disparities and age-related disparities in income, power, and health. This is especially the case for minority women (Brown, Jackson, & Faison, 2007). The Third Age as an identifiable phase may be new, but it remains embedded in existing outdated gender and age scripts and in enduring race and ethnic discrimination, producing disparate personal resources for those in their 50s, 60s, and 70s.

The life-course perspective also builds on the sociology of age to provide a way of linking social change to changes in individual lives. This conceptual framework is particularly instructive in light of the broad panorama of change in both the age and health structure of society leading to the development of a new Third Age stage of the life course, underscoring the social, cultural, and institutional features of our society that are out of step with this development. The life-course approach forces attention to the many interactive factors that influence health and effective functioning, including the links among social, demographic and institutional conditions, and individual biographies.

A life-course theoretical lens is especially useful in studying the Third Age precisely *because* these are times of remarkable dislocations in taken-for-granted rules and roles shaping life in the 21st century, with role entries and exits at different points in the life course undergoing fundamental transformations. These changes in the chronologization of the life course reflect (1) demographic changes in marriage, fertility, and longevity, (2) organizational changes in fundamental institutions such as schools, paid work, and pensions, (3) the changing economy and financial crisis, and (4) new initiatives in governmental policies and practices affecting job and retirement entry and exit portals, timing, and incentives.

The interplay between an individual's life history, the life course of the family unit, the larger community, business, and social policies, at a particular point in history, lies at the crux of life-course analysis. In addition, this perspective attends to the intersection of the multiple strands of the various careers that make up the life of the individual—the relationship, for example, between one's parenting or marital "career" and one's work career. What is new is that there are emerging Third Age career paths involving some mix of learning, service, and meaningful work.

THE THIRD AGE AS AN EMERGING INSTITUTION

Three things make something an institution: *language* that develops around it, taken-for-granted *customs*, and a body of *rules and laws* (Biggart & Beamish, 2003). All are in flux around life in the Third Age. Retirement is increasingly a "fuzzy transition": no longer the customary one-time, one-way, age-graded event (Kim & Moen, 2001; Moen & Peterson, 2009). And it most often occurs (at least for the first time!) before the customary "traditional" age of 65. Even as older workers are delaying retirement, they often find themselves retired through layoffs or buyouts earlier than expected, and often seek postcareer jobs.

The language around life in the Third Age is also problematic. In particular, Americans have no language for people who are retired from their career jobs but employed in a different job, working for themselves, or even sometimes doing the very same jobs they "retired" from! Neither do Americans have language to describe the civically engaged "retirees" whose "jobs," albeit unpaid, are possibly even more meaningful, useful, and fulfilling than the ones from which they retired. Furthermore, we no longer have a clear-cut definition of retirement. Brown, Jackson, and Faison (2007) argue that in some cases it is appropriate to use a combination of objective measures (such as receipt of a pension) and subjective measures (such as self-identifying as retired) to categorize individuals by retirement status today.

Recall that a key ingredient in the creation (or dismantling) of institutions like retirement is *legislation*. The normative lock-step life course—from education to employment to retirement (Kohli, 2007; Moen, 2003)—became the taken-for-granted arrangement defining educational, occupational, and pension policies, as well as the cultural backdrop of 20th-century American life. Legislative and regulatory policies and practices served to define the expected stages of life—education for the years of childhood and adolescence, employment the defining adult role, retirement effectively the transition to old age. The fact that women's lives, and many men's, were not so neatly ordered seemed beside the point. Recent federal policies, such as those prohibiting mandatory retirement and age discrimination, along with delaying social security eligibility, have sought to make continued full-time employment more attractive for older adults even as many outdated pension rules remain in place. Thus, different pieces of legislation create mixed messages, further advancing the deinstitutionalization of retirement. Complicating the Third Age project even further is the market collapse of 2009. Workers who lost a significant portion of their nest eggs (i.e., retirement savings) report delaying retirement (PEW Research Center, 2009).

Taken together, social forces have moved retirement from a taken-for-granted institutionalized passage to a Third Age project requiring a series of strategic selections in the form of role exits and entrances, along with their planning and timing (Moen & Peterson, 2009). But the Third Age remains circumscribed by available options, along with outdated beliefs about age, gender, and retirement that still color peoples' thinking. For example, while articles, books, and advertisements encourage third-agers to engage in *financial* planning and developing alternative sources of financial security, few messages encourage *lifestyle* planning around what one will actually *do* over the widening Third Age years (Cutler, 1997; Moen, Huang, Plassman, & Dentinger, 2006; Moen, Sweet, & Swisher, 2005).

Socially prescribed and legislated patterns of entry into or exit from particular life stages are one measure of the extent to which these stages have been institutionalized within society. Transitions that people take as "given"—like starting kindergarten or graduating from high school—come complete with guides for action—or "scripts." The cumulative impact of the socioeconomic, policy, and organizational trends described above along with existing research evidence points to contemporary retirement as having moved from a complete to an *incomplete* institution, with the Third Age yet to be institutionalized. The dislocations around both career paths and retirement make the strategic selection processes of Third Age workers and retirees all the more salient (Moen et al., 2005; Smith & Moen, 2003; Szinovacz & DeViney, 2000).

FUTURE STEPS: ISSUES TO CONSIDER

"Doing" the Third Age

There have been, to date, few studies of the life-course dynamics of Third Age women and men—the pathways to successful aging in terms of lifestyle, health, and psychosocial well-being, and the links to values, identity, and meaning. Bronfenbrenner (2005) suggests that the cognitive response of individuals is related to both characteristics of the person and features of the environment and the process that both shapes and binds the two over time. The Third Age is a time of significant changes in routines, roles, and relationships that may well affect how individuals perceive themselves and their abilities, as well as their construction of the meanings of their lives.

It is important to recognize that—and investigate how—individuals construct their own meanings surrounding this emerging life stage. Their definitions and meanings, in turn, have repercussions in terms of their strategic selections of roles and relationships as well as their identity, efficacy, outlook for the future, and physical/mental health.

Key Trends

Consider three life-course trends, calling for new research and new definitions, as well as new institutional arrangements to optimize life chances and life quality in the Third Age. First, Americans are spending and will be spending an increasing proportion of their lives *not* married. Increases in longevity along with divorce and widowhood, the postponement of marriage and remarriage, and choices to never marry mean that a growing portion of third-agers—especially women—will be single. Along with this demographic reality is another reality: marriage has been found to be a social support, conducive to individual health and well-being (Waite & Gallagher, 2000). Yet, millions of older Americans are without this form of social support. What kinds of relationships can provide similar kinds of support? What is the effect for third-agers spending a significant portion of one's life out of marriage? Does the timing of the transition to singlehood from divorce or widowhood affect individuals in the Third Age? Little is known about who nonmarried third-agers spend time with or go to for support.

A second life-course trend is the increasing proportions of our lives that will be spent in three-, four-, or even five-generation families. This means that third-agers will be involved in providing more caregiving— of older parents, aunts and uncles, disabled adult children, and grandchildren. It also means that third-agers will have a richer network of kin, both proximate and distant, and that this network can be called upon by and will call upon third-agers for advice and help when needed. A concept in sociology called "the strength of weak ties" (Granovetter, 1973) captures the fact that some relationships with even distant kin will be activated and reactivated as individuals move or as family circumstances and needs change. Matilda White Riley (1983) calls this form of kinship structure a "latent web of continually shifting linkages," an important topic for future research.

A third life-course trend: Americans spend an increasing proportion of their lives in retirement, and retirement from career jobs often occurs during the same period as children leave or have left the family nest. There is a real danger of social isolation of retired third-agers who live alone and are not connected to their communities, who have no children, whose children are geographically remote, or who as a result of divorce years earlier remain estranged from their children.

At the same time, there is emerging recognition that retired third-agers are an important but untapped resource. Communities, employers, and policy makers need to fashion new arrangements to exploit this valued resource, whether in the form of paid work or unpaid volunteer service. Paid work declines over the life course, particularly in response to changes in pension and other incentives, but these incentives are now moving in the direction of delaying full retirement. Unpaid civic engagement does not decline in the Third Age years (Moen & Altobelli, 2007), and public or community service as well as educational opportunities are attracting third-agers (Lawrence-Lightfoot, 2009; Manheimer, 2007; Morrow-Howell, Hinterlong, & Sherraden, 2001).

These three life-course trends have policy as well as research implications.

(1) *A broader definition of family.* Too often we think of families as mothers and fathers of young children. We need to reevaluate what it is that families do for individual members, how families change over the life course, and how we can fashion a definition that is inclusive, rather than exclusive, of the people who matter to us. This has broad implications—for residential zoning of houses, for example, for who gets admitted to see those in intensive care, or for who can be on health insurance "family" plans.

(2) *More supports for caregivers.* Gender remains a key factor in shaping the Third Age. Women are more likely than men to be active in caregiving as they age—for their own parents, particularly their mothers, or for their ailing spouses (Allen, 1994; Chesley & Moen, 2006). Women involved in caregiving are more likely than men to experience strain (Young & Kahana, 1989). Antonucci (1994) suggests that women not only have more close ties but also are more burdened by these intimate relationships than are men.

Social scientists have depicted the "nurturant role obligations" of women as wives and mothers as potentially interfering with self-care and, consequently, women's own health. Caregiving of older or chronically ill relatives can also produce role overload and strain or, conversely, a sense of purpose and meaning. Family caregiving is a tremendous social resource that permits independent living of dependent individuals or augments existing systems of formal care. But caregivers do not receive the resources and support that they need. Innovative research and policy development could fashion ways to ease the burden of caregiving and to facilitate purposeful and sustainable informal care.

(3) *Widening opportunities for meaningful engagement.* The typical life pattern for American men has consisted of 20 or more years

of preschool and schooling, 40 or more years of employment, and the remaining years spent in retirement leisure. For American women, on the other hand, the prime working years have been a combination and sequencing of unpaid domestic and paid labor. As women have moved into and remain in the labor force they have been adopting a modified version of the traditional male life course, but *combined* with their continuing family responsibilities. This means that the years of heaviest child-care responsibilities are also the years of heaviest investment in building a career, and the years of least child-care responsibilities are also the Third Age years around conventional retirement.

Robert Kahn (1994) describes the goodness of fit between the demands of the job and the abilities of the person who holds it, as well as the needs, goals, and aspirations and skills of workers and the requirements and opportunities of the job. The nature of this fit between the individual and his career job should affect whether workers choose to retire early, on time, late, or not at all. The idea of goodness of fit, what I call life-course fit (Moen & Huang, 2010; Moen et al., 2009), could be usefully applied to studies of roles and experiences in the Third Age. The Third Age project may well be a different experience for women than men, in part because of the historical difference in their attachment to the labor force. As described above, when men leave their jobs they are exiting from a role that has typically dominated their adult years. Women, on the other hand, commonly experience greater discontinuity, moving in and out of the labor force, in and out of part-time jobs in tandem with shifting family responsibilities (Moen & Chermack, 2005). Given occupational segregation by gender and their less stable employment histories, women are also less likely to be covered by a pension than are men, and those with pensions have incomes far lower than men's (Munnell & Sass, 2008).

Rethinking the lock-step pattern of education, employment, and retirement could lead to a variety of arrangements, including returning to school at various ages and a continuation of paid work in the Third Age in encore careers, often in more flexible ways and with fewer hours (Moen, 2007; Moen & Peterson, 2009). Alternative forms of civic engagement could emerge without age limits or boundaries. For example, the Peace Corps now welcomes applicants aged 18–86. Moreover, new forms of creative and purposeful learning are already emerging (Lawrence-Lightfoot, 2009; Manheimer, 2007).

CONCLUSION

The life course is now more fluid and variegated than age-graded and lock-step. Individuals, couples, and families make strategic selections in fashioning their own Third Age, but they do so hampered by (1) a risk economy, (2) life-course shifts in the timing and duration of schooling, marriage, childbearing, careers, and service, and (3) policies and practices better suited to the middle of the last century. Matilda White Riley (Riley, Kahn, & Foner, 1994) defined structural lag as the mismatch between out-dated institutional arrangements and the demographic realities of the Third Age: an aging workforce, a youthful retired force, a large, aging baby-boom cohort with aging parents. There are other major social forces also precipitating life-course "misfit" or lag between roles and realities: the absence of a living wage requiring two incomes for most families to remain in the middle class; a global economy where seniority no longer means security and retirement pensions and benefits are unraveling; the dismantling of social and community safety nets; a time-stretched work-force, with little time for civic engagement.

The changes we as a society are experiencing around the Third Age call loudly for a thoughtful reappraisal of existing life patterns. Even though the security and rewards of doing so are fast disappearing, taken-for-granted customs and institutionalized practices are predicated upon the career mystique emphasizing full-time dedication to paid work, from the time Americans leave school to the time they die or retire, whichever comes first (Moen & Roehling, 2005). What is key is that this myth and the policies and practices undergirding it stand in the way of creating *new, alternative life course and career flexibilities* for the Third Age. The challenge is not *how* to alter existing structures to widen Third Age options but *recognition of the need to do so.* This could lead to a reconfiguration of the life course in ways that create more options, greater life quality for both men and women in the Third Age and, eventually, at every stage of the life course.

REFERENCES

Allen, S. M. (1994). Gender differences in spousal caregiving and unmet need for care. *Journal of Gerontology: Social Sciences, 4,* S187–S195.
Antonucci, T. C. (1994). A life-span view of women's social relations. In B. F. Turner & L. E. Troll (Eds.), *Women growing older* (pp. 239–269). Thousand Oaks: Sage.

Biggart, N. W., & Beamish, T. D. (2003). The economic sociology of conventions: Habit, custom, practice, and routine in market order. *Annual Review of Sociology, 29,* 443–464.

Bronfenbrenner, U. (Ed.). (2005). *Making human beings human: Bioecological perspectives on human development.* Thousand Oaks: Sage.

Brown, E., Jackson, J. S., & Faison, N. (2007). The work and retirement experiences of aging Black Americans. In J. B. James & P. Wink (Eds.), *Annual review of gerontology and geriatrics. The crown of life: Dynamics of the early post-retirement period* (Vol. 26, pp. 39–60). New York: Springer.

Brückner, H., & Mayer, K. U. (2005). De-standardization of the life course: What it might mean? And if it means anything, whether it actually took place? *Advances in Life Course Research, 9,* 27–53.

Chesley, N., & Moen, P. (2006). Dual-earner couples' caregiving strategies, benefit use, and psychological well-being. *American Behavioral Scientist, 49*(9), 1248–1269.

Chirikos, T. N. (1993). The relationship between health and labor market status. *Annual Review Public Health, 14,* 293–312.

Crimmins, E. M., & Saito, Y. (2001). Trends in health life expectancy in the United States, 1970–1990: Gender, racial, and educational differences. *Journal of Social Science and Medicine, 52,* 1629–1641.

Cutler, D. M. (1997). Restructuring Medicare for the future. In R. D. Reischauer (Ed.), *Setting national priorities* (pp. 197–234). Washington, DC: The Brookings Institution.

Dannefer, D. (2003). Cumulative advantage/disadvantage and the life course: Cross-fertilizing age and social science theory. *Journals of Gerontology Series B-Psychological Sciences, 58*(6), S327–S337.

Dentinger, E., & Clarkberg, M. (2002). Informal caregiving and retirement timing among men and women: Gender and caregiving relationships in late midlife. *Journal of Family Issues, 23*(7), 857–879.

Elder, G. H., Jr., Johnson, M. K., & Crosnoe, R. (2003). The emergence and development of the life course. In J. T. Mortimer & M. J. Shanahan (Eds.), *Handbook of the life course* (pp. 3–19). New York: Plenum.

Elder, G. H., Jr., & Giele, J. Z. (Eds.). (2009). *The craft of life course research.* New York: The Guilford Press.

Freedman, M. (2007). *Encore: Finding work that matters in the second half of life.* New York: Public Affairs.

George, L. (1993). Sociological perspectives on life transitions. *Annual Review of Sociology, 19,* 553–573.

Granovetter, M. S. (1973). The strength of weak ties. *American Journal of Sociology, 78*(6), 1360–1380.

Han, S.-K., & Moen, P. (1999). Clocking out: Temporal patterning of retirement. *American Journal of Sociology, 105,* 191–236.

James, J., & Wink, P. (Eds.). (2007). *The crown of life: Dynamics of the early postretirement period* (Vol. 26). New York: Springer.

Kahn, R. L. (1994). Opportunities, aspirations, and goodness of fit. In M. W. Riley, R. L. Kahn, & A. Foner (Eds.), *Age and structural lag: Society's failure to provide meaningful opportunities in work, family, and leisure* (pp. 37–56). New York: John Wiley & Sons.

Kahn, R. L., & Antonucci, T. C. (1980). Convoys over the life course: Attachment, roles, and social support. In P. B. Baltes & O. G. Brim, Jr. (Eds.), *Life-span development and behavior* (Vol. 3, pp. 253–286). New York: Academic Press.

Kim, J., & Moen, P. (2001). Is retirement good or bad for subjective well-being? *Current Directions in Psychological Science, 10*, 83–86.

Kohli, M. (2007). The institutionalization of the life course: Looking back to look ahead. *Research in Human Development, 4*(3/4), 253–271.

Lawrence-Lightfoot, S. (2009). *The third chapter: Passion, risk, and adventure in the 25 years after 50.* New York: Farrar, Straus Giroux.

Leisering, L. (2003). Government and the life course. In J. T. Mortimer & M. J. Shanahan (Eds.), *Handbook of the life course* (pp. 205–225). New York: Kluwer.

Link, B. G. (2008). Epidemiological sociology and the social shaping of population health. *Journal of Health and Social Behavior, 49*, 367–384.

Manheimer, R. J. (2007). Allocation resources for lifelong learning for older adults. In R. A. Pruchno & M. A. Smyer (Eds.), *Challenges of an aging society: Ethical dilemmas, political issues* (pp. 217–237). Baltimore: The Johns Hopkins University Press.

Mayer, K. U. (2004). Whose lives? How history, societies and institutions define and shape life courses. *Research in Human Development, 1*, 161–187.

Moen, P. (2001). The gendered life course. In R. Binstock & L. George (Eds.), *Handbook of aging and the social sciences* (pp. 179–196). San Diego: Academic Press.

Moen, P. (2003). Midcourse: Navigating retirement and a new life stage. In J. Mortimer & M. J. Shanahan (Eds.), *Handbook of the life course* (pp. 267–291). New York: Kluwer Academic/Plenum.

Moen, P. (2007). Not so big jobs and retirements: What workers (and retirees) really want. *Generations, 31*(1), 31–36.

Moen, P., & Altobelli, J. (2007). Strategic selection as a retirement project: Will Americans develop hybrid arrangements? In J. James & P. Wink (Eds.), *The crown of life: Dynamics of the early postretirement period* (Vol. 26, pp. 61–81). New York: Springer.

Moen, P., & Chermack, K. (2005). Gender disparities in health: Strategic selection, careers, and cycles of control. *Journal of Gerontology, 60B*, 99–108.

Moen, P., & Chesley, N. (2008). Toxic job ecologies, time convoys, and work–family conflict: Can families (re)gain control and life-course "fit"? In K. Korabik, D. S. Lero, & D. L. Whitehead (Eds.), *Handbook of work–family integration: Research, theory, and best practices* (pp. 95–122). New York: Elsevier.

Moen, P., Elder, G. H., Jr., & Lüscher, K. (Eds.). (1995). *Examining lives in context: Perspectives on the ecology of human development.* Washington: American Psychological Association.

Moen, P., & Hernandez, E. (2009). Social convoys: Studying linked lives in time, context, and motion. In G. H. Elder, Jr. & J. Giele (Eds.), *The craft of life course research* (pp. 258–279). New York: Guilford Press.

Moen, P., & Huang, Q. (2010). Customizing careers by opting out or shifting jobs: Dual-earners seeking life-course "fit." In K. Christensen & B. L. Schneider (Eds.), *Workplace flexibility: Realigning 20th century jobs for a 21st century workforce* (pp. 73–94). Ithaca: Cornell University Press.

Moen, P., Huang, Q., Plassman, V., & Dentinger, E. (2006). Deciding the future: Do dual-earner couples plan together for retirement? *American Behavioral Scientist, 49*(10), 1422–1443.

Moen, P., Kelly, E., & Magennis, R. (2009). Gender strategies: Socialization, allocation, and strategic selection processes shaping the gendered adult life course. In M. C. Smith (Ed.), *Handbook of research on adult learning and development* (pp. 378–411). New York: Routledge/Taylor & Francis.

Moen, P., & Peterson, J. (2009). A third path? Multiplex time, gender, and retirement encores in the United States. In J. Kocka, M. Kohli & W. Streeck (Eds.), *Altern, Familie, Zivilgesellschaft und Politik (Aging, family, civil society, and politics)* (pp. 41–58). Nova Acta Leopoldina series. Stuttgart: Wissenschaftliche Verlagsgesellschaft.

Moen, P., & Roehling, P. (2005). *The career mystique: Cracks in the American dream.* Boulder, CO: Rowman & Littlefield.

Moen, P., & Spencer, D. (2006). Converging divergences in age, gender, health, and well-being: Strategic selection in the third age. In R. H. Binstock & L. K. George (Eds.), *Handbook of aging and the social sciences* (6th ed., pp. 127–144). Burlington: Elsevier Academic Press.

Moen, P., Sweet, S., & Swisher, R. (2005). Embedded career clocks: The case of retirement planning. *Advances in Life Course Research, 9*, 237–265.

Morrow-Howell, N., Hinterlong, J., & Sherraden, M. (Eds.). (2001). *Productive aging: A conceptual framework.* Baltimore: Johns Hopkins University Press.

Mortimer, J. T., & Shanahan, M. J. (Eds.). (2003). *Handbook of the life course.* New York: Kluwer Academic/Plenum Publishers.

Munnell, A. H., & Sass, S. A. (2008). *Working longer: The solution to the retirement income challenge.* Washington, DC: Brookings Institution Press.

O'Rand, A. (1996). The precious and precocious: Understanding cumulative disadvantage and cumulative advantage over the life course. *The Gerontologist, 36*, 230–238.

PEW Research Center. (2009). *Most middle-aged adults are rethinking retirement plans: The threshold generation* (by Rich Morin).

Phelan, J. C., & Link, B. G. (2005). Controlling disease and creating disparities: A fundamental cause perspective. *Journals of Gerontology, 60*, S27–S33.

Pillemer, K., Moen, P., Wethington, E., & Glasgow, N. (Eds.). (2000). *Social integration in the second half of life.* Baltimore, MD: The Johns Hopkins Press.

Quinn, J. F., & Burkhauser, R. V. (1990). Work and retirement. In R. H. Binstock & L. K. George (Eds.), *Handbook of aging and the social sciences* (pp. 308–327). New York: Academic Press.

Riley, M. W. (1983). The family in an aging society: A matrix of latent relationships. *Journal of Family Issues, 4*(3), 439–454.

Riley, M. W. (1987). On the significance of age in sociology. *American Sociological Review*, *52*(1), 1-14.

Riley, M. W., Kahn, R. L., & Foner, A. (Eds.). (1994). *Age and structural lag*. New York: Wiley.

Rook, K. S., Charles, S. T., & Heckhausen, J. H. (2006). Aging and health. In H. Friedman & R. C. Silver (Eds.), *Foundations of health psychology*. New York: Oxford University Press.

Ryder, N. B. (1965). The cohort as a concept in the study of social change. *American Sociological Review*, *30*(6), 843-861.

Settersten, R. A., Jr., (Ed.). (2003). *Invitation to the life course: Toward new understandings of later life*. Amityville, NY: Baywood.

Sewell, W. F. (1992). A theory of structure: Duality, agency, and transformation. *The American Journal of Sociology*, *98*(1), 1-29.

Shanahan, M. J., & Macmillan, R. (2007). *Biography and the sociological imagination*. New York: Norton.

Smith, D. B., & Moen, P. (2003). Retirement satisfaction for retirees and their spouses: Do gender and the retirement decision-making process matter? *Journal of Family Issues*, *24*, 1-24.

Szinovacz, M., & De Viney, S. (2000). Marital characteristics and retirement decisions. *Research on Aging*, *22*(5), 470-498.

Waite, L., & Gallagher, M. (2000). *The case for marriage: Why married people are happier, healthier, and better off financially*. New York: Doubleday.

Wethington, E. (2002). The relationship of work turning points to perceptions of psychological growth and change. *Advances in Life Course Research*, *7*, 111-131.

Young, R. F., & Kahana, E. (1989). Specifying caregiver outcomes: Gender and relationship aspects of caregiving strain. *The Gerontologist*, *29*, 660-666.

Chapter
2

The Third Age as a Cultural Field

Chris Gilleard and Paul Higgs

THEORIZING CULTURAL CHANGE IN THE ERA OF THE THIRD AGE

*P*eter Laslett is widely credited with introducing the term "the Third Age" into social gerontology during the mid-1980s (Laslett, 1987). Since then, it has become a pivotal concept in debates concerning the social and cultural nature of later life in contemporary Western society (Biggs, 2005; Gilleard & Higgs, 2000; Weiss & Bass, 2002). It remains, however, a term open to many interpretations. Each definition of the Third Age implies an ontology. In this chapter, rather than treating the Third Age as a "new stage of life," as Laslett (1987) did," or dismissing it as a shorthand term for the well-off elderly, as Bury (1998) and Blaikie (2002) have, we propose that the Third Age is more usefully conceptualized as a cultural field shaped by late-life consumption patterns, in which particular actors from particular cohorts participate more or less intensively than others. The nature and forms of this participation and the differing Third Age "lifestyles" that such participation supports help define the nature and form of the field itself. Underpinning this interpretation of the Third Age is the work of Karl Mannheim and Pierre Bourdieu.

We begin by considering the work of Karl Mannheim on generational location and generational styles. These we link to Pierre Bourdieu's cultural sociology and in particular his use of the terms "field" and "habitus." We consider the Third Age as an example of a cultural field, originating from the consumer-based lifestyles that emerged in the post-World War II period. In subsequent decades, these experiences and the practices associated with them expanded across class locations and life stages, destabilizing the social and cultural representations of aging and later life. We address the sources of this expansion and the vectors through which such developments took place before exploring the potential "upper limits" of this cultural field, as seen from the viewpoint of the first decades of the 21st century.

Mannheim: Generational Location and Generational Style

For Mannheim, the nature of a generation is determined by the confluence of the events of a historical period with a particular birth cohort, set in a particular social context (Mannheim, 1952/1997). This confluence of birth date and experience creates a "community of location" that forms the necessary, though not sufficient conditions for realizing a "generational unit." A generational location exists, therefore, as a distinct period of history that is experienced most acutely by members of a particular birth cohort. For Mannheim, youth was the critical period within the life course when such historical processes were most influential. But the combination of a particular stage of life and a particular period of historical change does not in itself create the conditions to define a generation. A further element is needed, namely participation in a "common destiny" (op. cit., pp. 47–49) that then creates a distinct generational "entelechy" or "style" (op. cit., pp. 51–53).

For many contemporary writers, baby boomers are just such a generational unit, formed by a community of location—membership of a cohort born in the 1940s whose members reached adulthood during the 1960s and who are facing retirement during the first decade of the 21st century (Phillipson, Leach, Money, & Biggs, 2008). Their common destiny is to have grown up and grown old in conditions of relative security, increased affluence, and at a moment of significant generational schism that made conscious the distinction between what was "old" in the sense of being old-fashioned and "out of date" and what was "new" in the sense of creating new lifestyles, new values, and new experiences.

However, Mannheim cautioned against speaking of generations "without any further differentiation [. . .] jumbling together purely biological phenomena and others which are the product of social and cultural forces [...] thus arriv[ing] at a sort of sociology of chronological tables (Geschichtstabellensoziologie)" (op. cit., p. 53). As he put it, "every new departure [...] has to operate in a given field which although in constant process of change is capable of description in structural terms" (op. cit., p. 55). It is this last point that commentators on the baby boom cohort/generation have tended to ignore. Representing the Third Age as a Mannheimian generational unit structured by birth cohort and historical location, such researchers have paid little attention to the social and cultural dynamics operating within that "community of location." The ascription of a generational identity to a population defined primarily by its demography is, we argue, an incomplete representation of Mannheim's conceptualization of "generation." Instead of treating the Third Age primarily in terms of its demographic identity—as a particular cohort—Mannheim's conception requires a more cultural and historical understanding. What is needed to transform a generational location (or cohort) into an "actual" generation or generational unit (which, in Mannheim's view, is both a cultural and historical phenomenon) is a shared engagement "with the tempo of social change" (op. cit., p. 51). The work of a later European sociologist, Pierre Bourdieu, helps us to better understand this connection.

Generational Fields and Generational Habitus: Bourdieu

Bourdieu's work offers a potentially fruitful direction to expand upon Mannheim's themes of a generational unit and its generational style. In particular, his concepts of the "cultural field" and the associated "habitus" that are enacted and internalized through participation in that particular cultural field are useful for understanding the fundamentally cultural nature of the Third Age (Bourdieu, 1977, 1993). The term cultural field is an example of an open concept whose definition exists only in relation to a particular theoretical system (Bourdieu & Wacquant, 1992). As such, it is not immutable, and is open to alternative uses within alternative theoretical systems.

According to Bourdieu (1993), a key element of any cultural field is the existence of an underlying logic that establishes and develops it. A cultural field emphasizes the range of possible practices that can be realized within it and focuses upon the position of the players within it, rather than the identities of the players themselves. While the emphasis in much of Bourdieu's work is on the contemporary domains of social space—particularly fields of culture—he recognizes the importance of a temporal dimension when cultural fields undergo "generational" transformations. As he notes, such generational transformations within any cultural field correspond to "social" rather than "biological" concepts of age. Hence, in terms of generational change, "young" generations may challenge the "old" whose members are themselves "biologically almost as old as [the members of] the 'old'" (Bourdieu, 1993, p. 59). Viewing the Third Age as a cultural field, therefore, is not so much about focusing upon the chronological age of the participants or players as it is about mapping the social space within which they participate, the new logics that are driving such participation, and the new sets of possibilities that are realized within the field.

Another of Bourdieu's "open concepts" that relates to our concept of the Third Age is the term habitus. It refers to a set of mostly unconscious practices and forms of experience that arise from and help shape the cultural fields in which they are co-assembled—so-called structuring structures. According to Bourdieu (1977), habitus are "history turned into nature." By this he means that lifestyles and everyday cultural practices embody the historical development of the field within which they emerged. We propose treating the Third Age as a cultural field emerging out of the distinctions/subcultures of the "cultural revolution" of the 1960s. Thus, we view the habitus of the Third Age as being fashioned within that period of change. What is important for understanding the contemporary field of the Third Age, however, is that these habitus continue to be enacted as practice well after their point of origin has passed. In the process, these habitus also change, and with that change comes a gradual transformation in the nature of later life.

Mannheim and Bourdieu: Achieving a Synthesis

By integrating Mannheim's theoretical framework of generational units and generational styles with Bourdieu's concept of cultural fields and their associated habitus, an alternative system of theorizing the Third Age emerges. This system is based neither on demography nor on the periodization of the life course, but on the emergence of particular cultural practices within a specific socio-historical period. We are not the first to propose such a synthesis. Edmunds and Turner (2002) suggested such a possibility in their book *Generations, culture and society*, but made little attempt to realize it within a coherent theoretical formulation.

Our argument is that we need to integrate Bourdieu's concept of a "cultural field" with Mannheim's idea of a "generational unit" in order to understand the Third Age as a "generational field." In this way, the Third Age is defined by its emergence within a particular historical period and realized more fully within particular birth cohorts who have created, carried, and redefined that field within their own life histories. Similarly, Bourdieu's concept of "habitus" can be equated with Mannheim's idea of a "generational style," defined by distinct practices and discourses that have helped fashion the generational field from which they have sprung. These practices and related discourse help distinguish the lifestyles of those reaching retirement age at the start of the 21st century from previous cohorts of retirees, differentiating the Third Age as a cultural field distinct from previous ways of growing old.

Bourdieu adds to the original Mannheimian formulation of the "problem of generation" in his emphasis upon the underlying logic that establishes and sustains a particular cultural field and the distinct set of opportunities that are realized within it. He also highlights the extent to which a generation is not reducible to membership of a fixed and finite population. A generational field has its own logic, and it is this logic and the opportunities (and struggles) that are engendered by it that determine its cultural identity within society. Together, both Mannheim and Bourdieu recognize that a cultural field or generational unit is a site, a social space, within which there is heterogeneity—hence the struggles to realize a potential position of cultural power—but also a shared rubric within which those struggles take place. Arguably, the Third Age is just such a contested site emerging under conditions of significant social change.

THE ORIGINS OF THE THIRD AGE AS A CULTURAL FIELD

Integrating Bourdieu's and Mannheim's work, we propose that the Third Age can be reconceptualized as a generational field expressed through historically determined social, cultural, and related consumerist practices— or generational habitus—which are realized more fully in the lives of people from particular birth cohorts. The Third Age can be considered a distinct cultural field most extensively expressed within the lifestyles of a particular generational location or cohort whose experiences and attitudes encapsulate a period of distinct and relatively rapid social change. It is a field, we suggest, that has emerged during the second half of the 20th century and is dominated, perhaps even defined, by cultural practices associated with both counterculture and consumerism,[1] practices and experiences that have evolved within a similar time frame to the life course of specific cohorts.

In this section, we describe the four principal vectors that have propelled and shaped this "generational field." The first and possibly most powerful vector is the rise of "consumerism" particularly within the youth of the post-World War II era. The second, and related to the first, is the growth in countercultural movements that explicitly rejected "old" ways of organizing life, work, and leisure, of seeking power and distinction, and of organizing social and personal relationships. The third, and perhaps least noted vector of change, has been the transformation in the social geography of life. This is most evident in the destruction of "old" (pre-World War II) neighborhoods that linked home, family, work, class, and ethnicity into a coherent whole and their replacement with new, modern but largely deracinated suburban communities in which homes become more singular differentiated social spaces and neighborhoods have had to work hard in order to recreate themselves. Finally, there is the changing nature of work, employment, and the workplace. Where once job choices reflected relatively homogenous distinctions between white and blue collar labor, where the workplace brought hundreds and thousands of people together in strongly gendered factory or office settings, and where intergenerational social mobility was limited, transformation in the nature, organization, and significance of work has undermined its role as a source of identity and community, eroding much of the culture, if not the economic basis, of class.

Consumerism

Turning to the first vector of consumerism, the dominant logic that operates within the field of the Third Age is based upon the mass consumerism of post-World War II society. During this period there was a shift from consumption to consumerism, derived from a significant rise in leisure, consumption expenditure, and the complexity of consumption. Individuals and households moved from simple, relatively unmediated acts of consumption to acts "which are deemed by the actor to provide satisfaction of something more than basic needs" (Ransome, 2005, p. 67). This was particularly evident in the lives of young people, creating the conditions for a distinct youth culture that could be realized and sustained across a much wider range of social locations than the early "prototypical" youth cultures evident in the first half of the 20th century (Fowler, 2008; Hine, 2000).

A key element in the distinctions sought by young people was the desire, shared across different social positions, not just to embrace the new, but also to establish a distance from the old ways of an older generation. New goods, new tastes, new fashions, new technologies, and new causes provided the vehicles by which young people separated their worlds from those of their parents. It was this generational schism and its emphasis upon the salience of youth and the new that laid the foundations for the subsequent emergence of the Third Age as a cultural field whose parameters of personal choice and individualized lifestyle created the opportunities for the continuing pursuit of "distinction" across the life course and that would lead to the destandardization of the modern life course (Anderson, 1985).

The cultural motifs of choice and lifestyle have themselves become institutionalized to the point that some commentators have argued that "social citizens" have been replaced by "citizen consumers" (Cohen, 2003). The opportunities for individuals in different class positions and at different stages of life to exercise consumerist choices have proliferated with the ever-widening extension of the market and the growing salience of leisure (Higgs et al., 2009; Rojek, 2005). Consumption has come to symbolize the virtues of choice, self-expression, autonomy, and pleasure that were emblematic for a generation who grew up during the "long sixties" (Marwick, 1998). Of course, these virtues are not completely self-selected, but neither are they imposed by the state. Whatever the choices that are made, they are choices shaped and stimulated by markets.

Identity Politics

The second vector of practice that shapes the generational habitus, and thus, the cultural field of the Third Age is the growth of the new social movements that are intertwined with consumerism. While seemingly at odds with consumer culture, the counterculture of the new social movements stressed the importance of personal development, cultural autonomy, and self-expression. Within these social movements, personal choices became political choices and national liberation movements joined with cultural liberation movements to assert the voice of autonomy and self-expression. Race, gender, sexual orientation, disability, and, for a short while, age movements united in a radical front crossing boundaries that had previously gone largely unchallenged (Aronowitz, 1992; Pichardo, 1997). The "new politics of recognition," as Nancy Fraser (1995) described it, was voiced more by students than by workers, young men, and women whose numerical significance was becoming a global phenomenon. For these students, and their youthful counterparts in the arts and the media, self-expression meant the freedom to reject all that was old, all that represented the old way of doing things. The political establishment, colonial authorities, and the owners of capital were symbolized as the old; those who were not old, not white, and not in charge found common cause in expressing a wish to be heard, a wish to replace old capital with new.

Community Transformed

The third vector, which is more salient in Europe than in the United States, relates to the transformation of communities as a result of postwar redevelopment. In the United States, as a result of the 1946 GI Bill offering low-cost housing loans to millions of veterans (Opdycke, 2007), there was a growth in new middle-class suburban developments oriented toward schools, shops, and private transport. In Europe, the clearances of prewar inner city housing stock took place a little later. As in the United States, these developments laid the foundations for new social housing that was designed not just for "young families" but for families ready to engage with the new technologies of home. The apartments and houses of the housing estates built in the 1960s were planned with washing machines and fridges, vacuum cleaners and TVs, and electric irons and electric cookers in mind. They were designed not to replicate prewar standards of living, nor reproduce prewar styles of living. Instead, they offered the majority of the population access to the new "modern" comforts of postwar society—a physical break with the old style of living and the opportunities to realize new lifestyles.

The new suburban developments and the new housing estates that replaced or restructured the prewar communities of propinquity created a new set of conditions in which household structures themselves could change. Those aged over 60 became increasingly able to live apart from their children, just as their children were able to live apart from them (Jones et al., 2008). The decline in the numbers of older people sharing a common household with their adult children, most evident between the 1930s and the 1970s, was in part made possible by such housing developments. The generational split that was being created in the arena of fashion, music, and the new media was also realized within individual households. Households occupied primarily by children, teenagers, and people of working age were most likely to benefit from these new modern amenities—leaving older households to occupy the positions of marginality within this new consumer society, a situation that has taken decades to disappear (Higgs et al., 2009).

The Changing Nature of Work

Last, and lagging behind many of these social and cultural changes, the change in the nature of work itself contributed to the reconceptualization of later life, providing the potential for the emergence of the Third Age as a cultural field. The transformation of working life in postwar, postindustrial Western society began as a cultural shift in attitudes toward work, a shift in perspective made possible by the general rise in living standards and the new stability provided by the postwar welfare state. Despite the continued growth in factories and factory workers and the continued persistence of coal mining, engineering, and shipbuilding, the centrality of the workplace was being hollowed out. Migrant workers were brought in to do jobs that the host population were reluctant to do. The prewar gendered segregation of the workplace was declining and the time spent at work was shrinking (Gershuny, 2000). Work was no longer an overwhelming homogenizing community nor a place organized around instilling fear and discipline. Careers were offered instead of jobs and the expansion and feminization of the public sector workforce altered the relationships of the "shop floor."

Alongside this hollowing out of work as a dominant enculturing force was the gradual disappearance of older workers. Between 1950 and 1980, the labor force participation in the United States of men aged 65 and above declined from nearly half (47%) to one quarter (25%). This decline was even steeper in Western Europe, where less than 10% of men aged over 65 were in employment (Costa, 1998, p. 29). This temporal constriction of work was not just a matter of retirement. The numbers of young people aged 16-24 who deferred starting formal employment to go to college also grew significantly in this period. The consequence was that people were spending fewer hours at work and lived more of their life without a workplace identity.

Both processes—the constriction of working time across the life course and the hollowing out of work as an enculturing force—have fostered alternative social spaces in which new lifestyles could be fashioned that relied less upon the fixities of home, family, and work. These new opportunities contributed to shaping a field of lifestyle and leisure that began with the youth of the 1950s and that has since evolved—both across the expanding life course of those born in the 1940s and in the lives of those born immediately before and after them. As work has become less secure, more flexible, and less a homogenizing experience, work-based identities no longer exercise the dominating influence on lifestyles. This has enabled adult lifestyles to be sustained more easily postretirement as they draw less upon work and more upon leisure, in sharp contrast to the loss of a work identity that many retired men in the 1950s considered such a personal tragedy (Townsend, 1963).

As the influence of community, work, and family on individual lifestyle declined, personal identity has become increasingly commodified. Rather than being experienced as a corrupting influence upon youth, the market seemed like an ally, a radical force equally opposed by the establishment, many of whose members continued to consider the working classes ill-suited to membership of the "leisure classes." Within these emerging markets and their novel practices of consumption, many of the habitus of the Third Age were being formed within a distinct generational location. Consumption as a way of expressing one's identity, of expressing generational defiance, of valorizing what is new and different, of exercising freedom of choice and self-expression shaped the rules of the field. Personal distinction, self-expression, and individual freedom that were so much vaunted by the youth of the 1960s have proved enduring marketing tropes that are applied to an ever-increasing array of products and services for adults of all ages, ranging from holidays, travel, and clothing to personal pensions, savings accounts, and retirement homes.

THE NATURE AND FORM OF CAPITAL(S) WITHIN THE THIRD AGE

In the previous section we outlined the principal vectors through which the Third Age has emerged as a cultural field influencing and shaping later life. In this section we consider the underlying dynamic that has driven and developed this generational field. Within the field that we consider marks out the Third Age, the dominant form of material capital is what is spent (consumption) rather than what is earned (income). The importance of this distinction has been highlighted by Bauman (2005). The dominant form of cultural and symbolic capital that is deployed within the Third Age is based upon lifestyle choice rather than ascribed identity. The dominant form of social capital operating within the field is derived as much from the extended horizontal networks of partners and friends as it is from the vertically aligned networks of kinship.

The linkages established between lifetime friends and lifetime "partners" overshadow previously privileged vertical forms of social capital based upon "family" and the spatially secured bonds of intergenerational solidarity. This does not mean that there are no exchanges between the generations; there is, of course, but it has become a less salient source of cultural capital. This, in brief, outlines the principal forms of capital that maintain the logic of the Third Age—consumption, leisure, and lifestyle exercised within chosen social networks that are no longer constrained in time or place.

The cultural and symbolic capital of the Third Age derives from the effective use of leisure—engaging in what Ekerdt (1986) has referred to as the "busy ethic," with its emphasis upon activity, exercise, travel, eating out, self-maintenance, and self-care. Distinction lies less in the area of work, in one's past or present contribution to the social product, and more in the arenas outside work—the creation of symbolically valued lifestyles. Work and leisure have become disconnected. Cultural capital flows more powerfully from the use and quality of individual leisure-time than from what work is done or how money is earned. The symbolic forms of capital that are legitimated within this field are those that support an active, agentic consumerism, in other words, consumption that expresses choice, autonomy, pleasure, and self-expression and that is focused on lifestyle. Equally, the absence of opportunities for these features can be seen as locating the origins of a "lack" of such "Third Age" capital.

The growing opportunities for personal choice that mass consumer society enables, requires the continuing expansion of material and cultural capital and its diversion from use value into proliferating systems of distinction. For Bourdieu, all cultural processes are forms of distinction, operating for the purpose of developing, maintaining, and reproducing social power. Arguably, the generational field that emerged in the postwar period was based upon achieving distinction by rejecting the "old" sources and forms of power, replacing them with new forms of cultural capital that could be established across class positions, but that also contained the possibility of creating new horizontal distinctions based upon lifestyles and subcultures. It was not simply a matter of "new" money; indeed, a "new spirit of capitalism" was introduced within this generational field—a free-spirited, radical capitalism that rejected the staid hierarchies of traditional modernity (Boltanski & Chiapello, 2005).

Capitalism has continued to evolve. The arenas of choice have expanded beyond the traditional boundaries of the market, incorporating aspects of the life world previously held to be the preserve of the family, the professions, or the state. Within this post-1960s culture, it is not youth *per se* that is bought and sold so much as ideologies of youthfulness and opportunity, symbolized by the consumerist quartet of virtues of choice, autonomy, pleasure, and self-expression. These virtues reemerge in new late-life "teenage-like" lifestyles, as retirement for many 60 odd year olds provides new opportunities rather than fewer opportunities to consume. Whether measured through the range and intensity of cultural leisure pursuits, the time spent shopping, expenditure on holidays, or the ownership of domestic information and communication technologies, the extent of participation in distinction seeking lifestyles is something new, which in many ways maintains another distinction that was particularly salient when this generational field was first formed—namely a distinction from that which is "old."

CHARTING THE LIMITS TO THE THIRD AGE

In some sense, the attributed community of "the old" forms a key boundary marking the limits of Third Age culture. The cultural field that is the Third Age is defined both by the continuities of choice before, during, and after working life and by the discontinuity of old age. Within this generational field there is a conscious absence of individualized strategies for practicing old age. Despite claims by writers such as Gullette (2004) that "aging identities" can and indeed should be actively constructed, participants in the Third Age reject old age as a collective choice. Instead of offering narrative security, the "community of old age" threatens to dissolve the lifestyles of autonomous individuals, turning them from active to passive consumers (Jones et al., 2008). Within the field of the Third Age, one reason why old age is culturally marginalized is because those who were old and seemingly outdated continue to be constituted as the "other," a past against which a generation has defined itself. As the signifier of that material and symbolic bankruptcy, old age is no longer a choice but a discourse to be rejected.

This conscious turning from old age defines a critical boundary for the Third Age which is achieved less by people masking or misrepresenting their chronological age as by denying it structural power, refusing to "learn to be old" (Cruikshank, 2003). The practices and discourses that constitute the habitus of the Third Age seek to empty age of personal meaning, treating it as "nothing but a number." The 60-year-old contemplating blepharoplasty, the 70-year-old pondering the merits of vibrators, or the 80-year old entering a marathon illustrate some of the more "avant-garde" practices of this cultural field. More common and mundane are people over 60 shopping, booking holidays, visiting the library or leisure center, taking up a second career, eating out, attending line dancing classes, watching satellite TV, phoning friends, or getting online to e-mail family members. The practices arising from such everyday micro-choices constitute the habitus, the ordinary lifestyles of the Third Age.

An equally critical boundary setting limits to the habitus of the Third Age is the inability to sustain a sense of individual distinction through consumption. While this may come about for a variety of reasons, and may be more easily reached by some than by others because of their limited access to financial, social, and cultural capital, a major instigator is the onset of significant physiological and mental frailty (Gilleard & Higgs, 2010). While adaptive technologies may help sustain the capacity to continue participating in consumer society (e.g., online shopping), active social policy can try to maintain a level playing field for the citizen, but not for the consumer for whom what matters is being able to be different.

FUTURE STEPS: ISSUES TO CONSIDER

Before considering the future of such a cultural reading of the Third Age, it may be helpful to state what, in our view, the Third Age is not. We do not see it as a form of identity conferred by being a member of a particular birth cohort. Nor do we think of it as a newly discovered stage of life or a cultural identity created by the media and the market. Equally, we do not think it advances our understanding to read the Third Age as simply reflecting ownership of a particular amount of physical, financial, or cultural capital. While all these elements are relevant to understanding the logic of the Third Age, they do not define it because they end up treating it as a status ascribed or achieved by some individuals and not by others, a structuring of difference. In this chapter, we have outlined a view of the Third Age in a more thoroughly cultural sense than previous researchers have done, something that is revealed in lifestyle rather than structured by identity. We began by considering Mannheim's use of a generational location as the foundation for the Third Age—a combination of particular birth cohorts living through a particular historical period, and developing a distinct "generational style" that members of these cohorts have carried through their adult lives. We linked these ideas of Mannheim to the work of Bourdieu and his notions of field and habitus. This led us to consider the Third Age as a cultural field, defined and realized through lifestyles of particular birth cohorts, notably those who were born in the 1940s. Their evolving lifestyles, we have argued, have come to form the habitus of later life and retirement. They operate within, and help give definition to, the evolving cultural field of the Third Age.

We locate the origins of this field in the experiences of post-World War II mass affluence, the development of age-defined subcultures, and the establishment of a distinctive generational consciousness that separated itself from the mentality of earlier generations. This field has been carried forward into later life most powerfully by particular birth cohorts and supported by an expanding range of lifestyle choices and sources of social distinction that resist, and by resisting, undermine the structuring identity of old age.

The Third Age is the outcome of this historical process. It continues to be shaped through several vectors—of consumerism, lifestyle, and subculture, the politics of the personal, and the decentering of work and community. As Bennett (1999) has pointed out, late modern lifestyles are constructed rather than given and are fluid rather than fixed. The field of the Third Age and the habitus that support and define it will continue to change as the participants of the field change and as technologies, markets, and capital evolve. While the necessity of consumption underpins the nature of the field, consumption and consumer practices will change. As Mannheim recognized, within any generational unit there exist conflicting tensions (and we would add, conflicting subcultures). Third Age consumerism, we believe, will encompass an ever-wider range of activities that are associated less with the signification of affluence than with the signs of valued lifestyles (such as green consumerism, eco-tourism, and conservation). The Third Age will remain an important social and cultural space in which such contestations and social transformations will be evident, supporting and sustaining an ever-wider range of subcultural lifestyles.

The second arena of change will be realized as the lives of the participants in the Third Age grow longer. This vertical expansion of the Third Age will lead to the further fragmentation and marginalization of old age. Social policy will focus more narrowly upon disability and poverty, while a more complex and contingent set of practices, operating largely within the market, will determine the resources required to support continuing participation in this field. New electronic and digitalized technology is likely to diversify the means by which people connect to and experience more individualized communities. This will leave those with the most limited access to financial, social, and symbolic capital to the marginalization represented by the ascribed community of old age. Age will be valued insofar as it creates entitlements, but increasingly contested when it results in exclusion.

Ignoring the Third Age as merely cultural froth on the surface of late modernity risks marginalizing gerontology itself alongside old age. If the importance of cohort dynamics, the periodization of late-life experience, the evolution of lifestyles and sub-cultures, and the agency of agelessness struggle to find expression within the discipline, gerontology will itself remain limited. By maintaining a focus that is dominated by disability, poverty, and lack, the potential richness of the discipline risks impoverishment. Aging is not confined to a specific period of life, nor should it be treated as the monopoly interest of a particular social group. Agedness should be questioned as a foundational determinant of ordinary lifestyle choices.

The Third Age has emerged as a cultural field that until now has been outlined in only the broadest of brush strokes. A richer and deeper understanding of the field is needed, of how time and resources are used in the construction and reconstruction of ordinary later lifestyles, of how later lifestyles are realized as well as how they fail, and of the complex negotiations around age and agedness that participation in this field requires. Whether one celebrates the opportunities the Third Age presents for a new sense of agency in later life, or berates the corrosiveness of the culture from which it springs and the "false consciousness" that it supports may be a matter of personal choice. Still, the Third Age is an important social reality that if dismissed can only impoverish our understanding of age and aging in contemporary societies.

NOTE

1. The role played by the 1960s counterculture in reshaping the nature and organization of capital has been discussed by Boltanski and Chiapello (2005). The point we wish to note here is that there is much evidence to show that the 1960s counterculture and consumer capitalism had more of a reciprocal rather than an antagonistic relationship with each other, forming part of the generational schism between those who had grown up in the pre- and the post-World War II era.

REFERENCES

Anderson, M. (1985). The emergence of the modern life cycle in Britain. *Social History, 10*, 69-87.

Aronowitz, S. (1992). *The politics of identity.* New York, NY: Routledge.

Bauman, Z. (2005). *Work, consumerism and the new poor.* Cambridge: Polity.

Bennett, A. (1999). Subcultures or neo-tribes? Rethinking the relationship between youth, style and musical taste. *Sociology, 33*, 599-617.

Biggs, S. (2005). Beyond appearances: Perspectives on identity in later life and some implications for method. *Journals of Gerontology Series B: Psychological Sciences and Social Sciences, 60*, S118-S128.

Blaikie, A. (2002). The secret world of sub-cultural ageing: What unites and what divides? In L. Andersson (Ed.), *Cultural gerontology* (pp. 95-110) Westport, CT: Auburn House.

Boltanski, L., & Chiapello, E. (2005). *The new spirit of capitalism.* London: Verso.

Bourdieu, P. (1977). *Outline of a theory of practice.* Cambridge: Cambridge University Press.

Bourdieu, P. (1993). *The field of cultural production.* Cambridge: Polity Press.

Bourdieu, P., & Wacquant, L. J. D. (1992). *An invitation to reflexive sociology.* Cambridge: Polity Press.

Bury, M. (1998). Ageing, gender and sociological theory. In S. Arber & J. Ginn (Eds.), *Connecting gender and ageing* (pp. 15-29). London: Sage Publications.

Cohen, L. (2003). *A consumers' republic: The politics of mass consumption in postwar America.* New York, NY: Alfred A. Knopf.

Costa, D. L. (1998). *The evolution of retirement.* Chicago: University of Chicago Press.

Cruikshank, M. (2003). *Learning to be old: Gender, culture and aging.* Lanham, MD: Rowman & Littlefield.

Edmunds, J., & Turner, B. S. (2002). *Generations, culture and society.* Cambridge: Polity Press.

Ekerdt, D. J. (1986). The busy ethic: Moral continuity between work and retirement. *The Gerontologist, 26*, 239-244.

Fowler, D. (2008). *Youth culture in modern Britain, c. 1920-c. 1970.* Basingstoke: Palgrave Macmillan.

Fraser, N. (1995). From redistribution to recognition? Dilemmas of justice in a post-socialist age. *New Left Review, 212*, 68-93.

Gershuny, J. (2000). *Changing times: Work and leisure in post-industrial society.* Oxford: Oxford University Press.

Gilleard, C., & Higgs, P. (2000). *Cultures of ageing: Self, citizen and the body.* London: Prentice-Hall.

Gilleard, C., & Higgs, P. (2010). Theorizing the fourth age: Aging without agency. *Aging and Mental Health, 14*, 121-128.

Gullette, M. M. (2004). *Aged by culture.* Chicago: University of Chicago Press.

Higgs, P., Hyde, M., Gilleard, C., Victor, C., Wiggins, R., & Jones, I. R. (2009). From passive to active consumers? Later life consumption in the UK from 1968-2005. *Sociological Review, 57*, 102-124.

Hine, T. (2000). *The rise and fall of the American teenager.* New York, NY: HarperCollins.

Jones, I. R., Hyde, M., Victor, C., Wiggins, D., Gilleard, C., & Higgs, P. (2008). *Ageing in a consumer society: From passive to active consumption in Britain.* Bristol: Policy Press.

Laslett, P. (1987). The emergence of the third age. *Ageing & Society, 7,* 113-160.

Mannheim, K. (1952/1997). The problem of generations. In M. A. Hardy (Ed.), *Studying aging and social change: Conceptual and methodological issues* (pp. 22-65). London: Sage Publications.

Marwick, A. (1998). *The sixties.* Oxford: Oxford University Press.

Opdycke, S. (2007). The spaces people share: The changing social geography of American life. In M. C. Carnes (Ed.), *The Columbia history of post World War II America* (pp. 11-35). New York, NY: Columbia University Press.

Phillipson, C., Leach, R., Money, A., & Biggs, S. (2008). Social and cultural constructions of ageing: The case of the Baby Boomers. *Sociological Research Online, 13*(3). Retrieved from http://www.socresonline.org.uk/3/4/4.html

Pichardo, N. A. (1997). New social movements: A critical review. *Annual Review of Sociology, 23,* 411-430.

Ransome, P. (2005). *Work, consumption and culture.* London: Sage.

Rojek, C. (2005). *Leisure theory: Principles and practice.* London: Palgrave.

Townsend, P. (1963). *The family life of old people.* Harmondsworth: Penguin.

Weiss, R. S., & Bass, S. A. (2002). *Challenges of the third age: Meaning and purpose in later life.* Oxford: Oxford University Press.

Chapter
3

The Political Economy of the Third Age

Kathrin Komp

THE POLITICAL ECONOMY OF AGING IN THE ERA OF THE THIRD AGE

*"T*oday, more than ever before, older people take the chance to actively shape their lives. They take responsibility for our country and for future generations. Without their voluntary engagement, our society would not function in many places. The Federal Ministry for Senior Citizens made it its goal to (...) spread this image of an active old age in the public" (von der Leyen, 2009). With these words the German Federal Minister for Family Affairs, Senior Citizens, Women and Youth described the current situation at a national congress for senior citizens. She, thereby, exemplified the perspective typical of the political economy of the Third Age. This perspective recently started to be applied in various countries.

The political economy of the Third Age adds a new twist to the classical political economy of aging. In its wider sense, political economy is the application of a political/ideological perspective to otherwise purely economic rationales for government activities (Lee, 2001; Weingast & Wittman, 2006). A central economic rationale is to bring input and output into an optimal relation to each other. A given input should be used to generate maximum output. A given output, on the other hand, should be realized with the smallest possible input (Barr, 2004; Cowell, 2006). Proponents of neoliberalism used this logic to problematize aging populations. They argued that population aging leads to a smaller working-age population,

51

and thus less input of workers into the welfare state. At the same time, it increases demands on pension and health care schemes, thus requiring more output of welfare states (Binstock, 1984; Jackson, 1991; Offe, 1996; Pierson, 2006). From an economic perspective, this situation is challenging: it combines less input with the need for more output. Proponents of neoliberalism, therefore, conclude that population aging drives the welfare state crisis, necessitating welfare cutbacks and welfare state restructuring (Offe, 1996; Pierson, 2006).

The political economy of aging criticizes such sweeping generalizations about the effects of aging populations. It objects that the group of older people is too heterogeneous to be captured in generalizations. The classical political economy of aging studied older people in welfare states, elaborating on inequalities along gender, and level of socioeconomic status (see, e.g., Minkler & Estes, 1999; Walker, 2006b). In the era of the Third Age, however, a new kind of inequality has emerged: the inequality between third-agers and fourth-agers. In the context of the political economy, third-agers are depicted as healthy retirees, who can be productive. In continental Europe, their productivity through activities such as volunteering and informal caregiving is stressed. In the United States, however, productivity through paid work after retirement is also focused on (see Chapter 9). Fourth-agers, in contrast, are understood as retirees in poor health, who are less capable of productive activities (Komp, Van Tilburg, & Broese van Groenou, 2009; Laslett, 1996).

In this chapter, I first develop an ideal–typical model depicting the political economy of the Third Age. This model shows that third-agers can increase the level of welfare in a country. The neoliberal evaluation of aging populations as a burden on welfare states, consequently, seems overly simplistic and pessimistic. The statement of the German Minister for Senior Citizens supports this perspective. Second, I discuss reasons why the ideal–typical model is being implemented only hesitantly. Finally, I present some lessons for gerontology as a scientific discipline that can be drawn from this chapter.

AN IDEAL–TYPICAL MODEL

The logic of the political economy of the Third Age can be explained in ideal–typical terms. Ideal types are images that result from a combination of characteristics. They are clear-cut and internally consistent. However, they do not always completely match reality. Instead, real cases usually represent ideal types to varying degrees (Weber, 1904/1973). In the following pages, I first define the third-ager as an ideal type of retiree. Then I characterize the relevance of third-agers for welfare states in ideal–typical terms.

The Third-Ager as an Ideal Type of Retiree

For political economy-oriented considerations, one can define the Third Age as an ideal type. To do so, one needs to group older people according to their most relevant characteristics. In the context of the political economy, the most relevant characteristics of older people are their health status and productivity. Figure 3.1 shows how older people can be grouped according to those characteristics. As a result, one obtains four ideal types, one of them being the "typical third-ager."

Figure 3.1 considers all older people, which it equates to the group of retirees (Kohli, 2007). Figure 3.1 then divides the group of older people into third- and fourth-agers. The Third Age is equated to the healthy life years after retirement, and thus time that can be used for productive activities. The fourth age is equated to the time retirees spend in poor health (Komp et al., 2009; Laslett, 1996). It stands for a period with little physical capability for engagement in productive activities.

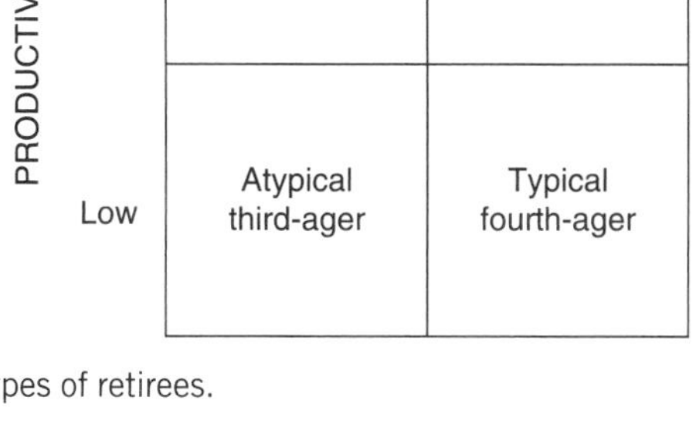

FIGURE 3.1   Ideal types of retirees.

The groups of third- and fourth-agers are further divided into a typical and an atypical group. Typical third-agers are assumed to be productive through a range of activities, extending from paid work to volunteering, informal caregiving, do-it-yourself, and care for oneself. Generally speaking, any activity that produces goods or services has to be considered as "productive" (Sherraden, Morrow-Howell, Hinterlong, & Rozario, 2001; Walker, 2006a). Political discussions, however, largely concentrate on older workers and only sometimes also mention older volunteers (Jegermalm & Jeppsson Grassman, 2009; Walker, 2006a). In their discussions, governments sometimes try to give the idea of being a third-ager a normative character. They can do this by stressing the responsibility older people have toward society. Consequently, being productive takes on the character of an obligation instead of a choice (Minkler & Holstein, 2008).

Typical fourth-agers are assumed to be unproductive due to poor health (Laslett, 1996). They lack the physical capability for productivity, which makes them unattractive for governmental programs seeking to increase productivity. Atypical fourth-agers are productive in spite of poor health. They can be seen as individuals who are productive despite being in poor health. These fourth-agers particularly soften the effect of population aging on the productivity level in a country. Welfare states could benefit from facilitating productive opportunities for fourth-agers. However, addressing them in such programs may not only be viewed as ineffective, it might also provoke moral concerns (Kohli, 1991). This could lead to opposition and a loss of votes in subsequent elections (Vis & Van Kersbergen, 2007).

The Relevance of Third-Agers for Welfare States

The relevance of third-agers for welfare states can be explained with the ideal types developed above. For the sake of simplicity, I will only use the typical third-ager and the typical fourth-ager in the explanations. In this context, I therefore consider atypical third-agers as those who governments hope will become typical third-agers if provided with proper incentives. I moreover consider atypical fourth-agers as a valuable resource for welfare states that governments do not react to. The relationship between typical third-agers, typical fourth-agers, and welfare states is portrayed in Figure 3.2.

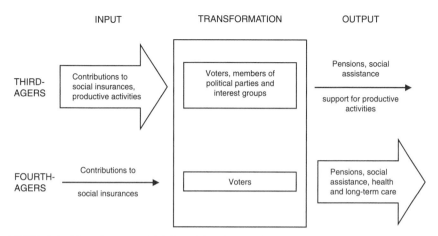

FIGURE 3.2   The relevance of third- and fourth-agers for welfare states.

Figure 3.2 is based on the economic rationale central to political economy. The left-hand side shows resources that governments can use for their activities (input). The right-hand side shows product that governments need to provide (output). The center shows the welfare state bringing input and output into an optimal relation to each other (transformation). This model is based on the idea that governments in welfare states redistribute resources in order to regulate risks stemming from market dependency (Svallfors, 2004). The upper part of the model gives the input, transformation, and output relating to third-agers. The lower part of the model gives the corresponding information for fourth-agers. The inclusion of fourth-agers in the model allows for comparisons and brings out the specificities of third-agers.

The input that third-agers provide is higher than that of fourth-agers. Third- and fourth-agers might contribute to social insurances. This can occur when contributions to social insurances end at a certain age, rather than with retirement. This is, for example, the case in some private insurance plans (Organisation for Economic Co-operation and Development, International Social Security Association, & International Organisation of Pension Supervisors, 2008). It might, moreover, occur when contributions continue throughout the entire life course such as in German mandatory health insurance (European Commission, 2007). It also occurs when social insurances are tax financed. Examples for such a mode of financing are the Spanish family allowances and the Austrian long-term care benefits (European Commission, 2007). In contrast to fourth-agers, third-agers also deliver input beyond social security contributions. This input takes the form of productive activities such as volunteering and informal caregiving (Van der Meer, 2006).

The transformation from input to output is more strongly influenced by third-agers than by fourth-agers. Both third- and fourth-agers influence governmental activities through voting (Goerres, 2008). Third-agers additionally shape governmental activities through their participation in political parties and interest groups. This participation is possible because of third-agers' good health. It is moreover facilitated by third-agers' interest in political activities. This interest has been reported to be strong in many countries (Goss, 1999; Karisto, 2007).

The output is more strongly oriented toward the demands of fourth-agers than those of third-agers. Both third- and fourth-agers receive pensions. These pensions can be public, private, or occupational (Myles, 2002). Where they are insufficient, they might be supplemented with social assistance payments (Gornick, Munzi, Sierminski, & Smeeding, 2009). In addition to pensions, fourth-agers receive health care and possibly also benefits from long-term care insurances. Long-term care insurances exist in several countries, including Germany, Austria, and Luxembourg, and in the northern Italian province Bolzano-Alto Adige (Autonome Provinz Bozen-Südtirol - Abteilung 24 Sozialwesen, 2008; European Commission, 2007; Pavolini & Ranci, 2008). In contrast to fourth-agers, third-agers might also receive governmental support in their productive activities. This support could aim at motivating older people to engage in productive activities or increase the time they spend on such activities (Jegermalm & Jeppsson Grassman, 2009; Vellekoop Baldock, 1999; Warburton, Paynter, & Petriwskyj, 2007).

Summing up, the relevance of third-agers for welfare states differs drastically from that of fourth-agers. Today's ideal–typical fourth-agers largely depict the stereotype of older people that was prominent in the 1980s. At that time, politicians portrayed older people as being unlikely to contribute to welfare states while extensively profiting from them (Binstock, 1984; Walker, 1990). Ideal–typical third-agers, on the other hand, turn this relationship upside down. They can contribute to welfare states on a large scale, while benefitting from them to a smaller degree than do fourth-agers. They moreover draw attention to the relationship between citizens and welfare states. While fourth-agers mainly interact with welfare states through the exchange of goods and services, third-agers can take a more active approach. When volunteering and providing informal care, they perform tasks that governments would otherwise have to organize themselves (Evers, 2005; Svetlik, 1993). When participating in political parties and interest groups, they moreover directly influence political processes. Fourth-agers, in contrast, rely on voting for a representative who acts on their behalf (Goerres, 2007).

A LONG WAY FROM THE IDEAL-TYPICAL MODEL TO REALITY

While policy makers usually acknowledge the existence of third-agers, they have not yet implemented all the ideas resulting from a political economy of the Third Age. There are various reasons for this neglect. Some reasons, such as path dependency and the redistribution of resources, are common to all welfare reforms (Alexander, 2001). Other reasons, such as the identification of third-agers, the welfare mix, and the moral economy of aging, are typical for the political economy of the Third Age. In the following section, I discuss these reasons in turn.

Path Dependency

The concept of path dependency describes how decisions are informed by previous decisions (Kay, 2005; Wilsford, 1994). On the one hand, it implies that established points of view are applied to new situations and new phenomena (Kay, 2005). In our case, this means that established perceptions of older people are applied to third-agers. Third-agers might thus be addressed as individuals in need of support, even though they are capable of providing support themselves. An example from Italy illustrates this: In 1993, the President of the Regional Council of Tuscany, Paolo Benelli, attended a meeting of the regional council of AUSER. AUSER is an association of older volunteers, which supports *inter alia* frail older people. During this meeting, Benelli underlined the contribution the social services provided by AUSER made to their older users' health and social integration. However, he never addressed the point that the people he was talking to, who were providing these services, were older people themselves (Anonymous, 1993). On the other hand, path dependency implies that established approaches for dealing with a situation are transferred to new situations (Scarbrough, 2000; Wilsford, 1994). In our case, this means that support programs for third-agers are likely to resemble established support programs for fourth-agers. Both aspects of path dependency hinder political activities that are sensitive toward the third-agers' specificities.

Redistribution of Resources

The adoption of a political economy of the Third Age entails a shift of priorities and activities in governmental activities. Consequently, resources need to be redistributed to support these new priorities and activities (Barr, 2004). For example, some of the finances and manpower used to support social care services and civic initiatives could be used to support productive aging activities. While individuals who receive more resources might support redistribution, those who are provided fewer resources will most likely disagree with the change. Their disagreement is particularly likely to hamper the process of redistribution in two cases: when a critical mass of people is concerned or when strong lobby groups coordinate efforts to support those viewed as being disenfranchised (Hacker, 2004; Pierson, 2006). Plans to allocate resources to support programs for third-agers might, therefore, create opposition.

This opposition becomes particularly complex when the needs of third-agers are posed against the needs of fourth-agers. This can occur when the resources that governments use to support productive aging activities are taken from budgets formerly used to support services for frail older people. Such redistribution is advantageous for policy makers, because it requires only a slight reallocation of budgets. It, thereby, puts comparatively weak pressure for justification on policy makers (Schyns, 2006). At the same time, however, it creates a complex network of opposition groups. This occurs in three ways. First, a great number of people are affected, which means that the opposition groups are especially large and potentially powerful. For example, if all retirees in Austria are affected, then this includes about 1.8 million people, which is more than 60% of the population aged 50 and over (Brugiavini, Croda, & Mariuzzo, 2005; Statistik Austria, 2009). Second, older people are generally perceived as deserving, which makes budget cuts affecting them morally controversial (Kohli, 1991, 2007). The controversy is likely to be even stronger if fourth-agers are affected by the cuts. Fourth-agers are considered deserving because they have a long history of paid work and also they face problems related to poor health. If this group faces diminished resources in any capacity, lobbyist groups are likely to coordinate strong oppositional support. Third, third-agers are often members of associations (Erlinghagen & Hank, 2006), in which they have forums to make their opinions heard. Summing up, redistribution of resources could potentially place the needs of third-agers at conflict with the needs of fourth-agers and create complex oppositional support mechanisms that may divide older adults as a group.

Identification of Third-Agers

The political economy of the Third Age depends on the differentiation between third-agers and fourth-agers. Correctly identifying third-agers among older people is essential for political intervention drawing on the political economy of the Third Age. It helps governments estimate how urgent such intervention is, it helps in the design of the intervention, and it is necessary when evaluating the effects of the intervention. Without an accurate way of identifying the young old, intervention based on a political economy of the Third Age can be difficult and imprecise at best.

In practice, the identification of third-agers is difficult for several reasons. First, older people are usually classified according to their age, not according to their characteristics (James & Wink, 2007; Neugarten, 1974; Settersten & Mayer, 1997). The only exception is informal care, where caregivers are often classified according to their relationship to the person in need of care (e.g., Papastavrou, Kalokerinou, Papacostas, Tsangari, & Sourtzi, 2007; Philip, 2001). The established system of classifying people would, therefore, have to be fundamentally changed so that third-agers are identified based on their unique characteristics, not their age. Second, the established measures used to evaluate the impact of population aging are also usually based on age. The best known of these measures, the old age dependency ratio, even links productivity to a certain age-group (Crown, 1985). It defines individuals aged 20–64 as "productive" and everyone above these ages as "unproductive." By dividing the number of unproductive individuals by the number of productive individuals, the dependency ratio indicates how many older people a middle-aged individual supports (Bruckner, 2009). In the era of the Third Age, this approach is especially problematic. It neglects to consider productivity after retirement and, thereby, overlooks the essence of a political economy of the Third Age. Adapting this measure to fit the idea of the Third Age, however, is challenging. The necessary data about healthy retirees in a population is not readily available. It would have to be calculated from suitable data sets (see Chapter 6 for suggestions on how this can be done).

Welfare Mix

The welfare mix describes the contribution of different kinds of actors for welfare production in a country. It usually considers the state, the market, voluntary associations (the third sector), and families as actors (Esping-Andersen, 1990; Evers, 1993). This focus on a multitude of actors is important for third-agers because their contributions to welfare production usually take the form of paid work, volunteering, and caregiving within the family (see, e.g., Hank & Stuck, 2008; Laslett, 1996; Morrow-Howell, Hinterlong, & Sherraden, 2001). The more attention governments give to the welfare mix, the easier it will be for them to implement policies based on a political economy of the Third Age.

While policy makers have paid increasing attention to the welfare mix over the last few years (see, e.g., Evers, 2005; Pavolini & Ranci, 2008; Powell & Barrientos, 2004), they still largely focus on paid work when it comes to productivity in old age. For example, governments and intergovernmental organizations such as the European Union and the World Health Organization have promoted active aging for more than a decade (Walker, 2002). In their discussions, they stressed aims such as increased productivity, health, and well-being. The list of activities that were relevant for those aims included paid work, volunteering, and informal caregiving (Walker, 2006a, 2009). In practice, however, paid work is at the center of governmental activities and remains the only productive activity supported in this capacity (Walker, 2009).

The Moral Economy of Aging

The moral economy draws attention to the social norms and moral assumptions underlying social interaction (Mau, 2004). In the moral economy of aging, the focus is on the norms and moral assumptions regarding old age. In the context of a political economy of the Third Age, the most important of these assumptions is that older people deserve to be unproductive and inactive, if they desire such a state. Older people contributed to society and the welfare state through decades of paid work. By the time they reach retirement, it is assumed that they have fulfilled the socially defined requirement of contributions to society (Kohli, 1991, 2007). Consequently, encouraging older people to contribute to the welfare state could be considered excessive and unfair. It could thus lead to protest, opposition, and the loss of votes in subsequent elections (Vis & van Kersbergen, 2007). Governments might therefore consider pursuing a political economy of the Third Age as risky and distance themselves from it for strategic reasons.

FUTURE STEPS: ISSUES TO CONSIDER

In the era of the Third Age, the political economy of aging gains in importance. It helps us get a better understanding of the impact that aging populations have on welfare states. When differentiating between the impact of third- and fourth-agers, we find that population aging does not necessarily place a strain on welfare states. Due to third-agers' engagement in productive activities, the effect of population aging on welfare states might just as well be neutral or positive. This challenges the neoliberal argument that population aging necessitates welfare state cutbacks (Pierson, 2006). It seems important that future studies in gerontology and political science consider the arguments made by the political economy of the Third Age. In this way, they could paint a more accurate picture of the welfare policies needed in the era of the Third Age.

Advancement of the political economy of the Third Age depends on two things. First, productive activities other than paid work have to be socially recognized. This perspective has been stressed under the rubric of "productive aging" for several years (see, e.g., Bass, Caro, & Chen, 1993). By now, the gerontological community seems to have accepted this perspective, while other scientific disciplines and policy makers still seem to lag behind. Future gerontological studies, therefore, need to continue stressing this issue. Second, third-agers need to be recognized as a social group with unique characteristics, not as an age group. Such a perspective makes their specificities more visible and governmental intervention more effective. The book at hand provides a foundation by which to promote this perspective. Future studies can further develop this perspective by exploring the challenges and opportunities its emergence implies. They can moreover facilitate its use by developing ways of identifying third-agers (see Chapter 6). Ideally, a variable identifying third-agers should be included in data sets.

Although it can help us reorient discussions about population aging to be more opportunity oriented rather than problem oriented, promoting the political economy of the Third Age also brings with it some risks. Labeling third-agers as "productive" and as a resource to welfare states impacts the image of fourth-agers. They are indirectly labeled as "unproductive" and described as a burden on welfare states (Phillipson, 2005). The political economy of the Third Age will, therefore, not necessarily resolve the negative image of older people. Instead, it might simply concentrate this negative image on fourth-agers. The result is likely to lance a new form of agism (Hagestad & Uhlenberg, 2005).

Such negative stereotyping of fourth-agers is not only undesirable, it also cannot be justified with the ideal–typical considerations presented in this chapter. It rarely happens that real persons perfectly correspond to an ideal type. In lieu thereof, they usually fall in between ideal types, combining characteristics of multiple types (Weber, 1904/1973). This could, for example, happen when an individual's health status fluctuates or when they repeatedly pick up and stop participating in productive activities. Moreover, this chapter focused on one kind of inequality only: the one between third- and fourth-agers. It did not consider other kinds of inequalities, for example across genders, levels of socioeconomic status, and degrees of urbanization. To make a more accurate statement about the situation of a person, all these kinds of inequalities need to be jointly considered. This is essential for future gerontological research.

In summary, the effects of population aging need to be reevaluated in the era of the Third Age. The political economy of the Third Age demonstrates how the effect of aging populations on welfare states might be opposed to what was previously assumed, especially neoliberalist conceptions. Population aging can have a positive effect on welfare states if productive activities other than paid work are also considered. However, we must be cautious so as not to create new forms of agism when applying this perspective.

REFERENCES

Alexander, G. (2001). Institutions, path dependence and democratic consolidation. *Journal of Theoretical Politics, 13*(3), 249–269.

Anonymous. (1993). Il Ruolo del Volontari dei Servizi Sociali [The Role of voluntary social services]. *Toscana - Consiglio Regionale, 9*, 214.

Autonome Provinz Bozen-Südtirol - Abteilung 24 Sozialwesen (2008). *Die Pflegeversicherung [The long-term care insurance]*. Bolzano: Autonome Provinz Bozen-Südtirol.

Barr, N. (2004). *The economics of the welfare state* (4th ed.) Oxford: Oxford University Press.

Bass, S. A., Caro, F. G., & Chen, Y. P. (Eds.). (1993). *Achieving a productive aging society*. Westport, CT: Auburn House.

Binstock, R. H. (1984). Reframing the agenda of policies on aging. In M. Minkler & C. L. Estes (Eds.), *Readings in the political economy of aging* (pp. 157-167). Amityville, NY: Baywood Publishing.

Bruckner, E. (2009). Employment population age-share differences: An international comparison of the economic impact of population aging. *Journal of Aging and Social Policy, 21*(1), 17-30.

Brugiavini, A., Croda, E., & Mariuzzo, F. (2005). Labour force participation of the elderly: Unused capacity? In A. Börsch-Supan, A. Brugiavini, H. Jürges, J. Mackenbach, J. Siegrist & G. Weber (Eds.), *Health, ageing and retirement in Europe—First Results from SHARE* (pp. 236-240). Mannheim: Mannheim Institute for the Economics of Ageing.

Cowell, F. (2006). *Microeconomics. Principles and analysis.* Oxford: Oxford University Press.

Crown, W. H. (1985). Some thoughts on reformulating the dependency ratio. *The Gerontologist, 25*(2), 166-171.

Erlinghagen, M., & Hank, K. (2006). The participation of older European in volunteer work. *Ageing and Society, 26*(4), 567-584.

Esping-Andersen, G. (1990). *The three worlds of welfare capitalism.* Princeton, NY: Princeton University Press.

European Commission. (2007). *Social protection in the member states of the European Union, of the European Economic Area and in Switzerland 2007. Comparative tables.* Cologne: European Commission.

Evers, A. (1993). The welfare mix approach. Understanding the pluralism of welfare systems. In A. Evers & I. Svetlik (Eds.), *Balancing pluralism. New welfare mixes in care for the elderly* (pp. 3-31). Aldershot: Avebury.

Evers, A. (2005). Mixed welfare systems and hybrid organizations: Changes in the governance and provision of social services. *International Journal of Public Administration, 28*(9), 737-748.

Goerres, A. (2007). Why are older people more likely to vote? The impact of ageing on electoral turnout in Europe. *British Journal of Politics and International Relations, 9*(1), 90-121.

Goerres, A. (2008). The grey vote: Determinants of older voters' party choice in Britain and West Germany. *Electoral Studies, 27*(2), 285-304.

Gornick, J. C., Munzi, T., Sierminski, E., & Smeeding, T. (2009). Income, assets and poverty: Older women in comparative perspective. *Journal of Women, Politics and Policy, 30*(2), 272-300.

Goss, K. A. (1999). Volunteering and the long civic generation. *Nonprofit and Voluntary Sector Quarterly, 28*(4), 378-415.

Hacker, J. S. (2004). Privatizing risk without privatizing the welfare state: The hidden politics of social policy retrenchment in the United States. *American Political Science Review, 98*(2), 243-260.

Hagestad, G. O., & Uhlenberg, P. (2005). The social separation of young and old: A root of ageism. *Journal of Social Issues, 61*(2), 343-360.

Hank, K., & Stuck, S. (2008). Volunteer work, informal help, and care among the 50+ in Europe: Further evidence for 'linked' productive activities at older ages. *Social Science Research, 37*(4), 1280-1291.

Jackson, W. A. (1991). On the treatment of population ageing in economic theory. *Ageing and Society, 11*(1), 59-68.

James, J. B., & Wink, P. (2007). *The crown of life: Dynamics of the early postretirement period. Annual Review of Gerontology and Geriatrics, Vol. 26.* New York: Springer Publishing.

Jegermalm, M., & Jeppsson Grassman, E. (2009). Caregiving and volunteering among older people in Sweden—Prevalence and profiles. *Journal of Aging and Social Policy, 21*(4), 352-373.

Karisto, A. (2007). Finnish baby boomers and the emergence of the third age. *International Journal of Ageing and Later Life, 2*(2), 91-108.

Kay, A. (2005). A critique of the use of path dependency in policy studies. *Public Administration, 83*(3), 553-571.

Kohli, M. (1991). Retirement and the moral economy of growing old: A historical interpretation of the German case. In M. Minkler & C. L. Estes (Eds.), *Critical perspectives on aging: The political and moral economy of growing old* (pp. 273-292). Amityville, NY: Baywood.

Kohli, M. (2007). The institutionalization of the life course: Looking back to look ahead. *Research in Human Development, 4*, 253-271.

Komp, K., van Tilburg, T., & Broese van Groenou, M. I. (2009). The influence of the welfare state on the number of young old persons. *Ageing and Society, 29*(4), 609-624.

Laslett, P. (1996). *A fresh map of life: The emergence of the third age* (2nd ed.). Basingstoke, New Hampshire: Macmillan.

Lee, S. (2001). Political economy. In R. J. B. Jones (Ed.), *Routledge encyclopedia of international political economy. Vol. 3: Entries P-Z* (pp. 1225-1230). London: Routledge.

Mau, S. (2004). Welfare regimes and the norms of social exchange. *Current Sociology, 52*(1), 53-74.

Minkler, M., & Estes, C. L. (Eds.). (1999). *Critical gerontology: Perspectives from political and moral economy.* Amityville, NY: Baywood Publishing.

Minkler, M., & Holstein, M. (2008) From civil rights to . . . civic engagement? Concerns of two older critical gerontologists about a "new social movement" and what it portends. *Journal of Aging Studies, 22*(2), 196-204.

Morrow-Howell, N., Hinterlong, J., & Sherraden, M. (2001). (Eds.). *Productive aging. Concepts and challenges.* Baltimore: Johns Hopkins University Press.

Myles, J. (2002). A new social contract for the elderly? In G. Esping-Andersen with D. Gallie, A. Hemerijk, & J. Myles, *Why we need a new welfare state* (pp. 130-172). Oxford: Oxford University Press.

Neugarten, B. (1974). Age groups in American society and the rise of the young old. *Annals of the American Academy of Political and Social Science, 415*(1), 187-198.

Offe, C. (1996). Democracy against the welfare state? In C. Offe (Ed.), *Modernity and the State. East, West* (pp. 147–182). Cambridge: Polity Press.

Organisation for Economic Co-operation and Development, International Social Security Association, & International Organisation of Pension Supervisors. (2008). *Complementary and private pensions throughout the world 2008.* Paris: Organisation for Economic Co-operation and Development.

Papastavrou, E., Kalokerinou, A., Papacostas, S. S., Tsangari, H., & Sourtzi, P. (2007). Caring for a relative with dementia: Family caregiver burden. *Journal of Advanced Nursing, 58*(5), 446–457.

Pavolini, E., & Ranci, C. (2008). Restructuring the welfare state: Reforms in long-term care in Europe. *Journal of European Social Policy, 18*(3), 246–259.

Philip, I. (Ed.). (2001). *Family care of older people in Europe.* Amsterdam: IOS Press.

Phillipson, C. (2005). The political economy of old age. In M. L. Johnson (Ed.), V. L. Bengtson, P. G. Coleman & T. B. L. Kirkwood (associate editors), *The Cambridge handbook of age and ageing* (pp. 502–509). Cambridge: Cambridge University Press.

Pierson, C. (2006). *Beyond the welfare state: The new political economy of welfare* (3rd ed.). Cambridge: Polity Press.

Powell, M., & Barrientos, A. (2004). Welfare regimes and the welfare mix. *European Journal of Political Research, 43*, 83–105.

Scarbrough, E. (2000). West European welfare states: The old politics of retrenchment. *European Journal of Political Research, 38*(2), 225–259.

Schyns, B. (2006). The role of implicit leadership theories in the performance appraisals and promotion recommendations of leaders. *Equal Opportunities International, 25*(3), 188–199.

Settersten, R. Jr., & Mayer, K. U. (1997). The measurement of age, age structuring, and the life-course. *Annual Review of Sociology, 23*, 233–261.

Sherraden, M., Morrow-Howell, N., Hinterlong, J., & Rozario, P. (2001). Productive aging. Theoretical choices and directions. In N. Morrow-Howell, J. Hinterlong & M. Sherraden (Eds.), *Productive aging. Concepts and challenges* (pp. 260–284). Baltimore: Johns Hopkins University Press.

Statistik Austria. (2009). *Jahresdurchschnittsbevölkerung seit 2001 nach fünfjährigen Altersgruppen und Geschlecht [Population as an annual average since 2001 per five-year age groups and gender].* Retrieved January 07, 2010, from http://www.statistik.at/web_de/statistiken/bevoelkerung/bevoelkerungsstruktur/bevoelkerung_nach_alter_geschlecht/023427.html .

Svallfors, S. (2004). Class, attitudes and the welfare state: Sweden in comparative perspective. *Social Policy and Administration, 38*(2), 119–138.

Svetlik, I. (1993). Regulation of the plural and mixed welfare systems. In A. Evers & I. Svetlik (Eds.), *Balancing pluralism. New welfare mixes in care for the elderly* (pp. 33–50). Aldershot: Avebury.

Van der Meer, M. (2006). Productivity among older people in the Netherlands: Variations by gender and the socio-spatial context in 2002–03. *Ageing and Society, 26*(6), 901–923.

Vellekoop Baldock, C. (1999). Seniors as volunteers: An international perspective on policy. *Ageing and Society, 19*(5), 581-602.

Vis, B., & van Kersbergen, K. (2007). Why and how do political actors pursue risky reforms? *Journal of Theoretical Politics, 19*(2), 153-172.

Von der Leyen, U. (2009). Grußwort [Greeting]. In Bundesarbeitsgemeinschaft der Seniorenorganisationen (Ed.), *Programmheft 9. Seniorentag, 08.-10. Juni 2009, Leipzig [Programme 9th Day for Senior Citizens, 08.-10. June 2009, Leipzig]* (p. 3). Bonn: Bundesarbeitsgemeinschaft der Seniorenorganisationen.

Walker, A. (1990). The economic 'burden' of ageing and the prospect of intergenerational conflict. *Ageing and Society, 10*(4), 377-396.

Walker, A. (2002). A strategy for active ageing. *International Social Security Association, 55*(1), 121-139.

Walker, A. (2006a). Active ageing in employment: Its meaning and potential. *Asia-Pacific Review, 13*(1), 78-93.

Walker, A. (2006b). Reexamining the political economy of aging: Understanding the structure/agency tension. In J. Baars, D. Dannefer, C. Phillipson & A. Walker (Eds.), *Aging, globalization and inequality. The new critical gerontology* (pp. 59-80). Amityville, NY: Baywood.

Walker, A. (2009). Commentary: The emergence and application of active aging in Europe. *Journal of Aging and Social Policy, 21*(1), 75-93.

Warburton, J., Paynter, J., & Petriwskyj, A. (2007). Volunteering as a productive aging activity: Incentives and barriers to volunteering by Australian seniors. *Journal of Applied Gerontology, 26*(4), 333-354.

Weber, M. (1973). Zur 'Objektivität' sozialwissenschaftlicher und sozialpolitischer Erkentnis [On the objectivity of insight from social science and social policy]. In M. Weber, *Gesammelte Aufsätze zur wissenschaftslehre [Collected essays on the theory of science]* (4th ed., pp. 146-214). Tübingen: J. C. B. Mohr. (Original work published 1904.)

Weingast, B. R., & Wittman, D. A. (2006). The reach of political economy. In B. R. Weingast & D. A. Wittman (Eds.), *The Oxford handbook of political economy* (pp. 21-25). Oxford: Oxford University Press.

Wilsford, D. (1994). Path dependency, or why history makes it difficult but not impossible to reform health care systems in a big way. *Journal of Public Policy, 14*(3), 251-283.

A Feminist Lens of the Third Age: Refining the Framework

Toni Calasanti and Neal King

A GENDERED LIFE COURSE IN THE ERA OF THE THIRD AGE

*T*he editors of this volume note the wide variety of uses of the Third Age concept. As it has diffused among disciplines and professions, it has resulted in exhortations of civic engagement (Laslett, 1987), studies of life satisfaction (James & Wink, 2007), and histories of consumerism (Gilleard & Higgs, 2009). Within this diversity, the bulk of scholarship conceives of the Third Age as a time of prosperity and health to celebrate and maximize through policy interventions. The notion sidesteps consideration of ageist exclusion itself and fails to attend to the effects of the accumulation of lifelong inequalities. It holds the most promise to those who want to preserve middle-aged vitality or who wish to *avoid* seeming old, frail, or withdrawn, and holds less promise to those of us who focus on understanding and ameliorating age inequality *per se*. This chapter explores ways in which the concept neglects feminist or critical gerontology and offers an alternative way to distinguish between the more prosperous and the more oppressed among old people. We conclude with suggestions for a research agenda on the Third Age more attentive to issues such as gender and other inequalities.

67

We do not mean to imply that the concept of the Third Age lacks merit. Rather, we note empirical challenges and the need for attention to the inequities that operate throughout life. We approach the assessment of social scientific concepts under the assumption that diverse approaches can be valid for different purposes. All categorizations collect diverse peoples under their labels, and all distinctions divide groups that share much in common. Scholars can always critique generalizations, labels, and divisions in empirical terms for these reasons. Even so, distinctions and groups are useful for analytic and political purposes, and bear defense in those terms. Distinctions among second, third, and fourth ages serve purposes other than the critique of age inequality, such that the relevance of those distinctions for feminist or critical gerontology remains unclear. The Third Age is one of several gerontological concepts (like successful aging and civic engagement) that have become popular in part for their promise to shield old people from the stigma of age and empower them to make contributions to their communities. But they may also draw the wrong distinction for a gerontology driven by the critique of ageism (see also Chapter 12, this book).

We elaborate this argument, first, with the empirical challenge— noting the public/private, careerist premise best fits relatively privileged workers with decades of steady, full-time labor-market activity. For other workers, the difference between work and retired life is not as clear as Third Age concepts suggest. We then focus on the inequities on which critical gerontology maintains its focus. We review research on the challenges faced by many retired people who might like to live up to Third Age ideals and show how these vary with social locations distinguished in terms of inequalities: gender, class, race, and age. With structural ageism squarely in mind, we advocate less attention to the construction of voluntary retirement as lifestyle and more attention to the constraints that prevent so many people from exercising such an option.

We do this in part to honor part of the original motivation of the concept, which aimed to improve the standing of old people in a society that was institutionalizing retirement for its most privileged groups. Laslett's (1987) stated intent was to describe a relatively prosperous time in the lives of a growing group, and to describe them in terms not tarnished by ageism, in order to suggest how members of this privileged group could best contribute to their communities. He noted a history of jaundiced, even hostile images of old age proffered by reformers, physicians, and the like: as illness, uselessness, and decay (p. 154). Laslett (1996) sought to focus instead on the value and productivity of the most privileged in their retired years. His elaboration of the concept more fully exhorted retirees to serve as guardians of culture and exemplars of voluntary citizenship (pp. 256–266). To this end, he defined the Third Age in terms of growing prosperity and lengthening lifespans at the national level.

Like many descriptive groupings, those of the Third Age come accompanied by caveats and cautions not to overgeneralize. Indeed, we take issue not with any one scholar's definition of this term but with those more commonly employed. Regardless of variation, some common premises appear across the Third Age literature:

1. The time between retirement and frailty is increasing; "the average person retiring today can anticipate living and being in good health at least 15 years beyond retirement" (James & Wink, 2007, p. xix).
2. This represents a new life stage, one characterized by good health and freedom from work or family obligations; "The post-retirement years are, for many, a time when there is no longer responsibility for childcare nor need for paid employment, the two obligations that would have structured much of preceding life" (Weiss & Bass, 2002, p. 3).
3. This lack of obligations and defined roles combines with good health to make this time of life "the age of opportunity for personal fulfillment" (James & Wink, 2007, p. xx).

Empirical Critique

Distinctions between the Second, Third, and Fourth Ages call attention to recent cohorts of retirees whose greater prosperity (and often earlier age of labor-force withdrawal) and health status allowed many to enter a lengthy period of leisure. Indeed, much of the discussion of the Third Age is predicated on a separation from paid work. But those distinctions rest upon observation of the institutionalization of retirement for well-paid, steadily employed breadwinners and do not describe other groups as well. And reference to the end of parenting obligations in lieu of retirement from paid employment, while providing a nod to gender concerns, fails to comprehend the continuity of care work—for children, grandchildren, and community—taken on disproportionately by women and especially poor women of color.

Early research on retirement proceeded in much the same way that investigations of men's and women's paid labor were conducted. Here, researchers employed a "job model" to explore men's experiences, which assumed that paid work is central in men's lives, influencing all other dimensions, including identity, and status relationships as well as family relationships. Researchers who explored women's paid work used a "gender" model that depicted family as central to women, with paid work influenced by this (Feldberg & Glenn, 1979). Thus "work" and "family" are construed as separate, unrelated realms, with paid work only important in men's lives. As a result, when the scholarly lens turned to retirement, men were assumed to face a difficult transition, while women—if examined at all—were thought simply to be returning to the families in which their identities were rooted.

Setting aside many possible objections to this depiction, we note that, once one takes health, income, and marital status into account, men generally show no ill effects from retirement (Beck, 1982)—an outcome that runs counter to the contention that work is central to their identity. Further, the importance of family to men's retirement satisfaction appears in the finding that being married (versus never married) appears to be far more crucial in explaining men's life satisfaction in retirement than women's, even though marital status has greater objective impact on women's retirement income (Calasanti, 1996). Positing the Third Age as a new life stage of unprecedented freedom in retirement reproduces rather than challenges the men-based, "separate spheres" assumptions that informed early research on the centrality of work and family.

Because much research on work and retirement defines work in terms of White, middle-class men's experiences, paid employment is taken to be very different from household work, both in terms of content and in how they might relate to one another. But the experiences of women who are retired reveal that these forms of work are not only separate but are both regarded as *work*. For instance, a study of 57 male and female retirees by the first author found that both men and women spoke of their retirement as a time of "freedom." But what this freedom meant varied tremendously based on gender, and demonstrated connections between these realms of work. Women's perceptions of work lives and retirement are of working at least two jobs; retirement entailed giving up labor-force activity but maintaining responsibility for domestic labor. Thus, women spoke of freedom in retirement as a relief from having to rush to complete domestic labor, or the chance to alter schedules such that they no longer needed to do laundry on particular days. By contrast, men spoke of no longer having to punch time clocks and of chances to try new activities—including domestic labor, returns to paid labor, hobbies, recreation, and other forms of culture (Calasanti, 1993) celebrated as characteristics of the Third Age. The ability of some (privileged) men to experience freedom in retirement rested on women's assumption of reproductive labor and domestic work (Calasanti & Slevin, 2001).

Work not only continues but can increase in retirement, in ways predicated on inequalities often obscured by notions of Third Age freedom. Consider the work lives of different groups, which complicate the notion of retirement on which the Third Age concept rests. In 2008, almost 1 million grandparents aged 65 or over maintained households in which their grandchildren lived (Administration on Aging, 2010). According to the U.S. Census Bureau (DeNavas-Walt, Proctor, & Smith, 2009), in 2007, 40% of grandparents whose grandchildren lived with them (a total of 2.5 million grandparents) were responsible for providing most of the basic needs of one or more of these grandchildren; and 1.5 million of these grandparents still worked for pay as well. Nine percent of all children in the United States live with their grandparents; of these, the majority live in their grandparent's home, indicating that in these multigenerational households, it is the grandparents who provide support. Finally, grandparents provide regular care for 30% of children under age 5 whose mothers work outside the home (DeNavas-Walt et al., 2009).

Care work can expand for potential third-agers in other ways as well. For instance, spouses make up one-quarter of informal caregivers for old people (Shirey & Summer, 2000). One can infer from research that these caregiving spouses are mostly old enough to enjoy the Third Age. In the first author's study, the average age of the spousal caregiver was 67 for women and 72 for men (Calasanti, 2006). And for many women of color, retirement means increased work for the broader community as they engage in race uplift (Calasanti & Slevin, 2001). Finally, a nationally representative 2009 survey finds that 36% of older parents (65+) reported that they have helped their children with childcare in the last year; 32% have helped with errands, housework, or home repairs (Pew Research Center, 2009). Thus, many people have failed to free themselves of the responsibilities of the Second Age.

The empirical challenge to the Third Age concept extends beyond noting the contiguity of work and retirement to finding that little distinguishes retirees from their younger counterparts. For instance, in a study of a nationally representative sample, Grafova, McGonagle, and Stafford find that, while those ostensibly living their Third Ages have generally seen increases in health and wealth, these two characteristics are related such that there is actually a "dispersion among the Third Age that ranges from those with good income and good health to those with failing health and limited income resources" (2007, p. 34). Likewise, McCullough and Polak highlight an absence of systematic variation in health and religiosity by retired status, such that "there may be no 'main effects' for the Third Age" on these measures of cultural engagement and well-being (2007, p. 189). James and Spiro find that "our [Health and Retirement Survey] data do not support the Third Age as a time of increasing well-being. Indeed, depression scores increase slightly across almost all waves of the data," findings that "are somewhat disturbing in the sense that retirement is a life phase meant to be the reward for a life well lived" (2007, p. 167).

Thus, the Third Age can appear to be a phantom phenomenon, visible mainly in the most privileged sector. Our critique extends beyond the descriptive shortcomings of the Third Age concept, however. Even taking into account the price one pays by grouping diverse people under any label, one can still assess its utility in terms of the larger purpose of the scholarship to inform political analysis and policy. Consideration at that level raises questions about the morals of Laslett's project and of feminist and critical gerontology *per se*.

Political Critique

Consider, for example, the political economic implications of the Third Age as a marketing scheme. Distancing themselves from Laslett's moralistic approach to old age, Gilleard and Higgs (2009) and Higgs and Jones (2008) have focused on spending patterns. They chart the rise of a consumer lifestyle among retired people and the hegemonic role of the Third Age in spurring this self-expression and the construction of individual agency (see also Chapter 2, this book). For Higgs and Jones (2008), study of the Third Age as a set of consumption patterns for the privileged is more worthwhile than focus on the inequities blurred or even hidden by the concept. They caution against ignoring that "the incomes and standard of living in the EU and North America have improved greatly over the past few decades" and distance themselves from the identification of older people as a "category of social policy needing intervention" (p. 26). For their purposes, the most relevant historical shifts and group differences are those that determine generation-specific discretionary spending rather than those that determine age-related inequality.

These analysts take a sophisticated, sociological approach to their study of late capitalism and the consumerist tendency to oppose individual agency to structural constraint (Gilleard & Higgs, 2009, p. 26). Our reservations about the assessment of consumerism offered by Gilleard and Higgs (2009, p. 29) include a concern for their tendency to focus on trends that have most to do with the populations of the EU and North America who had been the most privileged on the shop floor: The White men whose experiences of work seemed to be "hollowed out" by decreased homogenization. The road from class politics, to identity politics, to lifestyle politics (p. 31) will probably seem less remarkable to most other groups. We suggest different distinctions not because their analysis fundamentally fails but because our interest and focus are on age inequality *per se*. We therefore urge a distinction based not on chronological age or retired status of the household breadwinner, but on experience of ageist exclusion: "Old" is a social location of relative exclusion, whereas "adult" unmarked by age is a location of relative inclusion into networks of occupation and familial privilege. Social location on that map of age relations influences the extent to which the Third Age becomes a privilege to enjoy or an ideal out of reach and the repercussions of this Third Age for ageism itself. We thus study not consumer habits of the more privileged but instead the mechanisms underlying that prosperity, and which deny it to so many; and we explore age relations that create the stigma afflicting so many old people—consumers and otherwise. To these ends, we suggest an alternative framework which focuses on inequalities in households, labor-market participation, income, dependence on safety nets, consequent health outcomes, and rates and levels of retirement. Just as Antonucci, Ajrouch, and Birditt (2007) use Survey of Social Relations data to lend support to cumulative advantage theory, with its focus on inequalities by age, gender, race, and education, we review various reports of inequalities in old age to suggest that the distinctions between Second, Third, and Fourth Age are not the most relevant for the study of inequality.

Consider the issue of wealth in the Third Age. Official recognition of the number of poor over age 65 has doubled recently—not due to radical changes in circumstances but due to recognition that their numbers had been wrongly estimated before. Alternative poverty measures—which take medical expenses into account—find that 18.7% or almost 7.1 million old people are poor, compared to 9.7%, or 3.7 million, under the traditional measure (Associated Press, 2010). We are concerned not only with this level of poverty but also with group differences in access to Third Age lifestyles.

Together with the findings of continuity between Second and Third Age, such data suggest that distinctions that accrue across the life course, such as those based on social inequalities, may be more salient, especially when people enter the time designated as Third Age. That is, the postemployment era may indeed be a different period, but one marked by the intersections of these inequalities with those based on age relations. In this sense, we may re-vision the time before frailty marks one as "old," wherein people are faced with ageism, and to which they bring varying material and social resources—based on the intersections of gender, race, ethnicity, class, and sexuality—with which to resist being subjected to this form of inequality. Perhaps this is one of the number of possible reformulations of the Third Age that may be considered.

FOCUS ON SOCIAL INEQUITIES

Cumulative social inequalities based on gender, race, class, and sexuality influence later life by influencing access and earnings then intersect with ageism to affect exclusions from social life. For example, gender differences in labor-force remuneration persist despite women's increased employment rates. According to Census data, the female/male earnings ratio from 1960 until 1981 was fairly static, hovering at about 0.60. It rose to 0.70 by 1990; continued a slow rise to about 0.75 by the turn of the century, after which it fluctuated between 0.75 and 0.77 through 2008 (DeNavas-Walt et al., 2009).

Looking at race and ethnicity reveals similarly persistent economic inequalities, as race- and ethnicity-based distributions of income in the United States changed very little between 1972 and 2008 (DeNavas-Walt et al., 2009, p. 8). The impact of such systematic differences in earnings appears all the more starkly in a time of recession. During the economic downturn that began in 2007, real median household income in the United States fell for all racial and ethnic groups, yet important differences among groups remain: as of 2008, non-Hispanic White household income stood at 55,530 US$; that of Asians, at 65.637 US$; that of Hispanics (any race), 37,913 US$; and that of Blacks at 34,218 US$. During this same period, mean per capita income (derived by dividing total income of a particular group by total population of that group) also dropped for all racial and ethnic groups. Non-Hispanic Whites saw their income fall by 2.9%; for Blacks, 3.8% (32,244–31,313 US$); Asians, 2.4%

(31,050–30,292 US$); and Hispanics, (any race) 3.3% (16,203–15,674 US$).[1] Thus, while all groups saw significant decreases, those with the lowest incomes (Blacks and Hispanics) also saw the largest percentage decreases (DeNavas-Walt et al., 2009, Table 1, p. 7).

Recession also does not affect all classes equally, and the rich do in fact get richer. That is, income inequality has increased such that the shares of aggregate income going to the lowest, second, and middle quintiles all decreased (down 0.1%, 0.2%, and 0.2%, respectively); the fourth quintile remained unchanged, garnering 22.9% of income, and the share of aggregate income going to the highest quintile actually increased 0.5–49% (DeNavas-Walt et al., 2009, p. 11). Thus, this recession has exacerbated inequality and made the Third Age descriptor even less likely for future retirees.

Inequalities based on gender, race, ethnicity, and class take on greater salience as people age. Global competition and the spread of neoliberalism have combined to increase both the insecurity of employment and retrenchment of the welfare state. Workers face increasing odds of losing their jobs and difficulty finding comparable employment in later life (Johnson, 2009; Roscigno, 2010), while simultaneously being encouraged to take responsibility for funding their own retirement through the use of pensions, which, in turn, reflect the volatility of the global stock market (Phillipson, 2009). Phillipson and Vincent (2007) note that many of the risks associated with old age, such as the potential for poverty or loss of health, have not diminished with time. The major shift is rather in the retraction of the welfare state and its accompanying safety net, which has left individual families—and women in particular—increasingly responsible for providing care work and medical care, along with financial security.

The recession that began in 2007 presents an obvious structural caveat to a distinction between the Third and Fourth Ages. Family wealth has dropped precipitously, and "this sharp drop in total wealth immediately translated into an equally sharp increase in retirement income insecurity" (Weller, 2009, p. 1). But such retirement insecurity is neither new nor short-lived, and older people already had increased their labor market activity in part due to concerns about their ability to retire and have financial security (Johnson, 2009). Men's trend toward early retirement slowed in the 1990s and by 2000, employment levels for older male workers began to rise. Among men aged 65–69, labor force participation rates increased from 25% in 1993 to 34% in 2006. Women aged 55 have steadily increased their labor force participation rates over the last four decades. Similar to men's patterns, the largest increases for the older groups of women have occurred since the mid-1990s (Federal Interagency Forum on Aging-Related Statistics, 2008). As of 2008, 16.8% (6.2 million people) of those over age 65 are in the labor force, a full 21.5% of men and 13.3% of women in that age group (Administration on Aging, 2010).

Because the recession reflects global trends concerning work insecurity, a situation that is neither confined to the United States nor likely to disappear, it portends persisting constraints on long, healthy retirements—not only because of gender, race, and class inequalities in labor market outcomes, but because of ageism as well. Reporting on data drawn from the Bureau of Labor Statistics from 2007 to 2009, Johnson (2009) finds that the current recession's decline in labor force participation rates for men aged 25–54 is in contrast to the increase seen among older men, especially those aged 62–69, and all women. Indeed, older women's participation rose by 2.7%, the greatest increase during that two-year period (Johnson, 2009, Table 2, p. 28). At the same time, he finds that in 2009, "unemployment rates for older workers have reached record levels" in part because those who might be eligible for early retirement remain in the labor market (Johnson, 2009, p. 26). In July 2009, 2 million adults aged 55 and older were unemployed, more than twice as many as before the recession began in November 2007—the highest rate for women aged 55–64 since 1948. Among those of retirement age, the unemployment rate for men was 6.8% (about twice as high as before the recession) and 7.3% for women— again, an all-time high (Johnson, 2009, p. 26).[2]

What these data reflect is not simply an exacerbation of inequalities based on gender, race, and class but their intersection with age relations, a reality reflected in the fact that age discrimination claims jumped 25% from 2007 to 2008: from 19,103 to 24,582. These claims dropped but remain high in 2009, at 22,778 (U.S. Equal Employment Opportunity Commission, 2009). Some employers view older workers as more costly than younger workers as the former tend to have higher wages and higher benefit costs through contributions to pensions and health insurance. For these reasons, getting rid of older workers can be seen as a way to cut costs. As a result, over the last two decades, older workers have faced significant job displacement. Coupled with ageism in the labor market, they often face longer bouts of unemployment than do younger workers, while reemployment tends to occur in lower-paying jobs (Roscigno, 2010). Johnson (2009) notes that the consequences of unemployment in later life are especially serious. Not only does it take longer to become reemployed, increasing the difficulty of meeting household expenses at the time, but old workers also lose income and withholdings that count toward their Social Security and/or other pensions, and also usually end up in jobs that pay much less than previous occupations. As a result, they also will have lower incomes in retirement (p. 29). In short, the recession only highlights what has been true for older workers in general and particular groups of older workers for some time. That is, while workers are staying in the workforce longer, they are also among the most vulnerable workers.

Flippen and Tienda's (2000) longitudinal research on labor force pathways to retirement sheds light on the ways that race, ethnicity, and gender intersect with age to shape the paid work/retirement relationship. They begin with the observation that research conducted predominantly on White, middle-class men tends to document the importance of the availability of such incentives as social security and private pensions for retirement decision-making—and thus, we note, the path to the Third Age. For workers, mainly racial and ethnic minority group members and women "labor market constraints, poor health, and family caregiving obligations" are greater determinants (p. S14). Insecurity of employment among middle-aged women and racial/ethnic minority group members constrains and muddies their retirement decisions, making the prospects all the more ambiguous: "For these workers, retirement is not a single, irreversible event that represents the culmination of career employment, but rather a transition from employment to unemployment, retirement, or nonparticipation that may be temporary" (p. S26).

Racial and ethnic minority group members exhibit similar patterns of labor-market exit (Flippen & Tienda, 2000). They are more likely than Whites to be unemployed and out of the labor force in the cross-sectional analysis and also more likely to become unemployed over time. Once unemployed, Black and Hispanic older workers are less likely to find new jobs and thus face long-term joblessness or leave the labor force altogether discouraged. When gender is entered into the equation, Hispanic women emerge as particularly disadvantaged (p. S25).

The gender, race, and ethnic differences in employment pathways persist even when analysts control for human capital. Flippen and Tienda (2000) conclude that this points cumulative disadvantage, in which those who have difficulty with employment in their earlier years find themselves more vulnerable to job loss and other involuntary pathways out of the labor force in later life. They suggest that, as more minority group members enter old age, economic inequality among elders is also likely to rise (p. S26). For old people with low incomes and rates of steady employment, Third Age ideals may have scant relevance.

Scholars have long commented on the decline of retirement as a clear-cut shift in workers' lives. Before the turn of this century, for instance, between one-third and one-half of men reported that they did not permanently leave the labor force when they left their full-time jobs. Many reduced to part time, took temporary jobs, or re-entered full-time work, often more than once (Pampel, 1998; Quinn, Burkhauser, & Myers, 1990). Research has shown that race and ethnicity have shaped retirement such that, for instance, some older Black men see themselves as "nonretired"—they work less than 20 hours a week or not at all, but do not attribute the reduction in hours to being retired (Brown, 2009). Their higher disability rates—attributable in part to the physically demanding nature of their jobs as manual laborers—provide one explanation, and the instability of their jobs (and resultant lack of retirement benefits) provides another. Combined with their lower life expectancy, Black men spend larger parts of their lives in the labor market, suggesting that retirement is much more a White than Black experience (Hayward, Friedman, & Chen, 1996). The frequent disruptions to employment faced by other racial and ethnic minority-group members leads to similar differences in retirement, further shaped by gender. For example, Mexican Americans have similar patterns of labor-market instability and lack of access to pensions as Blacks. Men but not women among them are more likely to call themselves retired if they receive retirement income, while women are more likely to see retirement as an activity status (Zsembik & Singer, 1990).

The Third Age is thus most relevant to the most privileged in what many term the Global North; and globalization challenges its permanence—through its impacts on transfer and insurance programs of the welfare state, global markets for labor and pension funds. The results of the patterns of employment, unpaid work, and income that we have reviewed include differences in health and health care, which also affect the ability to realize the ideals of Third Age engagement. Lower-skilled jobs increase the likelihood of exposure to toxins; racial and ethnic minority group members are more likely to occupy such jobs, as well as physically demanding jobs that increase their risks (Brown, 2009). Work and health are related such that those who work unstable or low-paid jobs have few benefits and lower access to health care, which influences their access to higher wages. In preretirement years, Blacks and Hispanics are less likely than Whites to have either employer-based health insurance and more likely to have access only through public, means-based programs. They also receive care in less optimal settings and cannot benefit from continuity of it (Williams, 2004). Racial differences in health persist regardless of income, or education (Brown, 2009), such that minority groups are more likely to enter the Third Age in poor physical health. Indeed, if frailty is a marker of the Fourth Age, they may skip the Third Age altogether.

Even among those receiving Medicare, race differences obtain. Research using the Medicare Current Beneficiary Survey finds that minority-group members appear less likely to be using antidementia drugs than are non-Hispanic Whites, even when controlling for socioeconomic status, health-care access and utilization, or comorbidities. In short, they are not receiving equivalent treatment for dementia despite receipt of what are presumably comparable benefits under Medicare (Zuckerman et al., 2008). Black Medicare beneficiaries are likewise less likely than Whites to receive the most common procedures, either due to delays in diagnosis or failures to manage chronic conditions. They also receive fewer medical procedures and lower-quality medical care than Whites do, even under similar conditions of income, insurance, disease, and medical facility (Williams, 2004).

FUTURE STEPS: ISSUES TO CONSIDER

The variations in old age that we have reviewed give us perspective on the Third Age and the role that discussion on it can play in the advocacy of critical gerontology. Many gerontologists assume advocacy roles; and much of the Third Age literature urges both a wider recognition of the Third Age and that retirees embrace their opportunities. Despite attention by some scholars to variations in actual experiences of this time of life, Third Age theory focuses attention on the distinctions between this "new" stage, the worklives that preceded it, and the frailty of the Fourth Age. The latter becomes the "new" old age—in such a way that the Third Age serves as the age that is not "old." Indeed, James and Wink posit that one key reason for the emergence of the Third Age lies in its distance from old age: "society's attitudes toward old age and aging appear to be changing as large numbers of people are defying aging stereotypes. 'Old age will not begin until 80' appears to be the view," they note, of the baby boom generation entering retirement (2007, p. xix). Obviously, attitudes are affected by resources to scholars exploring the meaning of the Third Age must be attentive to the relative distribution of resources among those who have opportunities associated with the Third Age and those who do not.

Henretta (2008, p. 403) argues, however, that "the potential of the Third Age does not reside just in the resourcefulness of individuals in managing their own transition to meaningful activity. It resides primarily in social structural arrangements that foster or hinder a creative retirement." Such structural arrangements embed inequalities based on age, gender, race, class, and sexuality that affect this hypothesized stage of life: not only in terms of potential for, and meaning of it, but even the nature of what we desire from retirement. Hence, one of the tasks facing those who advocate for a Third Age conceptualization of postretirement, predecline, is to address the roles of labor markets, government interventions, and health and other industries in shaping outcomes.

The Pew Research Center (2009) reports disconnect between anticipated futures and what has actually occurred. The Pew group found that younger people (aged 18–64) expect to spend much more time in their postretirement lives, traveling for pleasure, pursuing hobbies, doing volunteer work, and starting second careers than retired people actually do. The largest benefit that those 65+ report is having more time to spend with family, which might suggest that gerontologists should emphasize continuity over shifts toward consumption, creativity, or reinventing selves, as they reckon the impact of hitting retirement age. In response to an open-ended question, 28% of the Pew sample specified the chance to spend more time with family as what they valued most about old age, while 25% reported that they would value time with grandchildren. Research into activities thought to be associated with the Third Age must explore not only new forms of engagement, but also the renewal of such everyday activities as spending time with loved ones.

Weiss and Bass (2002, p. 4) describe the Third Age as a "freedom from the demands of earlier life" such as employment and care work, and divide old people along the lines of retirement and physical infirmity (the Fourth Age). By contrast, and in view of the ways in which class, race, and gender affect distributions of labor-force participation and income, we urge a distinction in terms of experience of ageism. Observing along those lines, any shift toward greater freedom appears tenuous, and increasingly so in the present globalized economy. The notion of "freedom from work and family" then appear to be distinct and better descriptors of privileged groups and thus as based on White, middle-class, gendered norms, which are in turn rooted in a Victorian separation of public and private spheres. Hailing the Third age as "golden years" that disprove stereotypes of decline seems a well-intentioned intervention, but distracts from the inequalities of later life that bear the most direct attention. A viable research agenda would include investigation of the extent to which those categorized as Third Agers experienced ageism to the same extent as those not able to access a Third Age.

By analogy, we avoid the common, scholarly use of "older" to characterize old people. The well-intentioned aim is to refrain from stigmatizing those whom we describe but the effect is to maintain the stigma of anyone who would counts as old—those who have entered the Fourth Age, in Laslett's typology. The more direct challenge to ageism is to confront the equation of old with anything derogatory, and/or to raise questions about why people find frailty and dependency more repulsive among old people than they do among other populations, such as children. The question, then, is does the Third Age have room for anyone who is not completely independent?

Laslett's original task, one maintained in many definitions of the Third Age, was to encourage and empower people in their 60s and 70s toward fuller engagement with employment, volunteer work, and other communal and civic pursuits. Minkler and Holstein (2008) have critiqued both the "successful aging" and "civic engagement" literatures, expressing "unease . . . about other 'grand narratives' such as productive and successful aging . . . which also impose totalizing ideals about the meaning of a good old age" (p. 197) that ignore diversity. They note that "the possibility for choice is not equally distributed" (p. 201). They cite the desire to do less, for a life less frenetically paced (p. 198), for a life less like the impressively busy Third Age. Researchers need to question the extent to which the Third Age is defined by what has been called a "busy ethic" as opposed to less strenuous activities.

Laslett was aware of such reservations and provided caveats about his list of old people's responsibilities, where he asked not to be read as enjoining pursuits for which old people are unprepared or disinclined (1996, p. 265). His larger message is clear, nevertheless: The Third Age is a time for old people to find ways to engage with others and to maintain the cultural heritage from which they have benefitted. Discussions on the inequalities that shape access to such activities and the resources on which they depend are simply not as important in such discussions. Following Gilleard and Higgs (2009, p. 26), and King and Calasanti (2009), we suggest further study of constructions of agency and choice in the Third Age.

Final Thoughts

Animated but not obviously guided by a direct concern for ageism, the study of the Third Age creates opportunity to see how well people fit its ideals and suggests what interventions might help. This focus on prosperous reinvention directs attention from those who cannot or do not wish to fit, and presumes models of work and retirement based upon the experiences of the most privileged earners. As is apparent in the suggestions above, one size does not fit all and closer specification of the meaning of the Third Age will enhance its explanatory value. Even among those who might enjoy this time of freedom, relative wealth, and health in retirement, there are pockets of old people who either cannot participate or do not want to participate in the ways described. From this standpoint, the emphasis on third-agers as a standing rebuke to stereotypes of old age seems problematic, especially for those in the Fourth Age (i.e., the "real" old people) because this discourse offers no direct challenge to the ageism that underlies the stereotypes and resulting exclusion. An interesting research question would be to explore how people transition out of the Third Age and what factors are involved.

Drawing the distinction between young–old and old–old distances the researcher from the many groups who find their access to a Third Age impeded by the structural inequities that intersect with the very ageism that the Third Age discourse was originally developed to mitigate. Celebration of the prosperity of those in the Third Age deflects ageism onto those who are unable to resist frailty or otherwise fit depictions of third-agers. Calls for greater attention to diversity within any grouping are laudable gestures toward complexity; and so the recognition that old people vary in their health, incomes, levels of social engagement, and so on is helpful to those wishing to design more precise modes of recognition and intervention. But this advocacy of a "new life stage" that many cannot or do not attain distracts from the most immediate bases of age inequality and the other inequalities that intersect with it. Obviously, there is additional work to do and it will be up to those who read the contributions from this anthology to undertake required research on the Third Age.

NOTES

1. Hispanics tend to have larger families and thus their per capita income is lower than Blacks', while their household income is actually a bit higher.

2. In addition to the lack of seniority and union protection, Johnson speculates that older men take longer than younger men to get new jobs and thus spend more time unemployed. Older women do not, however, spend a lot more time unemployed than do younger women (Johnson, 2009, p. 28), which may owe to the fact that they tend to take lower-paying jobs in the first place, making age less of a factor in reemployment.

REFERENCES

Administration on Aging. (2010). *A profile of older Americans: 2009.* Retrieved March 2010, from http://www.aoa.gov/AoAroot/Aging_Statistics/Profile/2009/

Antonucci, T. C., Ajrouch, K. J., & Birditt, K. (2007). Social relations in the Third Age: Assessing strengths and challenges using the convoy model. In J. B. James & P. Wink (Eds.), *Annual review of gerontology and geriatrics (The crown of life: Dynamics of the early postretirement period)* (Vol. 26, pp. 193–210). New York, NY: Springer.

Associated Press. (2010, March 2). *Gov't adopts formula that doubles elderly poor.* Retrieved March 2010 from http://www.npr.org/templates/story/story.php?storyId=124254998

Beck, S. H. (1982). Adjustment to and satisfaction with retirement. *Journal of Gerontology, 37*(5), 616–624.

Brown, E. (2009). Work, retirement, race, and health disparities. In T. C. Antonucci & J. S. Jackson (Eds.), *Annual review of gerontology and geriatrics (Life-course perspectives on late-life health inequalities)* (Vol. 29, pp. 233–249). New York, NY: Springer.

Calasanti, T. M. (1993). Bringing in diversity: Toward an inclusive theory of retirement. *Journal of Aging Studies, 7*(2), 133–150.

Calasanti, T. M. (1996). Gender and life satisfaction in retirement: An assessment of the male model. *The Journals of Gerontology Series B: Social Sciences, 51B*(1), S18–S29.

Calasanti, T. M. (2006). Gender and old age: Lessons from spousal caregivers. In T. M. Calasanti & K. F. Slevin (Eds.), *Age matters: Re-aligning feminist thinking* (pp. 269–294). New York, NY: Routledge Press.

Calasanti, T. M., & Slevin, K. F. (2001). *Gender, social inequalities, and aging.* Walnut Creek, CA: AltaMira Press.

DeNavas-Walt, C., Proctor, B. P., & Smith, J. C. (2009). Income, poverty, and health insurance coverage in the United States, 2008. *Current Population Reports.* Retrieved March, from http://www.census.gov/prod/2009pubs/p60-236.pdf

Federal Interagency Forum on Aging-Related Statistics. (2008). *Older Americans: Key indicators of well-being.* Retrieved from http://www.agingstats.gov

Feldberg, R. L., & Glenn, E. N. (1979). Male and female: Job versus gender models in the sociology of work. *Social Problems, 26*(5), 524–538.

Flippen, C., & Tienda, M. (2000). Pathways to retirement: Patterns of labor force participation and labor market exit among the pre-retirement population by race,

Hispanic origin, and sex. *The Journals of Gerontology Series B: Psychological Sciences and Social Sciences, 55*(1), S14–S27.

Gilleard, C., & Higgs, P. (2009). The third age: Field, habitus, or identity? In I. R. Jones, P. Higgs, & D. J. Ekerdt (Eds.), *Consumption & generational change: The rise of consumer lifestyles* (pp. 23–36). New Brunswick, NJ: Transaction Publishers.

Grafova, I., McGonagle, K., & Stafford, F. P. (2007). Functioning and well-being in the third age: 1986–2001. In J. B. James & P. Wink (Eds.), *Annual review of gerontology and geriatrics (The crown of life: Dynamics of the early postretirement period)* (Vol. 26, pp. 19–38). New York, NY: Springer.

Hayward, M. D., Friedman, S., & Chen, H. (1996). Race inequities in men's retirement. *The Journals of Gerontology Series B: Psychological Sciences and Social Sciences, 51B*(1), S1–S10.

Henretta, J. C. (2008). The potential of retirement. *The Gerontologist, 48*(3), 401–404.

Higgs, P., & Jones, I. R. (2008). *Medical sociology and old age: Towards a sociology of health in later life.* New York, NY: Routledge.

James, J. B., & Spiro, A. (2007). The impact of work on the psychological health and well-being of older Americans. In J. B. James & P. Wink (Eds.), *Annual review of gerontology and geriatrics (The crown of life: Dynamics of the early postretirement period)* (Vol. 26, pp. 153–173). New York, NY: Springer.

James, J. B., & Wink, P. (2007). *Annual review of gerontology & geriatrics (The crown of life: Dynamics of the early postretirement period)* (Vol. 26). New York, NY: Springer.

Johnson, R. W. (2009). The recession's impact on older workers. *Public Policy & Aging Report, 19*(3), 1, 26–31.

King, N., & Calasanti, T. M. (2009). Ageing agents: Social gerontologists' imputations to old people. *International Journal of Sociology and Social Policy, 29*(1/2), 38–48.

Laslett, P. (1987). The emergence of the third age. *Ageing and Society, 7*(2), 133–160.

Laslett, P. (1996). *A fresh map of life: The emergence of the third age* (2nd ed.). Cambridge, MA: Harvard University Press.

McCullough, M. E., & Polak, E. L. (2007). Change and stability during the third age: Longitudinal investigations of self-rated health and religiousness with the Terman sample. In J. B. James & P. Wink (Eds.), *Annual review of gerontology and geriatrics (The crown of life: Dynamics of the early postretirement period)* (Vol. 26, pp. 175–192). New York, NY: Springer.

Minkler, M., & Holstein, M. B. (2008). From civil rights to … civic engagement? Concerns of two older critical gerontologists about a "new social movement" and what it portends. *Journal of Aging Studies, 22*(2), 196–204.

Pampel, F. C. (1998). *Aging, social inequality, and public policy.* Thousand Oaks, CA: Pine Forge Press.

Pew Research Center. (2009). Growing old in America: Expectations vs. reality. *Social & Demographic Trends,* June 29, 2009. Retrieved from http://pewsocialtrends.org/pubs/736/getting-old-in-america

Phillipson, C. (2009). Reconstructing theories of aging: The impact of globalization on critical gerontology. In V. L. Bengtson (Ed.), *Handbook of theories of aging* (2nd ed., pp. 615–627). New York, NY: Springer.

Phillipson, C., & Vincent, J. (2007). Globalisation and ageing. In J. E. Birren (Ed.), *Encyclopedia of gerontology* (2nd ed., Vol. 1, pp. 630–635). Boston: Academic Press.

Quinn, J. F., Burkhauser, R. V., & Myers, D. A. (1990). *Passing the torch: The influence of economic incentives on work and retirement.* Kalamazoo, MI: W.F. Upjohn Institute for Employment Research.

Roscigno, V. J. (2010). Ageism in the American workplace. *Contexts, 9*(1), 16–21.

Shirey, L., & Summer, L. (2000). Caregiving: Helping the elderly with activity limitations. *Challenges for the 21st century: Chronic and disabling conditions* No. 7. Retrieved from http://www.agingsociety.org/agingsociety/pdf/Caregiving.pdf

U.S. Equal Employment Opportunity Commission. (2009). *Age discrimination in employment act (ADEA) charges.* Retrieved from http://www.eeoc.gov/eeoc/statistics/enforcement/adea.cfm

Weiss, R. S., & Bass, S. A. (Eds.). (2002). *Challenges of the third age: Meaning and purpose in later life.* Oxford: Oxford University Press.

Weller, C. E. (2009). Pension design in the crisis. *Public Policy & Aging Report, 19*(3), 1, 3–6.

Williams, D. R. (2004). Racism and health. In K. E. Whitfield (Ed.), *Closing the gap: Improving the health of minority elders in the new millennium* (pp. 69–79). Washington, DC: Gerontological Society of America.

Zsembik, B. A., & Singer, A. (1990). The problem of defining retirement among minorities: The Mexican Americans. *The Gerontologist, 30*(6), 749–757.

Zuckerman, I. H., Ryder, P. T., Simoni-Wastila, L., Shaffer, T., Sato, M., & Zhao, L. (2008). Racial and ethnic disparities in the treatment of dementia among Medicare beneficiaries. *The Journals of Gerontology Series B: Psychological Sciences and Social Sciences, 63*(5), S328–S333.

Part II

Methodological Approaches for Third Age Research

Chapter
5

Demographic Approaches and Their Potential Application in Third Age Research

J. Scott Brown and Scott M. Lynch

DEMOGRAPHIC RESEARCH IN THE ERA OF THE THIRD AGE

*D*emography is the study of population structure and dynamics and their influence on individual behaviors. Historically, "population structure" referred to a population's size, as well as its age and sex distribution at a given moment in time, while "population dynamics" referred to the three mechanisms by which population structure may change: fertility, mortality, and migration (see Nam, 1994). Over the last half-century, demographers have begun to investigate aspects of population structure beyond size, age, and sex composition, as well as the dynamics involved in producing changes in this more detailed composition. Included among these new areas of interests are three major areas of study: economic demography, family demography, and medical demography (e.g., Bumpass, 1990; Espenshade & Serow, 1978; Harris, 2010). This emergent interest is sensible given that the economy is a key institution for shaping population dynamics, the family is the key social unit in which population dynamics—like fertility—play out, and health is both a major outcome of, and antecedent to, economic and family position.

Demography's expanded focus on economy, family, and health, as well as its simultaneous interest in population-level and individual-level processes, implies that it may offer some important insights into thinking about the emergence and existence of the "Third Age." The Third Age, defined as the period of life after an individual exits the labor force and prior to the onset of health impairments that restrict an individual from remaining actively engaged in social life (Weiss & Bass, 2002), is typically thought of as an individual-level phenomenon. That is, individuals are thought to experience the Third Age, but major demographic changes have brought the Third Age into existence, and it is the supposed existence of this Third Age for large portions of the population that has garnered attention in the contemporary gerontological literature. In particular, we contend that three major demographic shifts have facilitated the emergence of the Third Age at the individual level: (1) the demographic transition, (2) the rise in income inequality—or more accurately the growth in wealth facilitating earlier retirement ages, and (3) epidemiologic transitions. In this chapter, we discuss these three demographic processes in terms of their implications for the emergence of the Third Age, and we discuss some relevant demographic methods and perspectives for studying this period more systematically than has been done in extant literature.

THE DEMOGRAPHIC TRANSITION

The Demographic Transition is a label attached to observed changes in two of the three major population dynamics demographers study: fertility and mortality. Specifically, most populations in developed countries experienced a fall in mortality rates, leading to large increases in life expectancy at birth, followed by a delayed fall in fertility rates. Most currently industrialized countries experienced this transition over the course of the 19th and early 20th century (see Thompson, 1929).

This transition tends to accompany a society's shift from a primarily agrarian subsistence to an industrialized one (Davis, 1945). In the pretransition phase, an agrarian society experiences high fertility levels and high mortality levels. Agrarian existence necessitates large family sizes, because children are potential resources as farm laborers and because having more children provides an individual with greater assurance that at least one child might survive to provide care and shelter to a parent who survives into old age. Importantly, having both high fertility and high mortality rates results in relatively stable populations that experience at most either slow growth or slow decline.

The onset of industrialization pushes a society into the transition phase by changing the relationships among population structures and individual motivations. Most notably, rapid changes that accompany industrialization result in a relatively rapid reduction in mortality rates—a phenomenon we will discuss momentarily. However, individual motivations regarding fertility are slower to change. This delay results in a period in which fertility rates remain similarly high to those in the pre-transition period, but where mortality is substantially lowered. As individual fertility motivations "catch-up" with the social and economic realities of industrialized society in which children are no longer seen as an asset as they once were in agrarian life, fertility rates decline. Thus, societies enter the posttransition phase, which is characterized by more evenly balanced low fertility and delayed mortality. The result is slower population change.

In the interim between falling mortality rates and falling fertility rates, a transitioning society experiences rapid population growth, and the age distribution begins to shift (Blacker, 1947). Rapid population growth first occurs because the old-age population grows due to falling mortality. During this phase, the "population pyramid"—a horizontal bar graph representing the number of males and females in the population at each age—rectangularizes, so that the proportion of the population in each age group begins to equalize. As fertility falls toward the end of the transition phase, the rectangular population "pyramid" begins to invert, reflecting a decline in the number of persons at younger ages. The net, posttransition result—ignoring migration—is that the population "ages," and eventually, the size of the population may decline depending on the level of fertility experienced posttransition and the rate at which mortality stabilizes.

The fall in mortality experienced at the beginning of The Demographic Transition provides the "first leg" of a three-legged stool needed to facilitate the emergence of a Third Age: Falling mortality leads to growth in the old-age population, which provides a pool of elders who may possibly experience such a life-course stage. However, economic and health change are required to provide the other two legs of the "stool."

EPIDEMIOLOGIC TRANSITIONS

The first epidemiologic transition (see Myers, Lamb, & Agree, 2003) provides a major change in population structure that facilitates the emergence of a Third Age. This transition historically accompanies industrialization and represents a qualitative change in the health and mortality of a population. Specifically, for currently industrialized countries prior to industrialization in the 19th and early-20th centuries, most health problems and mortality resulted from various contagious diseases. Beginning in the late 19th century and continuing through the first half of the 20th century, increased urbanization led to increases in public health initiatives, such as improvements in water supply, sewage disposal, and trash collection systems. In addition, in this period better understanding and treatment of communicable disease processes and better preventive medical efforts, including the development of vaccines for childhood illnesses, resulted in drastic reductions in the incidence, spread, and severity of most communicable diseases, especially those with particularly high mortality rates. Indeed, success of these efforts was so significant that a once serious illness—smallpox—was essentially eradicated globally in the late 1970s (World Health Organization, 2010).

The result of these reductions in contagious disease mortality was an expansion of the old-age population and a shift in the major causes of death from acute to chronic diseases, such as heart disease, cancer, stroke, and complications from Type II diabetes. A consequence in the growth in the old-age population was a shift in emphasis in medicine and public health efforts toward understanding and treating chronic illnesses, producing a second epidemiologic transition beginning in the 1960s.[1] Beginning in the 1960s, old-age mortality rates began to fall precipitously perhaps as our ability to treat chronic illnesses—and their accompanying physical limitations—increased.

Today, populations that have completed these epidemiological transitions (or are well into the second) are characterized by healthier old-age populations. This health improvement has provided the second "leg" of the stool required for the emergence of a Third Age as a major stage in the life course. Yet, without major political-economic change at the population level, a Third Age could not emerge.

POLITICAL-ECONOMIC CHANGE

At the same time that major change has occurred in two of the key population dynamics (fertility and mortality), as well as qualitative change in the health of the older population, major changes in the political economy of developed countries has also changed. In the United States, in 1900, life expectancy at birth was 47 years of age (Noymer & Garenne,

2000). Average retirement age at that time—that is, the age at which individuals permanently ceased working at their primary job—was around 70 years of age (Pollock, 2006), and retirement was often a function of ' either death or poor health, both of which limit the possibility of a life-course stage in which elders are healthy yet retired.

Over the last century, however, the average age at retirement has fallen drastically: by the year 2000, retirement age was just over 60 years of age (Gendell, 2001). How was such a reduction in the average retirement age made possible? The answers to this question are complex, and a large body of research has emerged in attempt to understand it. Key components of this change have been the explosion of wealth in developed countries and policy that has facilitated financial security in retirement, especially since the 1940s (in the United States).

The shift from an agrarian to an industrialized economy brings with it a change in the type of labor needed, in particular a greater need for labor in the manufacturing sector. Because of demographic changes in the age structure of the population, a manufacturing labor shortage emerged following World War II leading to competition for labor and the emergence of defined-benefit pension plans that promised permanent, life-long retirement pay/compensation after a specified number of years of service. In addition, in the United States, in response to old-age poverty produced by the Great Depression, Social Security emerged, which guaranteed a fixed income for elders who were deemed "too old" to work. Social Security policy—specifically, a defined "retirement age" at which individuals were able to collect public retirement benefits—helped spur a reduction in the age at which defined-benefit plans "kicked-in" to provide retirement pay, facilitating earlier retirement. This eligibility age has, so far, not kept pace with the second epidemiologic transition. In other words, the average retirement age has not adjusted upward to reflect improvements in the health of elders.

The results of the combination of the three demographic legs of the stool are: (1) reductions in old-age mortality, (2) improvements in health for elders, and (3) a falling retirement age—have led to the suspected emergence of a "Third Age" in the life course of individuals. Figures 5.1 and 5.2 graphically represent the emergence of this Third Age.

Figure 5.1 shows the state of a hypothetical population prior to the existence of a Third Age—that is, a population as it appears before experiencing demographic, economic, and retirement transitions. The figure shows the survival curve for the population (solid line), as well as the

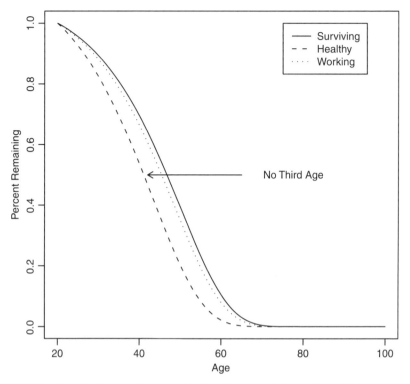

FIGURE 5.1   Hypothetical pre-demographic transition population with no third age.

proportion remaining healthy (dashed line) and working (dotted line) across age. As the figure shows, by about age 50, half of the population has died. At that age, almost all survivors are still working, and the proportion remaining healthy is considerably lower than the proportion working, indicating that many in poor health continue to work, most likely out of necessity. Given these curves, there is no possibility for a Third Age. To see this, consider that, at any age (a vertical slice through these curves), there is no healthy and retired subset of the population.

Figure 5.2 shows the survival, health, and working curves after transition. In this figure, it is clear that life expectancy is much longer than in the first figure: roughly half of the population remains alive at age 75. Furthermore, of those surviving, most are healthy. In contrast, the curve representing the proportion remaining working is substantially lower than previously with respect to the survival and health curves. These

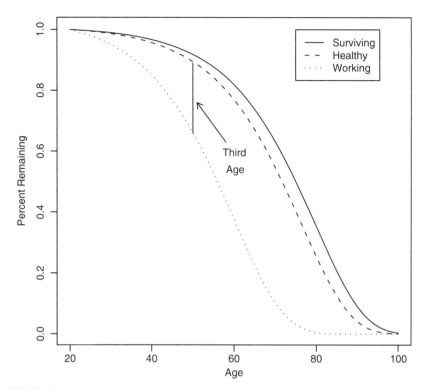

FIGURE 5.2 Hypothetical post-demographic transition population with third age.

conditions make a Third Age possible. For example, at age 50, the vertical line shows that some 20% of the population remains healthy but is not working. More generally, the gap between the healthy and working curves from ages 20 and above shows the proportion of the population that may potentially experience a Third Age. This proportion appears to be substantial.

THE IMPORTANCE OF INEQUALITY

Figure 5.2 notwithstanding, the concept of the Third Age is tenuous. Complicating the demographic story are (1) inequality in retirement benefits/ earnings, (2) non-unidirectional change in health at older ages, and (3) complex work patterns among older adults. While many economic policies related to retirement, at least to some extent, are progressive, the inequalities that dominate the working period of life are reflected in economic differentials during retirement. Thus, for many large and economically disadvantaged minority groups (e.g., many racial minorities in the United States), the ability to retire at younger ages may not exist. Therefore, the pattern shown in Figure 5.2 may not be relevant for significant portions of any given population.

Likewise, heterogeneity in health and disability patterns creates inconsistencies with the overall demographic pattern. Specifically, transitions into and out of poor health are common and make "productive" life unpredictable. This health transition may be one reason an individual retires in the first place—they are no longer dependable workers. Recovery of good health may induce such individuals to return to work rather than remain in a "Third Age" state of healthy and retired, and this tendency to return to work is likely related to the economic standing of the retired individual (i.e., there is considerable endogeneity between economic inequality and health status among older adults).

Further complicating this issue are the diverse work patterns of older adults who are near to retirement or who have recently retired. For example, some older adults retire from their primary occupation before they reach age eligibility for public pension benefits. Often, these elders "bridge" this employment/retirement gap through jobs where they are frequently underemployed (i.e., their education, experience, and/or salary history are well above the qualifications for the new "bridge" occupation). Complete separation from employment is also not the case for many retired individuals who obtain postretirement part-time positions to remain active and/or to supplement retirement income. As such, some postretirement employment patterns are also related to economic inequality.

For each of these substantive reasons, the aggregate demographic pattern shown in Figure 5.2 may not reflect the reality of life for significant portions of populations in developed nations. This issue is well known in traditional demographic research, and so, we shift our discussion to those areas of population research and methodology that address issues with some similarities to examinations of the "Third Age."

ACTIVE LIFE EXPECTANCY AND RELATED DEMOGRAPHIC RESEARCH

Demographers have long been interested in issues of mortality, disability, and health across the life span. The earliest work in this area was focused on finding an overall shape for the distribution of mortality and understanding variation in this distribution (Gompertz, 1825). As methods developed to answer these questions, one methodological innovation, the demographic life table, proved especially useful in summarizing these distributions. More importantly, as demographic interests turned toward more nuanced understandings of the shape of mortality and the mechanisms behind the distribution of deaths, life table methods were expanded beyond the simple transition between the two basic population states of living versus dead. Such expansions allowed demographers to partition death into mortality due to different disease mechanisms (i.e., the multiple-decrement life table) as well as to examine more transient state spaces such as general health or disability (i.e., the multistate, or increment–decrement, life table). Over the last half-century, this latter focus has resulted in a considerable literature examining the periods of life that are spent in variously measured states of good or ill health across a multitude of socio-cultural contexts. It is with this particular substantive focus where traditional demographic work and the concept of the Third Age most closely align.

Disability and Active Life Expectancy

While Total Life Expectancy (TLE) is defined as the average number of years that a person surviving to a particular age can expect to live, Active Life Expectancy (ALE) is defined as the average number of years that a person surviving to a particular age can expect to live in a healthy or non-disabled state. As should be quickly apparent, the Third Age, when defined as the period of life after an individual exits the labor force and prior to the onset of health impairments that restrict an individual from remaining actively engaged in social life, is essentially a subportion of the larger healthy state that demographers define with ALE. More precisely, though the onset of the Third Age is differentiated from the more general notion of active life by the event of exiting the workforce, the exit from the Third Age and the transition out of the active life state are fundamentally similar. Indeed, the primary difference between exit from these two similar states is in the addition of a single transitioning out possibility from the Third Age versus the period of active life—death or the onset of significant impairment indicates a transition out of either of these states; reentry into the workforce also indicates a transition out of the Third Age but has no effect on transition into or out of active life. Thus, from a demographic perspective, one can think of the Third Age as a conditional form of active life, and therefore, a fundamentally demographic state.

A key issue in both demographic work measuring health and activity states and in understanding the Third Age is how activity and/or health are defined. ALE, for example, is but one measure of healthy and/or active states in demographic work, and several alternative measures have been used in the literature. ALE, which is also known as Disability-Free Life Expectancy (DFLE), differentiates state space by the presence/absence of significant disability most frequently assessed via reported impairment with one or more Activities of Daily Living (ADL). This measure has been successfully used across a broad range of cultural contexts (see, e.g., Robine, Jagger, Clavel, & Romieu, 2005), and is sometimes examined instead as its compliment—Disabled Life Expectancy (DLE). Healthy Life Expectancy (HLE) is also widely used in demographic work (see, e.g., Lynch & Brown, 2010) and differs from ALE by defining state spaces using self-reported health rather than disability status. A derivative measure of this form, Health-Adjusted Life Expectancy (HALE), has been similarly utilized in a broad array of comparative work (see, e.g., Mathers et al., 2001).

Conceptualizations of the Third Age, however, tend to discuss "active engagement" when describing the active or healthy aspect of the Third Age state. Given the similarity between the terms "active engagement" and active life, one might propose that the disability measures used to indicate active life are also appropriate for measuring the Third Age. However, some issues call into question such a proposition. For example, the ADL used in typical ALE research are the most basic of social functioning activities and are associated with abilities to do tasks within one's own dwelling (Katz, Ford, Moskowitz, Jackson, & Jaffe, 1963). As such, a person who is capable of these tasks may or may not be capable of "active engagement" outside the home. ADL are also focused on personal care tasks and provide very little information on one's ability to interact in social settings. Thus, using typical disability statuses from the ALE literature may not be appropriate.

Two alternatives for defining the healthy aspect of the Third Age are available. If the semantic parallel between "active engagement" and active life is desirable, then one might utilize other less severe levels of disability or impairment to differentiate active versus disabled states. Instrumental Activities of Daily Living (IADL), which measure one's ability to engage in activities outside of the home and social interaction such as shopping or telephone use, could be used as alternative measures of disability status in Third Age research. Functional Limitation measures (Nagi, 1976; Rosow & Breslau, 1966), which measure the ability to perform specific physical tasks such as climbing stairs or lifting heavy objects, may also provide more appropriate definitions for the health dimension in Third Age studies. On the other hand, a more global self-perception of being in good health may more accurately capture the ability of an individual to actively engage. Thus, using the self-rated health measure consistent with the HLE literature may be optimal. Additionally, given that its absence from most ALE and HLE research is a critique of that literature, the role of cognitive impairment in defining the health portion of the Third Age will need to be addressed.

Demographic Methods in Third Age Research

To date, the only attempt to assess the Third Age empirically using demographic methods (Carr, 2009) has done so via an adaptation of Sullivan's version of the period life table (Sullivan, 1971). Sullivan's life table methodology involves the construction of a standard single-decrement period life table where the person-years (the total amount of time lived by a population typically within a one-year age interval— i.e., each surviving person contributes one person-year; each person who dies during the interval contributes less than a year) are apportioned into person-years lived in a healthy state and person-years lived in a disabled state, usually based on vital statistics mortality data and health data from nationally representative surveys. These person-year values are then easily converted into the more easily readable form of life expectancies for total (TLE), active (ALE), and disabled (DLE) life.

   Carr's adaptation for use in Third Age research generates values of Third Age Life Expectancy (TALE) to describe the age-distributed Third Age population (2009). Similar to more typical applications of Sullivan's life table method, person-years are apportioned into the period spent within the Third Age and the period after one has exited this state. The key difference lies in how the state space of the Third Age is defined. Whereas with ALE the state is defined as the absence of disability, defining TALE requires both a disability threshold as well as some level of disengagement from work. Carr defines this state using the combined thresholds of the absence of severe disability measured as having no ADL *and* working less than 20 hours per week. This difference in the construction of states in TALE as compared to the more traditional ALE measure, however, generates interesting questions regarding the limits of such demographic measures. In particular, TALE is unique from other life expectancy measures in that it (1) is a state with complex dimensionality and (2) has complex exits that are not unidirectional.

More traditional measures of ALE or HLE define the state of being "active" or "healthy" as unidimensional. To be "active" or "healthy," one must be observed to have no (typically ADL) disability or to report neither fair nor poor health, respectively. In other words, a state threshold is set within a single measure or single scale. With TALE, however, simultaneous thresholds in disability and work status are required to define the state. Whether this is methodologically problematic is not clear. It is likely that having more dimensional complexity makes measures like TALE more sensitive to definitional variations than traditional measures. For example, though minor variations are observed, ALE has been shown to be relatively stable across varying levels of ADL severity (see Lynch, Brown, & Harmsen, 2003). A more complex measure such as TALE, however, may magnify such minor differences with variations in how the working dimension is defined. Testing of the effects of definitional variation in both dimensions of TALE is needed.

Perhaps of greater concern methodologically is the complexity of exit from the Third Age state. In traditional ALE approaches, an individual is considered to be in the healthy state until the onset of significant impairment. When data allow (i.e., when panel data are available), multistate life table methodologies are employed that allow for transitions into and out of the disabled state to occur. In most cases, however, panel data are not available, and cross-sectional methods such as Sullivan's method are required. In Sullivan's method, transitions into and out of the disabled state are assumed not to occur (or alternatively, are assumed to occur in a perfectly balanced fashion—i.e., the same number of people transition from healthy to disabled as transition from disabled to healthy, and the number of people transitioning from healthy or disabled to death is proportionally balanced).

Since the construction of TALE is a straightforward adaptation of Sullivan's method, these same assumptions apply. However, entry into and exit from the Third Age state is likely to occur with greater frequency. Simply put, the transition rates in the disability dimension of TALE match those for ALE, but TALE also has the added transition possibilities associated with its work dimension (e.g., workforce reentry due to financial need or the need to obtain health-care coverage for a spouse who is not eligible for government health-care provisions, etc.). These heightened transition rates would not be problematic for multistate methods using panel data. However, since panel data that allow for detailed measurement of work status (beyond simple measures of working versus not working) and detailed measurement of disability of health status do not appear to exist, Carr (2009) was forced to adapt Sullivan's method. Since the validity of Sullivan's method for health expectancy calculations in dynamic situations has been called into question (Barendregt, Bonneux, & Van der Maas, 1994; see Mathers & Robine, 1997, for a defense of Sullivan's method), one should view Carr's TALE results with some caution. Ultimately, panel data are needed that will allow for adequate assessment of these transitions, and additionally, that will allow for comparison of Carr's Sullivan-based results to assess the validity of that method for assessing Third Age life expectancies.

A Final Methodological Caution

One final note of caution is warranted when using demographic approaches to examine the Third Age. The Third Age is fundamentally a state produced through the individual processes of health maintenance and work status. In other words, literature on this period of life is focused on the "third-ager" as an individual with productive potential given relatively good health and increased free time in retirement. Demographic methods, however, produce population summaries that aggregate individual processes. More specifically, the output from demographic analytical tools essentially consists of population averages. For example, the graphical representations in Figures 5.1 and 5.2 show curves that represent the *average* proportions surviving, working, and healthy across age. The patterns in these figures may or may not represent the actual lived experience of individuals in those populations. Indeed, there are nearly an infinite number of combinations of individual health, retirement, and mortality experiences that could yield the observed aggregate patterns. As such, Third Age researchers should be very cautious when utilizing such demographic tools, since the output displayed in Figure 5.2 could be produced from a population where many (or perhaps even most) individuals do not experience any significant time being both healthy and retired.

FUTURE STEPS: ISSUES TO CONSIDER

The field of Demography can offer much both substantively and methodologically as Third Age research continues to develop. Research on the Third Age suffers to a great extent from a lack of clarity of measurement.

Conceptually, the notion of the period of life after an individual exits the labor force and prior to the onset of health impairments that restrict an individual from remaining actively engaged in social life seems relatively clear. However, operationalizing the measurement of labor force exit and restrictive health impairments is less definitive in Third Age research, which often uses age as a proxy of both (e.g., Midwinter, 2005; Timmer & Aartsen, 2003). Demographic research on ALE and related measures of healthy or unimpaired life may be informative in the quest to clearly define the latter concept in Third Age research. Future research should examine the effects of using different demographic measures of health/disability (e.g., ALE vs. HLE) on estimates of the number and age range of individuals in the Third Age. Likewise, more attention needs to be focused on the precision of measurement of retirement status and how varying definitions of "working" may alter the Third Age population pattern. Given the heterogeneity and inequality inherent in both health and labor force participation, careful attention should also be given to the effects of varying definitions of the Third Age for advantaged versus disadvantaged groups.

Methodologically, research on the Third Age is a natural fit with demography. Carr's work (2009) in adapting Sullivan's life table method for the empirical examination of Third Age research questions is an excellent example of how demographic methods can be effectively utilized in this area. Still, several methodological challenges remain. Definitional ambiguity of the two key concepts that define the Third Age, exit from the workforce and activity limiting health impairment, needs to be clarified before the full potential of demographic research on the Third Age can be realized. Likewise, the demographic method adapted by Carr is useful primarily in situations where detailed longitudinal data on the same individuals followed over long periods is unavailable, as is currently the case for data needed in empirical examinations of Third Age questions. Such demographic methods, though useful, also come with serious limitations, and these limitations may be especially important when examining more complex and potentially more volatile states such as being in the Third Age. Panel data with detailed work and health information are greatly needed for the best demographic methods to be applied in the Third Age research.

Major population shifts that are of interest to demographers typically involve substantial changes across all ages of a population rather than just being focused within a small age segment of the population as is the typical focus of Third Age researchers. What then might demographers and other social scientists anticipate resulting from this emergent Third Age population shift? Riley and Riley (1994a, 1994b) provide us with one intriguing possibility. They observed that the life course in industrial societies is organized generally around the relationship of individuals to work. Riley and Riley described how the industrial life course is age segregated or divided into a "tri-partition" corresponding roughly to prework, work, and postwork periods. The prework period consists of preparation for work including social and human capital investments, the work period is the period of active labor force participation and wealth accumulation, and the postwork period is viewed as a period to disengage from the labor force and divest wealth for various purposes (e.g., leisure, healthcare, etc.). The emergence of an extended postretirement period of life lived free from health impairments may not be consistent with this structuring of the life course (see Carr, 2008). Riley and Riley (1994b) suggest that a reformulation of the life course might occur such that rather than occurring consecutively as they currently do, the activities that make up the current age-segregated periods may move to intermittent or concurrent occurrence—an integrated life course. In other words, they envisioned the possibility that an individual might enter and leave the workforce at varying intervals/ages to either reinforce educational training for career enhancement or occupational change or partake of extended periods (though brief compared to retirement) of exit from education and the labor force. It is not inconceivable that the emergence of the Third Age is but the beginning of such a fundamental societal and population change, though this is not the only possibility (e.g., the Third Age could be eliminated altogether by policies that increase the retirement age to be consistent with the demographic changes in health and mortality observed over the last century resulting in a continued, albeit extended, tri-partitioned life course). Third Age researchers should examine these possibilities as would demographers by expanding their focus to include a broader age range (e.g., are we observing more intermittent work and education patterns in young adulthood and/or in mid-life?).

The bottom line, simply stated, is that demography and research on the Third Age are fundamentally a good fit. We should anticipate a great deal more demographic thought making its way into the examination of the Third Age, as well as the more frequent use of demographic tools by Third Age researchers.

NOTE

1. Some consider this second epidemiologic transition to be part of the first, but Myers, Lamb, and Agree (2003) demarcate it as a second transition, and we have adopted their terminology.

REFERENCES

Barendregt, J. J., Bonneux, L., & Van der Maas, P. J. (1994). Health expectancy: An indicator for change? *Journal of Epidemiology and Community Health, 48,* 482–487.

Blacker, C. P. (1947). Stages in population growth. *Eugenics Review, 39,* 88–102.

Bumpass, L. L. (1990). What's happening to the family? Interactions between demographic and institutional change. *Demography, 27*(4), 483–498.

Carr, D. C. (2008). Redefining the role of older adults in society: Does the "Third Age" promote a successful alternative to the tripartitioned life course? *Journal of Societal and Social Policy, 7*(1–2), 37–51.

Carr, D. C. (2009). *Demography, ideology, and stratification: Exploring the emergence and consequences of the Third Age* [Doctoral Dissertation]. Networked Digital Library of Thesis and Dissertations.

Davis, K. (1945). The world demographic transition. *Annals of the American Academy of Political and Social Sciences, 237,* 1–11.

Espenshade, T. J., & Serow, W. J. (1978). *The economic consequences of slowing population growth.* San Diego, CA: Academic Press.

Gendell, M. (2001). Retirement age declines again in 1990s. *Monthly Labor Review, October,* 12–21.

Gompertz, B. (1825). On the nature of the function expressive of the law of human mortality, and on a new mode of determining the value of life contingencies. *Philosophical Transactions of the Royal Society of London, 115,* 513–585.

Harris, K. M. (2010). An integrative approach to health. *Demography, 47*(1), 1–22.

Katz, S., Ford, A. B., Moskowitz, R. W., Jackson, B. A., & Jaffe, M. W. (1963). Studies of illness in the aged. The index of ADL: A standard measure of biological and psychosocial function. *Journal of the American Medical Association, 185,* 914–919.

Lynch, S. M., & Brown, J. S. (2010). Generating multistate life table distributions for highly-refined subpopulations from cross-sectional data: A Bayesian alternative of Sullivan's method. *Demography, 47*(4), 1053–1077.

Lynch, S. M., Brown, J. S., & Harmsen, K. G. (2003). The effect of altering ADL thresholds on active life expectancy estimates among older persons. *The Journal of Gerontology: Social Sciences, 58,* S171–S178.

Mathers, C. D., Murray, C. J. L., Lopez, A. D., Salomon, J. A., Sadana, R., Tandon, A. et al. (2001). Estimates of healthy life expectancy for 191 countries in the year 2000: Methods and results. *Global Programme on Evidence for Health Policy Discussion Paper, No. 38.* World Health Organization.

Mathers, C. D., & Robine, J. M. (1997). How good is Sullivan's method for monitoring changes in population health expectancies. *Journal of Epidemiology and Community Health, 51,* 80-86.

Midwinter, E. (2005). How many people are there in the Third Age? *Ageing and Society, 25,* 9-18.

Myers, G. C., Lamb, V. L., & Agree, E. M. (2003). Patterns of disability change associated with the epidemiologic transition. In J. M. Robine, C. D. Jagger, C. D. Mathers, E. M. Crimmins, & R. M. Suzman (Eds.), *Determining health expectancies* (pp. 59-74). New York, NY: John Wiley.

Nagi, S. Z. (1976). An epidemiology of disability among adults in the United States. *Millbank Memorial Fund Quarterly, 54,* 439-467.

Nam, C. B. (1994). *Understanding population change.* Itasca, IL: F.E. Peacock Publishers.

Noymer, A., & Garenne, M. (2000). The 1918 Influenza epidemic's effects on sex differentials in mortality in the United States. *Population and Development Review, 26*(3), 565-581.

Pollock, A. J. (2006). Retirement finance: Old ideas, new reality. *AEI Outlook Series.* Retrieved May 19, 2010, from http://www.aei.org/outlook/24940

Riley, M. W., & Riley, J. W. Jr. (1994a). Age integration and the lives of older people. *The Gerontologist, 34,* 110-115.

Riley, J. W. Jr., & Riley, M. W. (1994b). Beyond productive aging: Changing lives and changing structures. *Ageing International, 21*(2), 15-19.

Robine, J. M., Jagger, C., Clavel, A., & Romieu, I. (2005). Disability-free life expectancy (DFLE) in EU countries from 1991 to 2003. *European Health Expectancy Monitoring Unit Technical Report, 2005_1.*

Rosow, I., & Breslau, N. (1966). A Guttman Health Scale for the aged. *Journal of Gerontology, 21,* 556-559.

Sullivan, D. (1971). A single index of mortality and morbidity. *HSMHA Health Reports, 86,* 347-354.

Thompson, W. S. (1929). Population. *The American Journal of Sociology, 34*(6), 959-975.

Timmer, E., & Aartsen, M. (2003). Mastery beliefs and productive leisure activities in the Third Age. *Social Behavior and Personality, 31,* 643-656.

Weiss, R. S., & Bass, S. A. (Eds.). (2002). *Challenges of the Third Age: Meaning and purpose in later life.* New York, NY: Oxford University Press.

World Health Organization. (2010). *Smallpox. WHO Factsheet.* Retrieved May 19, 2010, from http://www.who.int/mediacentre/factsheets/smallpox/en/

Chapter
6

The Third Age as a Socio-Demographic Variable for Cross-Country Comparisons

Kathrin Komp and Jürgen H.P. Hoffmeyer-Zlotnik

CROSS-COUNTRY COMPARISONS IN THE ERA OF THE THIRD AGE

*T*he Third Age is a country-specific phenomenon. Its emergence relates to social structures and is discussed differently across countries (Gilleard & Higgs, 2007; Karisto, 2007; Komp, Van Tilburg, & Broese van Groenou, 2009; Laslett, 1996). Country comparisons of the Third Age can, therefore, generate unique insight. They can help us to separate country-specific from universal characteristics of the Third Age.

While the value of cross-country comparisons of the Third Age is undisputable, such studies have been sparse until now. Most previous studies developed the concept of the Third Age, laying the foundation for empirical research (e.g., Gilleard & Higgs, 2007; Laslett, 1996). Very few studies have taken an empirical approach in studying third-agers, and instead, often present conceptual considerations or mere descriptions of a single country (e.g., Grafova, McGonagle, & Stafford, 2007; Jones et al., 2008; Karisto, 2007; Midwinter, 2005). One reason for the lack of country-comparative research is the challenge of creating a set of criteria for identifying third-agers in different countries. Many characteristics that are used to identify third-agers, such as retirement, health, and family care,

are understood differently across countries (Hoffmeyer-Zlotnik & Wolf, 2003).

This chapter lays the foundation for country-comparative research on third-agers. It does this by introducing a socio-demographic variable that can be used to identify third-agers. This variable is particularly useful for quantitative studies, which can test the models and hypotheses developed in previous conceptual and qualitative studies. In order to introduce a socio-demographic variable identifying third-agers, we start by presenting two different understandings of the Third Age. Subsequently, we discuss ways of identifying third-agers according to those understandings with data at the microlevel and macrolevel.

THE THIRD AGE AS A SOCIO-DEMOGRAPHIC VARIABLE

The Third Age can be seen as a socio-demographic variable in cross-country comparisons. Socio-demographic variables define population groups whose members are in similar situations and show similar opinions and behaviors. Well-known examples for such variables are age, gender, income, and educational level (Braun & Mohler, 2002; Wolf & Hoffmeyer-Zlotnik, 2003). The use of these variables in cross-country comparisons is challenging, because their relevance, measurement, and distribution can differ across countries (Wolf & Hoffmeyer-Zlotnik, 2003).

The concept of life phases provides a framework for viewing the Third Age as a socio-demographic variable. Life phases are longer-lasting situations that divide the time span from birth to death into distinct categories (Settersten & Mayer, 1997). They correspond to social roles and activities (Mayer, 2004; O'Rand, 2003), thus creating the homogeneous population groups that are typical for socio-demographic variables. The model predominantly used, distinguishes four life phases: (1) youth, which is the time of education and socialization, (2) middle age, which is the time of paid work, (3) early old age, which covers the healthy life years after retirement ("the Third Age"), and (4) late old age, which covers the last years of life spent in poor health (Neugarten, 1974; Settersten & Mayer, 1997).

The predominant model with four life phases uses a work-centered perspective, defining life phases according to their relation to paid work. It understands the Third Age as the time that older people could additionally spend on paid work, if retirement were delayed. Such a perspective is particularly important in studies of the effect of population aging on the workforce and on pension systems. When older people's activities and possibilities are studied, however, this approach falls short. Especially women can have vast caregiving responsibilities which structure their lives (Bracke, Christiaens, & Wauterickx, 2008). Laslett (1996) therefore proposed that unpaid caring tasks within the family should be recognized as equal to paid work. In such a work-and-care-focused perspective, the Third Age appears to be a time of possibilities. The Third Age is a time in which there is freedom from physical impairment and from the restrictions created by paid work and by informal caregiving. However, the work-centered and the work-and-care-focused perspectives have one major drawback: they make the Third Age difficult to measure. No survey and no official statistics include information on the Third Age as those perspectives define it. Many researchers, therefore, simplify the concept of the Third Age by equating it to an age-bracket (James & Wink, 2007; Neugarten, 1974; Settersten & Mayer, 1997). The age brackets commonly used start between 55 and 65 years and end between 74 and 79 years of age (e.g., James & Wink, 2006; Morris & Caro, 1997; Neugarten, 1974). The upside of this approach is that information on age is readily available. However, the downside is that age tells us little about an individual's situation (Settersten & Mayer, 1997). An age bracket cannot, therefore, serve as an indicator for the Third Age. It can only serve as a rough approximation. Consequently, we propose that a work-centered or work-and-care-focused perspective on the Third Age is more appropriate. We now discuss how third-agers can be identified when adopting these perspectives.

The Work-Centered Perspective

From a work-centered perspective, the Third Age describes healthy retirees. Country-comparative research on the Third Age, therefore, needs to consider possible country-differences related to the concepts of retirement and health status. We present ways to measure retirement and health in succession.

Retirement can be measured in several ways. First, it can be measured using employment status (Bescond, Chataignier, & Mehran, 2003; Gustman, Mitchell, & Steinmeier, 1995). Employment status usually differentiates the categories "retired," "employed and self-employed," "in education," "homemaker," "ill or disabled," and "unemployed or looking for work." This measurement makes the identification of retirees easy, as they are summarized in a separate category. Where respondents can pick several categories of the employment status, the category marked as the most important should be used. However, the use of employment status for identifying retirees raises the question whether homemakers, unemployed, and disabled people reach a status equal to retirement at some point. The question about the status of homemakers is particularly relevant in Southern and Continental European countries, where women often refrain from paid work in order to care for the family and do household chores (Billari & Kohler, 2004; Trifiletti, 1999). The question about the status of disabled and unemployed people is particularly relevant in Continental European countries, where disability and long-term unemployment pensions are (mis)used as alternative pathways to retirement (Organisation for Economic Co-operation and Development, 2006). We recommend using the mandatory retirement age in a country as the cutoff point for those groups of people. From the mandatory retirement age on, they might receive pension benefits due to earlier employment or periods of education (European Commission, 2007). At this point, they reach a situation resembling retirement (Komp et al., 2009). In countries where no mandatory retirement age exists, the average effective retirement age can be used as a cutoff point.

Second, retirement can be measured as the receipt of pension benefits (Bowlby, 2007). This measurement is less ambiguous than the employment status, as it only has two answer categories: "yes" and "no." However, there are different kinds of pensions, namely public, occupational, and private ones (Myles, 2002). Individuals can receive more than one kind of pension and they might start receiving them at different points of time. It is also possible that individuals work while receiving pension benefits (Hayward, Hardy, & Liu, 1994). We recommend setting the cutoff point where pension benefits exceed the income from paid work.

Third, retirement can be measured using the number of contracted or actual working hours (Bowlby, 2007; Gustman et al., 1995). When using this measure, one needs to make two decisions. First, one needs to decide which number of working hours one wants to use as the cutoff point to separate working from not-working individuals. The International Labour Organization, for example, recommends considering individuals with as little as one working hour per week as "working" (International Labour Organization, 1987). Second, one needs to decide how to separate retirees from other individuals who do not spend any time working, such as unemployed people and children. Such a separation can be reached by employing an additional criterion for retirement, such as the employment status "retiree" or the receipt of pension benefits. The combination of working hours with an additional criterion for retirement seems particularly useful in two cases. First, it seems useful when many individuals of all age groups do not spend any time working. This occurs, for example, in Continental European countries due to structural unemployment (Bussemaker & Van Kersbergen, 1999). Second, it seems useful when many older people spend time working. This situation is particularly common in countries such as the United Kingdom and the United States, where old-age pensions are often insufficient to cover everyday expenses (Choi, 2001; Hayward et al., 1994).

The onset of poor health can be determined with subjective or objective measures. When adopting a subjective measure, respondents are asked to describe their own health status (Baron-Epel & Kaplan, 2001). The possible answers differ between surveys, and researchers need to determine a cutoff point between good and poor health that suits the data and their study. When an objective determination of health is preferred, there are several measures that can be employed. The most common ones are a list of the diagnosed diseases, a list of impairments in (instrumental) activities of daily living, or physical limitations that were found during a health assessment in the framework of the data collection (Katz, 1983; Mackenbach, Avendamo, Andersen-Ranberg, & Aro, 2005; Visser, Deeg, & Lips, 2003). Like the subjective measures, the objective measures of health also require a decision about where to set the cutoff point between good and poor health.

The Work-and-Care-Focused Perspective

The work-and-care-focused perspective is an extension of the work-oriented one. It modifies the work-oriented perspective by placing unpaid caring tasks within the family on par with paid work. It, therewith, sees third-agers as healthy retirees without unpaid caring tasks within the family. The following section discusses how unpaid caring tasks within the family can be measured. This measurement can be added to the ones of retirement and health status described above when identifying third-agers from the work-and-care-focused perspective.

Unpaid caring tasks within the family are difficult to delimit. On the one hand, there are country differences in the understanding of family. Northern Europeans, for example, see immediate kin as family, while

Southern Europeans also include more distant relatives (Bien & Quellen-berg, 2003). Family care might, thus, be provided to various family members, from one's grandchildren to one's grandparents (Attias-Donfut, Ogg, & Wolff, 2005). On the other hand, caregiving within the family occurs in numerous forms, ranging from hands-on caring activities to the responsibility for a person in need of care (Laferrère & Wolff, 2006). Many of these tasks go unnoticed, because they are considered natural and self-evident for women. This perspective on unpaid caring tasks within the family is particularly well pronounced in Continental and Southern Europe (Philip, 2001; Trifiletti, 1999).

In order to measure unpaid caring tasks within the family, one can consider two possibilities. First, one can measure the time spent on caring tasks (Laferrère & Wolff, 2006). This approach requires a decision about which activities the task of caring embraces and who is included as "family." Given the variation in the way these concepts are interpreted from one country to the next, it might be necessary to use country-specific answers to these questions. Second, one can focus on the legal responsibility for persons in need of care. This responsibility is usually given when one's children are underage. In countries where long-term care insurance exists, for example, in Austria and Germany, such responsibility can also be placed on individuals other than one's underage children. It can, for example, be placed on one's spouse or parents when they are in need of care for a longer period of time (Komp et al., 2009). The upside of con-sidering the legal responsibility for care is that the measurement is rela-tively easy and unambiguous. The downside is that it might not capture all informal care provided within families (Laferrère & Wolff, 2006).

MEASURING THE THIRD AGE AT THE MICROLEVEL

When measuring the Third Age at the microlevel, we are focusing on indi-vidual third-agers. Research at this level could, for example, study the social network of third-agers or how third-agers spend their leisure time (see Chapter 7 of this book which describes time-use studies). The advan-tage of microlevel studies is that they can compare subgroups in a popu-lation. They can, for example, be used to examine differences between men and women or between ethnic groups.

There are rich data for microlevel studies available. These data are usually collected in surveys and available in data sets. The data sources we describe below contain sufficient information to identify third-agers according to the work-centered and the gendered perspective. They moreover contain enough information for cross-sectional and for longitudinal studies on the Third Age. Cross-sectional studies describe the situation at one point of time. They could, for example, study whether there are more men or women among the third-agers in a given year. Longitudinal studies, in contrast, describe the development over time. They could, for example, investigate how long people remain third-agers (Hooyman & Kiyak, 2008).

In the following pages, we describe easily accessible international data sets that can be used to study the Third Age at the microlevel. Then, we explain how the Third Age can be measured with these data. Finally, we demonstrate the measurement for selected countries.

Data Sources at the Microlevel

We identified two data sources as most useful for country-comparative studies of the Third Age at the microlevel: the European Social Survey (ESS) and a group of data sets that can be combined with the Survey on Health, Ageing and Retirement in Europe. The first data source is the ESS. It includes socio-demographic data and information on institutions, attitudes, beliefs, and behaviors (in a rotating module). The socio-demographic data available include information on the respondents' health, employment status, and family situation. They, therefore, provide the information necessary for identifying third-agers when employing either the work-centered or the work-and-care-centered perspectives. The ESS has released data every other year since 2002. In every wave, it draws a different sample from the population aged 15 years and over (Lynn, Häder, Gabler, & Laaksonen, 2004). As a result, it only allows for both, cross-sectional studies at the individual level and longitudinal studies at the country level. The ESS collected data in numerous European countries, increasing from 22 in the first wave to 31 in the fourth wave. What makes the ESS stand out is its high data quality, which the ESS team aims to collect in a "methodologically bullet-proof study" (ESS, 2009). Those efforts are visible in socio-demographic data needed to identify third-agers. The data are harmonized across countries, which makes cross-country comparisons particularly easy. The ESS data are available free of charge under http://www.europeansocialsurvey.org.

The second data source is a group of data sets that can be combined with the Survey of Health, Ageing and Retirement in Europe (SHARE).

SHARE is a cross-national panel database, containing information on health, socioeconomic status, social and family networks of individuals aged 50 years and over. It contains the information necessary to identify third-agers—that is, health, employment status, and family situation. Consequently, it provides particularly rich data to choose from. Due to its panel design, SHARE allows for longitudinal studies. This makes it more versatile for country-comparative research on the Third Age than the ESS. Until now, data have been collected in 2004 and 2006, and retrospective interviews have been conducted in 2008 and 2009. A downside of SHARE is that it only includes individuals aged 50 and over. This means that we could miss out on third-agers below 50 years of age. This is particularly probable where the effective retirement age is low, for example, among women in Austria and the Slovak Republic (Organisation for Economic Co-operation and Development, 2009). Only one of these countries, namely Austria, is included in the SHARE sample. Besides Austria, 11 other European countries were included in the first wave of SHARE. The second wave included 13, and the third wave included 14 European countries. The SHARE data can be obtained free of charge from http://www.share-project.org.

SHARE was designed with two other data sets as models. Those data sets are the English Longitudinal Study of Ageing (ELSA) and the Health and Retirement Study (HRS) from the United States. Consequently, the three data sets contain similar data and can easily be combined. The initial fieldwork for ELSA started in 1998. Since then, four waves of data have been collected and supplemented with life history interviews. The ELSA data are available via the Economic and Social Data Service http://www.esds.ac.uk/longitudinal/Introduction.asp. HRS started out as two separate studies: the early HRS and "Assets and Health Dynamics of the Oldest Old" (AHEAD). The early HRS contained information on individuals making their transition from work to retirement, collecting data every other year from 1992 on. AHEAD contained information on individuals aged 70 and over, collecting data every other year from 1993 onward. In 1998, the studies were merged, creating the HRS as we know it today (Health and Retirement Study, 2008). The HRS data are available via http://hrsonline.isr.umich.edu/index.php.

Besides ELSA and HRS, there also are a number of other surveys that are harmonized with SHARE. These surveys are single-country surveys which were designed using ELSA, HRS, and SHARE as models. However, most of these surveys were set up only recently, so that data were not always readily available when this chapter was written (January 2010).

Those surveys include, for example, the Mexican Health and Aging Study, the Korean Longitudinal Study on Aging, the Japanese Health and Retirement Study, the Chinese Health and Retirement Longitudinal Survey, and the Longitudinal Aging Study in India (Meijer, Zamarro, & Fernandes, 2008).

The two data sources we focus on, namely ESS and SHARE, contain different variables one can use to identify third-agers. We compiled a list of those variables in Table 6.1, with SHARE representing the survey itself as well as the group of data sets that can be combined with SHARE. Table 6.1 shows that both the ESS and SHARE contain all variables necessary for identifying third-agers. The variables related to involvement in paid work are identical in both data sets. SHARE, however, captures health status and involvement in informal caregiving in more variables than the ESS. Regarding involvement in informal caregiving activities, the ESS focuses on care for minors, while SHARE also collects information on informal caregiving for inter alia the spouse and parents. Regarding the health status, the ESS focuses on subjective overall health and subjective overall limitations in activities of daily living. SHARE additionally collects information on specific diseases, symptoms, and limitations in instrumental and noninstrumental activities of daily living. Moreover, it measures the respondents' grip strength and walking speed while collecting the data.

TABLE 6.1   Variables in International Surveys That Allow for Identifying Third-Agers

	PAID WORK	INFORMAL CARE	HEALTH
ESS	▪ Employment status ▪ Contracted working hours ▪ Actual working hours	▪ Age of children in household	▪ Self-rated overall health ▪ Activities of daily living
SHARE	▪ Employment status ▪ Contracted working hours ▪ Actual working hours	▪ Age of children ▪ Children in household ▪ Time and frequency provided care ▪ Household member receives benefits from long-term care insurance	▪ Self-rated overall health ▪ Specific diseases and symptoms ▪ (Instrumental) activities of daily living ▪ Measurement of grip strength and walking speed

Note: ESS = European Social Survey; SHARE = Survey of Health, Ageing and Retirement in Europe.

This makes SHARE preferable where exact measurements are required and only older people need to be studied. The ESS, in contrast, is preferable when rough measurements are sufficient and when information on the total population is required.

If the data sources presented do not cover the countries or the time span one is looking for, one can revert to national survey data as a last resort. Such data can be collected in surveys covering all age groups (e.g., the German ALLBUS) or in surveys focusing only on older people (e.g., the Dutch Longitudinal Aging Study Amsterdam). However, these surveys have the disadvantage that they are usually not harmonized across countries. This means that a different set of variables might have to be used in every country, which compromises cross-country comparisons. Strict country comparisons are, therefore, not possible with national survey data.

An Example of Third Age Research at the Microlevel

Microlevel data hold vast possibilities for Third Age research. However, identifying third-agers with microlevel data also requires some preparatory work. We illustrate this preparatory work by using an example. In this example, we compare men and women with regard to the percentage of third-agers in the population aged 15 and over. When identifying third-agers, we adopt the work-and-care-focused. Our results, therefore, tell us whether men or women have a bigger chance for spending their later life without obligations and restrictions.

For our example, we used data from wave 4 of the ESS, which were collected in 2008. In the data set, we identified third-agers based on fulfillment of three conditions. First, they must be retired. This means that all individuals who stated they were "in paid work," "in education," "unemployed," or "in community or military services" are labeled as "not third-agers." Homemakers below the mandatory retirement age in a country are also labeled as "not third-agers." From this age on, they are entitled to receive pension benefits that place them in a situation comparable to that of retirees (Szinovacz & DeViney, 1999). This leaves retirees, homemakers above the mandatory retirement age and individuals who describe themselves as "permanently sick or disabled" in the pool of possible third-agers. Second, individuals must be healthy to be identified as third-agers. We operationalize this in two ways: individuals should not have named being "permanently sick or disabled" as their main activity and they should not have declined when asked whether they were hampered in their "daily activities in any way by any longstanding illness, or disability, infirmity, or mental health problem." Individuals who did not fulfill this condition are labeled "not third-agers." This second step leaves retirees and homemakers above the mandatory retirement in the pool of possible third-agers. Third, individuals must be free from legal obligations to provide care in order to be considered a third-ager. We operationalize this as not being a parent to a minor. Consequently, everybody with children underage is labeled "not third-agers." This third step leaves retirees and homemakers above the mandatory retirement age who do not have children underage in the pool of possible third-agers. From this final pool of individuals, we still need to remove individuals with missing values on any variable that is necessary for determining whether they are third-agers. This leaves us with the final differentiation between "third-agers" and "not third-agers" in our data set. An SPSS syntax file with these computations can be downloaded from http:// kathrin-komp.eu/downloads.htm.

To display the results of our computations, we weighted the cases in our sample with a population weight and calculated the percentage of third-agers in the population aged 15 years and over, per country and gender. We chose three countries from the ESS and present their results in Figure 6.1: Latvia, Belgium, and Portugal. Among the countries in our

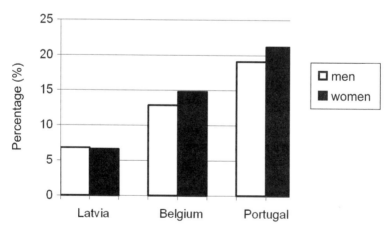

FIGURE 6.1   Percentage of third-agers in the population aged 15 years and older, calculated with microlevel data. *Note*: This figure was calculated from ESS data from wave 4, collected in 2008.

sample, those countries have the highest, the lowest, and an intermediate percentage of third-agers.

Figure 6.1 describes the percentage of third-agers across gender and countries. The percentage of third-agers in the population aged 15 years and older lies between 7% and 22% among men and women in all countries presented. It is higher among women than among men in Belgium and Portugal and vice versa in Latvia. It is, moreover, higher in Portugal than in the other two countries, with Latvia having the lowest share. Studies utilizing this approach when identifying third-agers can determine the percentage of third-agers with, for example, gender differences in care obligations and workforce participation and with country-specific retirement regulations.

MEASURING THE THIRD AGE AT THE MACROLEVEL

When measuring the Third Age at the macrolevel, we focus on populations of third-agers. A typical question studied at this level would be how many third-agers there are in a country. Alternatively, macrolevel studies can be used to describe the average third-ager in a country. From this perspective, one can, for example, study whether the average individual in a country can expect to be a third-ager at some point. The usability of macrolevel research, however, ends, when we shift the focus to phenomena below the country-level (Coleman, 1990). It is, for example, not possible to examine differences in the attitudes of third-agers and non-third-agers using macrolevel data.

Macrolevel research can draw on extensive data sets. Those data sets are usually presented in tables, with one number given per country and year. It is noteworthy that those tables often contain information on a great number of countries and points of time. This makes them particularly suitable for large-scale cross-country comparisons and for longitudinal studies at the country level. Large-scale country comparisons can, for example, study the character of the Third Age according to continents or types of welfare states (Esping-Andersen, 1990; Mayer, 2001). Longitudinal studies can be used to identify factors that influence the development of the Third Age in a country (e.g., retirement regulations; see Komp et al., 2009) and factors that are influenced by this development (e.g., the size of senior-oriented markets). However, there also is a disadvantage. Macrolevel data usually do not contain any information on informal caregiving. This means that third-agers cannot be identified from the gendered perspective when macrolevel data are used.

In the following pages, we present particularly rich sources for international macrolevel data. Moreover, we describe how the Third Age can be measured with these data. Finally, we calculate the Third Age with macrolevel data for selected countries and years.

Data Sources at the Macrolevel

Macrolevel data necessary to measure the Third Age across countries can be particularly easily obtained from three sources: the World Health Organization (WHO), Eurostat, and the Organisation for Economic Co-operation and Development (OECD). The WHO has a freely accessible database with health-related information on their homepage under http://www.who.int/whosis/en/index.html. This database holds information on healthy life expectancy in 2003 in almost all countries worldwide. Eurostat is the statistical office of the European communities. Available at http://epp.eurostat.ec.europa.eu, it provides free access to data on age groups in the population and on the healthy life expectancy ("healthy life years' expectancy") in Member States of the European Union for up to 12 years. The OECD calculates the average effective age of retirement for its publications. Data are available free of charge at http://www.oecd.org/dataoecd/3/1/39371913.xls. If these three data sources do not render enough data for a planned analysis, they can be supplemented with data from national statistical offices. However, this approach can create inconsistencies between countries: while data from the international data sources are harmonized across countries to some degree, the data from the national statistical offices do not need to be collected and presented in the same way.

Using data from the WHO, Eurostat, and the OECD, one can measure the Third Age using the work-centered and the age-based perspectives. The measurement of the Third Age in both perspectives is fairly uncomplicated. When applying the age-based perspective, one simply needs to count the number of individuals in the chosen age bracket. When applying the work-centered perspective, one can subtract the average effective retirement age in a country from the healthy life expectancy in that country. A positive difference means that the average individual in this country can expect to spend time as a third-ager. A difference smaller or equal to zero means that the average individual in this country cannot expect to spend any time as a third-ager. However, the difference does not give any information on variation within a country. It is, therefore, possible that some individuals within that particular country spend time as a third-ager, even if the average individual in that country cannot expect to do so.

An Example of Third Age Research at the Macrolevel

Third Age research at the macrolevel is easy to conduct and to interpret. We demonstrate this by calculating the time the average individual in a country spends as a third-ager. When doing this, we adopt the work-centered perspective. The results of our calculations can, for example, be used to determine whether governments might profit from programs supporting paid work in old age.

For our example, we calculated the time—an average individual can expect to spend as a third-ager by subtracting the average retirement age from the healthy life expectancy. We derived data on the average effective retirement age from the OECD and data on the healthy life expectancy at age 65 from Eurostat. Figure 6.2 shows the results for five countries for

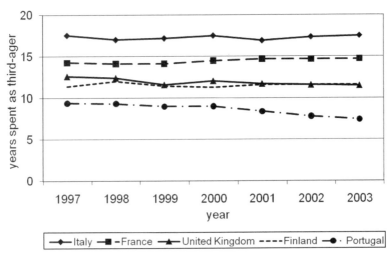

FIGURE 6.2   Years the average individual spends as a third-ager, calculated with macrolevel data. *Note:* The calculations for this figure used data from the OECD and Eurostat.

the years 1997–2003. Among the countries on our sample, those countries had the highest, lowest, and intermediate values.

Figure 6.2 shows considerable country differences in the amount of years the average individual spends as a third-ager: in Italy the value is about 18 years, in Portugal it is about 9 years. In all countries except for Portugal, the number of years stayed relatively stable over the time period of observation. In Portugal, we see a slight decline from the year 2000 onward. Studies employing this way of identifying third-agers could now try to explain the country differences and the development over time in Portugal with, for example, retirement regulations or the health-care system in a country.

FUTURE STEPS: ISSUES TO CONSIDER

Until now, research on the Third Age has focused on single countries rather than examining country differences. Moreover, it has mainly presented conceptual considerations. The next step to advance our knowledge should, consequently, include empirical research, such as quantitative cross-country comparisons. This chapter explains when such comparisons can be useful and how they can be approached.

In this chapter we underlined that different research questions might require the utilization of different perspectives on the Third Age. We described two such perspectives: a work-centered and a work-and-care centered one. Both perspectives might render different, possibly contradictory results. It is, therefore, imperative that one chooses a perspective on the Third Age that fits the question one strives to answer. Moreover, it is essential that future studies and discussions explicate which perspective on the Third Age they adopt. This information makes it easier to accumulate knowledge about the Third Age across different studies.

One major issue inhibiting quantitative cross-country comparisons on the Third Age is the availability of suitable data. Microlevel data sets contain all the information necessary for identifying third-agers. However, this information is spread over different variables. Scholars first need to combine these variables before they can start with quantitative analyses of the third-ager. Especially inexperienced scholars would benefit if this preparatory work was eliminated. This could be done by including a generated variable identifying life phases, and therewith third-agers, in microlevel data sets. The use of macrolevel data, on the other hand, is limited by the absence of information on informal caregiving. Without this piece of information, third-agers cannot be identified using the gendered perspective. It would, therefore, be desirable that macrolevel data sets added information on caregiving to the list of topics covered.

Despite some shortcomings in the data available, quantitative cross-country comparisons of the Third Age are already possible. Cross-country research will help us differentiate country-specific from universal characteristics of the Third Age. It should, therefore, be included in the agenda for gerontology in the era of the Third Age.

REFERENCES

Attias-Donfut, C., Ogg, J., & Wolff, F.-C. (2005). European patterns of intergenerational financial and time transfers. *European Journal of Ageing, 2*, 161-173.

Baron-Epel, O., & Kaplan, G. (2001). General subjective health status or age-related subjective health status: Does it make a difference? *Social Science and Medicine, 53*, 1373-1381.

Bescond, D., Chataignier, A., & Mehran, F. (2003). Seven indicators to measure decent work: An international comparison. *International Labour Review, 142*, 179-211.

Bien, W., & Quellenberg, H. (2003). How to measure household and family. In J. H. P. Hoffmeyer-Zlotnik & C. Wolf (Eds.), *Advances in cross-national comparison. A European working book for demographic and socio-economic variables* (pp. 279-294). New York, NY: Wiley.

Billari, F. C., & Kohler, H.-P. (2004). Patterns of low and lowest-low fertility in Europe. *Population Studies, 58*, 161-176.

Bowlby, G. (2007). Defining retirement. *Perspectives on Labour and Income, 8*, 15-19.

Bracke, P., Christiaens, W., & Wauterickx, N. (2008). The pivotal role of women in informal care. *Journal of Family Issues, 29*, 1348-1378.

Braun, M., & Mohler, P. P. (2002). Background variables. In J. A. Harkness, F. J. R. Vijver, & P. P. Mohler (Eds.), *Cross-cultural survey methods* (pp. 99-113). New York, NY: Wiley.

Bussemaker, J., & Van Kersbergen, K. (1999). Contemporary social-capitalist welfare states and gender inequality. In D. Sainsbury (Ed.), *Gender and welfare state regimes* (pp. 15-46). Oxford: Oxford University Press.

Choi, N. G. (2001). Relationship between life satisfaction and postretirement employment among older women. *The International Journal of Aging and Human Development, 52*, 45-70.

Coleman, J. S. (1990). *Foundations of social theory*. Cambridge, MA: Harvard University Press.

Esping-Andersen, G. (1990). *The three worlds of welfare capitalism*. Princeton, NJ: Princeton University Press.

European Commission. (2007). *Social Protection in the Member States of the European Union, of the European Economic Area and in Switzerland. Situation on 1 January 2007.* Office for Official Publications of the European Communities, Luxembourg.

European Social Survey. (2009). *Methodology.* Retrieved on January 31, 2010, from http://www.europeansocialsurvey.org/index.php?option=com_content&view=article&id=77&Itemid=349.

Eurostat. *Healthy life years at age 65, by gender* [Data file]. Retrieved on December 02, 2009, from http://epp.eurostat.ec.europa.eu/portal/page/portal/product_details/dataset?p_product_code=TSDPH220.

Gilleard, C., & Higgs, P. (2007). The third age and the baby boomers: Two approaches to the social structuring of later life. *International Journal of Ageing and Later Life, 2,* 13-30.

Grafova, I., McGonagle, K., & Stafford, F. P. (2007). Functioning and well-being in the third-age: 1986-2001. In J. B. James & P. Wink (Eds.), *The crown of life: Dynamics of the early postretirement period. Annual review of gerontology and geriatrics* (pp. 19-38). New York, NY: Springer.

Gustman, A. L., Mitchell, O. S., & Steinmeier, T. L. (1995). Retirement measures in the Health and Retirement Study. *The Journal of Human Resources, 30,* S57-S83.

Hayward, M. D., Hardy, M. A., & Liu, M.-C. (1994). Work after retirement: The experiences of older men in the United States. *Social Science Research, 23,* 82-107.

Health and Retirement Study. (2008). *Sample Evolution: 1992-1998.* Retrieved on February 02, 2010, from http://hrsonline.isr.umich.edu/sitedocs/surveydesign.pdf.

Hooyman, N. R., & Kiyak, H. A. (2008). *Social gerontology: A multidisciplinary perspective.* Upper Saddle River, NJ: Pearson Education.

International Labour Organization. (1987). *Guidelines on the implications of employment promotion schemes on the measurement of employment and unemployment, endorsed by the Fourteenth International Conference of Labour Statisticians (October-November 1987).* Retrieved on January 31, 2010, from http://www.ilo.org/wcmsp5/groups/public/—dgreports/—integration/—stat/documents/normativeinstrument/wcms_087602.pdf.

James, J. B., & Wink, P. (Eds.). (2007). *The crown of life: Dynamics of the early post-retirement period. Annual review of gerontology and geriatrics.* New York, NY: Springer.

Jones, I. R., Hyde, M., Victor, C., Wiggins, R., Gilleard, C., & Higgs, P. (2008). *Ageing in a consumer society: From passive to active consumption in Britain.* Bristol: Polity Press.

Karisto, A. (2007). Finnish baby boomers and the emergence of the third age. *International Journal of Ageing and Later Life, 2,* 91-108.

Katz, S. (1983). Assessing self-maintenance: Activities of daily living, mobility, and instrumental activities of daily living. *Journal of the American Geriatrics Society, 31,* 721-727.

Komp, K., van Tilburg, T., & Broese van Groenou, M. (2009). The influence of the welfare state on the number of young old persons. *Ageing and Society, 29,* 609-624.

Laferrère, A., & Wolff, F.-C. (2006). Microeconomic models of family transfers. Applications, *Vol. 2*. In S.-C. Kolm & J. Mercier-Ythier (Eds.), *Handbook of the economics of giving, altruism and reciprocity* (pp. 889–970). Amsterdam: North-Holland.

Laslett, P. (1996). *A fresh map of life: The emergence of the third age* (2nd ed.). London: MacMillan Press.

Lynn, P., Häder, S., Gabler, S., & Laaksonen, S. (2004). *Methods for achieving equivalence of samples in crossnational surveys: The European Social Survey experience. Institute for Social and Economic Research, Working Paper 2004-2009.* Colchester: University of Essex.

Mackenbach, J., Avendamo, M., Andersen-Ranberg, K., & Aro, A. R. (2005). Physical health. In A. Börsch-Supan, A. Brugavini, H. Jürges, J. Mackenbach, J. Siegrist, & G. Weber (Eds.), *Health, ageing and retirement in Europe. First results from the survey of health, ageing and retirement in Europe* (pp. 82–88). Mannheim: Mannheim Research Institute for the Economic of Ageing.

Mayer, K. U. (2001). The paradox of global social change and national path dependencies. Life course patterns in advanced societies. In A. Woodward & M. Kohli (Eds.), *Inclusions and exclusions in European societies* (pp. 89–110). London: Routledge.

Mayer, K. U. (2004). Whose lives? How history, societies, and institutions define and shape life courses. *Research in Human Development, 1*, 161–187.

Meijer, E., Zamarro, G., & Fernandes, M. (2008). Overview of available aging data sets. In A. Börsch-Supan, A. Brugavini, H. Jürges, A. Kapteyn, J. Mackenbach, J. Siegrist, & G. Weber (Eds.), *First results from the survey of health, ageing and retirement in Europe (2004-2007). Starting the longitudinal dimension* (pp. 24–29). Mannheim: Mannheim Research Institute for the Economic of Ageing.

Midwinter, E. (2005). How many people are there in the third age? *Ageing and Society, 25*, 9–18.

Morris, R., & Caro, F. G. (1997). The young old, productive aging, and public policy. In R. B. Hudson (Ed.), *The future of age-based public policy* (pp. 91–103). Baltimore: Johns Hopkins University Press.

Myles, J. (2002). A new social contract for the elderly? In G. Esping-Andersen with D. Gallie, A. Hemerijk, & J. Myles (Eds.), *Why we need a new welfare state* (pp. 130–172). Oxford: Oxford University Press.

Neugarten, B. (1974). Age-groups in American society and the rise of the young-old. *Annals of the American Academy of Political and Social Science, 415*, 187–198.

O'Rand, A. (2003). The future of the life course. Late modernity and life course risks. In J. T. Mortimer & M. J. Shanahan (Eds.), *Handbook of the life course* (pp. 693–701). New York, NY: Kluwer.

Organisation for Economic Co-operation and Development. (2006). *Live longer, work longer.* Paris: Organisation for Economic Co-operation and Development.

Organisation for Economic Co-operation and Development. *Average effective age of retirement in 1970-2007 in OECD countries* [Data set]. Retrieved on December 02, 2009, from http://www.oecd.org/dataoecd/3/1/39371913.xls.

Philip, I. (Ed.). (2001). *Family care for older people in Europe*. Amsterdam: IOS Press.

Settersten, R. A. Jr., & Mayer, K. U. (1997). The measurement of age, age structuring, and the life course. *Annual Review of Sociology, 23,* 233–261.

Szinovacz, M. E., & DeViney, S. (1999). The retiree identity: Gender and race differences. *Journal of Gerontology: Social Sciences, 54B,* S207–S218.

Trifiletti, R. (1999). Southern European welfare regimes and the worsening position of women. *Journal of European Social Policy, 9,* 49–64.

Visser, M., Deeg, D. J. H., & Lips, P. (2003). Low vitamin D and high parathyroid hormone levels as determinants of loss of muscle strength and muscle mass (sarcopenia): The Longitudinal Aging Study Amsterdam. *The Journal of Clinical Endocrinology & Metabolism, 88,* 5766–5772.

Wolf, C., & Hoffmeyer-Zlotnik, J. H. P. (2003). Measuring demographic and socioeconomic variables in cross-national research. In J. H. P. Hoffmeyer-Zlotnik & C. Wolf (Eds.), *Advances in cross-national comparison. A European working book for demographic and socio-economic variables* (pp. 1–13). New York, NY: Wiley.

Time-Use Studies: A Method for Exploring Everyday Life in the Third Age

Stella Chatzitheochari and Sara Arber

TIME-USE RESEARCH IN THE ERA OF THE THIRD AGE

O ver the past decades, we have seen a significant shift in social gerontology from approaches that were built around the ideas of exclusion, disengagement, and dependency of older people toward a new paradigm that viewed life after retirement as an expanded phase of high involvement in leisure activities. This paradigmatic shift was brought about by a series of social and demographic transformations in Western societies that led social gerontologists to radically alter their conceptions of what it meant to be a mature adult after the relinquishment of previous work and family roles. The emergence of retirement as a social institution, the decrease in the retirement age, and the increase of healthy years' expectancy after exit from the labor market were seen as contributing to the emergence of a new distinctive period of well-being before the subsequent health deterioration during the last years of life (Laslett, 1987; Neugarten, 1974). Taking into account the increased opportunities for participation and the different socialization experiences and diverse needs and interests of new generations, authors suggested that this time of healthy retirement would be one of extended and self-fulfilling leisure. The emergence of this new life-course stage was understood as

127

a uniquely modern phenomenon, constituting a key development in the transformation of later life and of the entire life-course structure in Western societies (Gilleard & Higgs, 2000; Weiss & Bass, 2002). Generally referred to as the Third Age, a term first employed by Laslett in his seminal contribution to the field (Laslett, 1987), the theoretical idea of high involvement following retirement soon gained normative power and became synonymous with the concept of "successful aging" (Rowe & Kahn, 1997). As a result, active aging became a key goal for many Western governments and is being vigorously promoted by national, local, as well as supranational policies (Department of Work and Pensions, 2005; European Commission, 2002).

However, despite the plethora of theoretical discussions about active aging and the Third Age, it appears that empirical research in the field has not advanced at the same pace and has not always been conducted in an entirely satisfactory and systematic manner (Wahl, Tesch-Römer, & Hoff, 2007). Everyday life constitutes one of the areas that have not received much attention in aging research, primarily due to the lack of availability of large-scale representative data sets. Indeed, most previous studies on the topic have relied on small nonrepresentative samples, often comprising less than 200 participants (Gauthier & Smeeding, 2003). As a result, social scientists' knowledge on older people's everyday lives remains surprisingly limited (Hill, Herzog, & Juster, 1999).

It is therefore pertinent for social scientists to make use of methodological tools that will enable a better understanding of daily life experiences and realities after retirement. Time-use surveys constitute a potentially useful methodological tool for Third Age research, providing insight into a variety of issues relating to everyday life in older age. Despite the number of time-use studies conducted worldwide that has grown steadily since the 1990s, and recent methodological advancements in data collection which have rendered time-use data sets the most reliable source of information on daily life and activity patterns, there have been few attempts by researchers studying aging to analyze such data in order to examine postretirement lifestyles (Fast & Frederick, 2004; Frederick & Fast, 2004; Gauthier & Furstenberg, 2002; Gauthier & Smeeding, 2003).

This chapter aims to introduce time-use research methodology to researchers working in the field of aging and suggests that social gerontology can benefit from insightful time-use analysis in the era of the Third Age. With an impressive pool of time-use data currently available for developed as well as developing countries (Harvey, 2001, p. 1), it is possible to address a wide range of important questions. For example, the extent to which predictions of generalized active leisure participation have eventuated for recent cohorts of retirees can be examined. An understanding of activity patterns of different social groups during the healthy retirement years and an identification of potential barriers to leisure participation are also possible with time-use analyses.

In the first part of this chapter, we provide an introduction to the most important methodological aspects of time-use research methodology and discuss their advantages over conventional methods of data collection on everyday life. In the second part of this chapter, we present an analysis of British time-use data from 2000 in order to demonstrate the potential of this methodology. Our chapter concludes with suggestions for future analyses of time-use data that can complement social gerontology's understanding of the phenomenon of aging in the era of the Third Age.

METHODOLOGICAL APPROACHES FOR EXAMINING ACTIVITY PATTERNS AND EVERYDAY LIFE

The study of how people spend their time goes back to the beginning of the 20th century, and today constitutes a rapidly expanding and politically influential area of research (Bryson, 2007, p. 152). There are two different methodologies for data collection on time allocation at a large-scale level: through the inclusion of questions relating to time use in interviewer-administered conventional surveys and through the use of self-completed time diaries by participants.

Simple questions on individuals' time allocation are often included in social surveys in order to gather information on the frequency and/or duration of certain prespecified activities during a specific time period. For example: How many hours did you work last week? How much time do you spend watching television during a typical week? How many times did you go to the theater during the last three months?

A clear disadvantage of this methodological approach is that questions are asked regarding only a limited number of activities and a holistic account of everyday life is not provided. However, the most important problem relates to the accuracy of the estimates obtained with this approach. While at first it may seem like a simple calculation task, recalling details about time spent on a certain activity involves several steps of cognitive processing that are difficult to perform within a few seconds. For instance, a person who is being asked how many hours he/she spent at work last week has to search his/her memory for all episodes of work in the previous week, separating episodes of work from other activities that were taking place at the same time and adding up all the episode lengths across days in the last week correctly (Robinson & Godbey, 1997, p. 59). Such cognitive tasks are difficult to perform correctly in a short time even in the case of routine daily activities. Indeed, a number of validation studies have found results obtained by such stylized questions regarding time participation in certain activities to be significantly overestimated (Chase & Godbey, 1983) and, in some cases, to have a sum of more than 24 hours per day or 168 hours per week (Verbrugge & Grube-Baldini, 1993). This likely bias of estimates derived from stylized estimates has been well documented (Gershuny, 2005; Robinson, Chenu, & Alvarez, 2002), casting doubt on their relative validity.

Time-use research currently represents the most reliable and widely employed methodology in the study of everyday life (Ver Ploeg et al., 2000, p. 37). What differentiates time-use surveys from conventional surveys that gather information on individuals' time allocation is the use of a time diary for data collection. Time diaries gather information on the chronological structure and nature of individual time and provide a holistic account of the organization of daily life that is not feasible by conventional surveys that mainly produce longer-term time-use estimates. Overall, the time-diary approach presents several advantages over other methods of data collection. The following section provides a description of some aspects of time-use methodology while at the same time referring to potential time-use analyses that can be conducted in Third Age research.

TIME-USE METHODOLOGY

The first surveys that employed time diaries as data collection instruments were conducted in the interwar period in the United States and the Soviet Union (Andorka, 1987, p. 149). However, the great upsurge of time-use surveys began in the 1960s with the Multinational Time-Budget Research Project that collected data on people of working age in 12 Western countries (Szalai, 1972). Following this study, a regular collection of time-use data started taking place in a considerable number of countries, guided by the idea that such data would fill in a number of gaps in the statistical information available in the social domain. Since the mid-1990s, we have been witnessing a steady growth in the number of stand-alone time-use studies. An impressive pool of harmonized time-use data for a large number of developed and developing countries is currently available and can be analyzed to answer a broad range of social science and policy-related questions.[1]

The Time Diary

The time-use diary has been characterized as a "micro-behavioral technique" which offers a complete account of individuals' daily behavior over a limited period of time (Robinson & Godbey, 1997, p. 64). Despite the fact that some of its features tend to vary among different time-use surveys, its heart is always preserved: a self-reported description of activities across the full 24 hours of the day is collected along with an assignment of the starting and stopping times of each activity (Stinson, 1999, p. 5).

Figure 7.1 provides an example of three hours of a time diary completed by a female retiree. In addition to gathering information on the main activity of the diarist for each 10-minute block, the diary also collects information on whom the respondent was with, where the activity took place, and whether the respondent was doing anything else at the same time. An impressive level of micro-measurement detail is thus achieved and a holistic narrative account of daily life is produced, giving access to the nature, sequence, and context of human activity.

The originality of this technique lies in the fact that it "capitalizes on the most attractive measurement properties of the time variable" (Robinson & Godbey, 1997, p. 97). The diary covers the full 24 hours of a day and all daily activities are potentially recorded, adding up to 1440 minutes. The diary also respects the "zero-sum" property of time, that is, time is a metric with a fixed upper limit and that if time in one activity increases, it must be zeroed out by decreases in other activities. At the same time, the fact that respondents are asked to provide a sequential account of their daily activities corresponds to the way they may store their events in memory, thus aiding accurate recall and increasing the validity of the data. Indeed, a series of cross-validation studies that made use of spouse activity reports, video-recorded observations, shadow observations, and random hour accounts has provided evidence on the validity and reliability of time estimates from diary data (Robinson & Godbey, 1977, pp. 74–77).

Another important advantage of time-diary methodology is that, by allowing diarists to record their activities in their own words (this is

	What were you doing?	What were you doing at the same time?	Where were you?	Were you with anybody?				
Morning Time, a.m.	Please record your main activity for each 10-minute period	What is the most important activity you were doing at the same time?	eg. at home, at friends, in the car, walking etc.	alone/unknown people	Children up to 9 yrs old	Children aged 10 or more	Other Hhd members	Other people you know
7.00-7.10	Sleeping							
7.10-7.20	→							
7.20-7.30	Had a shower		At Home	+				
7.30-7.40	Made Breakfast		→	→				
7.40-7.50	Ate Breakfast		→	→				
7.50-8.00	Did the washing up		→	→				
8.00-8.10	I got dressed		→	→				
8.10-8.20	I went for a walk		Walking	→				
8.20-8.30	→		→	→				
8.30-8.40	Bought a newspaper		→	→				
8.40-8.50	Waiting for the bus		→	→				
8.50-9.00	Got the bus		On the Bus	→				
9.00-9.10	→		→	→				
9.10-9.20	Watch Television	Discussing with my husband	At Home				+	
9.20-9.30	→	On the phone with my daughter	→				→	
9.30-9.40	→		→				→	
9.40-9.50	→		→				→	
9.50-10.00	→		→				→	

FIGURE 7.1   Fraction of a time-use diary filled in by a female retiree.

most often the case in national time-use surveys), it leaves room for daily practices that become prevalent for the population to be identified over time, a good example here being the use of internet. The analysis of time-use data sets from the last decades could thus allow Third Age researchers to identify new activity practices that have become popular over time for newer cohorts of retirees.

Depending on the purposes and the economic budget of the survey, a lot of variation exists regarding diary administration, the format of the diary, and the period of time surveyed. However, what is most important is that the higher reliability of time-diary data compared with time estimates derived from conventional surveys has been evidenced to be irrelevant to the survey design followed in time-use studies (Robinson, 1985).

Activity Coding

Respondents own descriptions of activities in the time-use diary (in the cases where an open-ended diary approach is used, as in Figure 7.1) are subsequently grouped into meaningful activity codes for analysis. Detailed activity codes can be further aggregated into broader activity categories, such as paid work, unpaid work, leisure, and personal care, according to a set of accepted classification criteria or according to the researcher's theoretical assumptions and analysis aims. It is important to note that the same criteria for activity coding are employed by different countries in order for comparability to be possible (see Horrigan et al., 1999 for a summary of coding schemes used in time-use research).

In the case of research on the Third Age, this comparability is important in order to understand cross-national differences in activity patterns and the effects of cultural context and different welfare regimes on everyday life experiences after retirement. The availability of harmonized comparable data from previous decades also makes possible a pseudo-cohort analysis to examine life-course influences in leisure patterns and to evaluate whether there has been indeed a historical change in the social category of older age and its daily experience as claimed in theoretical literature.

Sampling Issues

Time diaries collect data on relatively short periods, ranging from one day to the maximum of a week. However, the sampling of one weekday and one weekend day is the most common strategy, as it achieves an optimal balance between sufficient time coverage and reasonable response burden (Osterberg, 2000). Given that use of time on weekends and weekdays is of a substantially different nature, it is important for both to be sampled. For Third Age research, the availability of data for both weekends and weekdays appears to be of particular interest as it allows researchers to examine whether weekend days retain a different character after retirement of whether time-use patterns and activity practices during weekends and weekdays tend to become similar after the relinquishment of previous work roles. Researchers interested in producing longer-term time-use estimates, may construct synthetic weekly time estimates by weighting days accordingly.

It is becoming more common for time-use surveys to sample all respondents within a household rather than sampling only one household member. The availability of time-use data on all persons of the same household greatly enhances the value of diary data for understanding intra-household behavior, giving researchers the opportunity to study the household as a unit in its own right. In the case of Third Age research this allows the modeling of the contextual influences of the household on daily activities through the use of multilevel modeling techniques.

Complementary Data Collection Instruments

Apart from the time diary, time-use surveys also make use of several other data collection instruments, such as individual and household question-naires. Depending on the survey's purposes, a variety of information ranging from standard socio-demographic variables to subjective feelings and social values may be gathered. This allows for many different questions to be answered. For social gerontologists, the availability of information on social values can contribute to a better understanding of different leisure preferences after retirement. Information on subjective feelings is also important as it allows for the issue of satisfaction arising from different leisure activities to be addressed, contributing to quality-of-life research and encouraging a greater understanding of the meaning older people attach to different types of activities.

Finally, the inclusion of stylized questions on participation in certain activities that do not occur weekly for many people, such as taking a holiday or going to the theater, is also important as it complements the information provided by the time diary and contributes to the production of a full map of human activity and leisure behavior.

Response Rates

A common criticism of time-use surveys relates to the lower response rates they achieve compared to conventional surveys as a result of the burden of diary completion. It is common for time-use surveys to receive a response rate of approximately 60%, and as survey nonresponse is commonly taken as an indicator of the quality of survey data (Abraham, Maitland, & Bianchi, 2006), concerns have been expressed regarding the bias that such nonresponse rates introduce to the estimates obtained from time-use surveys. However, nonresponse is a source of bias only to the extent that those who respond to the survey are different from those who do not with respect to the characteristics of interest (Abraham et al., 2006) and recent studies have provided evidence that nonresponders of time-use surveys cannot be identifiable according to any socio-demographic indicator (Abraham et al., 2006; Gershuny, 2002; Robinson & Godbey, 1997), which indicates that biases introduced by nonresponse are not strongly related to the commonly used social research explanatory variables (Sullivan, 2006, p. 44). This seems to convincingly refute claims regarding nonresponse bias in time diary estimates, providing further evidence for the reliability of the data collection instrument.

Overall, time-use research methodology constitutes a reliable and accurate methodological tool with numerous advantages over conventional social surveys, and can be analyzed in many different ways to complement social gerontology's understanding of different facets of everyday life.

LEISURE PATTERNS OF OLDER PEOPLE IN THE UNITED KINGDOM: A TIME-USE ANALYSIS

Having discussed the methodological advantages and characteristics of time-use methodology, we will present a time-use analysis to further elucidate the potential of this methodology for aging research through an exemplar. The analysis presented here capitalizes on British time-use data from 2000 and examines the relationship of individual social characteristics with participation in "active" and "passive" leisure activities. Given that the idea of the Third Age has been linked with participation in "active" leisure pursuits (Gilleard & Higgs, 2000; Laslett, 1987), this analysis enables us to explore the socio-demographic characteristics of British older people who can be characterized as "third-agers" and examine whether there exist social inequalities with regard to participation in "active" leisure pursuits.

Data

We analyze data from the 2000 UK Time Use Survey (UKTUS) (see *2000 TUS Technical Report*, Office for National Statistics, 2003). The survey was conducted by the Office for National Statistics (ONS) between June 2000 and September 2001 and three-stage multistage sampling procedures were followed in order to obtain a representative sample of areas, households, and individuals in the United Kingdom.

The time period surveyed by the UKTUS diary was 24 hours and all individuals over the age of 8 in sampled households were asked to fill in the diary for two prespecified days: a weekday and a weekend day. The format of the time diary was identical to that of Figure 7.1: the 24-hour period was broken down into 144 ten-minute slots in which participants were asked to provide descriptions of their primary and secondary activities in their own words. During the subsequent activity coding procedure, respondents' descriptions were grouped into approximately 250 activity categories.

A total of 11,677 individuals completed 20,981 diaries and the UKTUS achieved a response rate of 62% and 72%, at the household and diary level, respectively, resulting in a net diary response rate of 45%. Such response rates are considered typical for time-use surveys and evidence has been provided by recent studies that these low rates do not introduce significant nonresponse bias in time-use surveys' estimates (Abraham et al., 2006; Gershuny, 2002; Robinson & Godbey, 1997).

We conduct our analysis on a subsample of 696 men and 919 women over 64 years old. Data are weighted by an individual-level ungrossed weight provided in the ONS survey files in order to correct for nonresponse. Activity duration estimates refer to the average time spent on each activity reported as primary over the two surveyed diary days. Our analysis examines the relationship of "active" and "passive" leisure lifestyles with gender, health status (self-assessed), social class (NS-SEC 3-class version classification), educational level, and age.

Distinguishing Between "Passive" and "Active" Leisure Activities

To examine the social characteristics of both a passive indoor and an active Third Age lifestyle, we need to distinguish between "active" and "passive" leisure activities from the time-use activity codes. We grouped the approximately 250 activity categories of the UKTUS into seven general activity categories: domestic work, personal care, caring for children/

other members of the household, socializing with others, passive leisure, active/Third Age leisure, and an "other" category consisting of a few nonclassifiable codes.

Table 7.1 provides information on the average time spent on their seven different activities by British older adults over the two diary days by gender. Both men and women spent the same amount of time on caring for other household members and for personal care activities. Women spend more time doing household tasks while men spend more time in leisure pursuits. "Passive" forms of leisure constitute a dominant activity for both sexes. However, men spend approximately half an hour more in "passive" leisure pursuits than women. In contrast, very few minutes are spent on average on active leisure/Third Age activities, men spending 27 minutes and women spending 17 minutes.

The "active" leisure category consists of seven activity subcategories that were identified in the activity codes of the UKTUS: (1) engagement with arts, (2) entertainment, (3) hobbies in the countryside, (4) physical exercise, (5) voluntary work, (6) use of personal computers and the internet in general, and (7) formal studying in the library, for university or some other organized course.

Most of these seven "active" leisure activities are not "home-based," require some degree of advanced planning, and are cognitively more demanding and engaging than more passive forms of leisure, like, for example, television viewing or reading the newspaper. In this sense participation in these activities indicates a more engaged and active retired person, that is, a "third-ager" as described in relevant literature (Laslett, 1987). On the other hand, the category of passive "leisure" consists

TABLE 7.1 Mean Time Spent on Different Activities Over the 2 Days

ACTIVITIES	MEN	WOMEN
Personal care	11 h 25 min	11 h 25 min
Domestic work	3 h 7 min	3 h 50 min
Social activities	1 h 51 min	1 h 41 min
Caring for others	13 min	13 min
Active leisure	27 min	17 min
Passive leisure	5 h 36 min	5 h 2 min
Other	13 min	13 min

Note: Source: UK 2000 Time Use Survey; n = 1615; weighted.
The estimates refer to activities reported as primary by respondents.

mostly of indoor, less interactive, and generally "low-demand" activities and the majority of codes within this passive leisure category refer to mass-media consumption.

It is important to also examine the participation rates and average time spent on "active" and "passive" leisure pursuits by participants only, in Table 7.2.

Participation rates in "active" leisure pursuits are low for both sexes across the two diary days (Table 7.2). Among men the highest participation rates are found for physical exercise (12%), use of computers (8%), voluntary work (8%), and outdoor entertainment activities (8%). Women overall have lower participation rates in all seven activities. With the exception of the use of computers where women have very low participation (2%), there is the same rank order of activities as in the case of men. At the same time, when focusing solely on participants there are generally high active leisure durations, which essentially means that the small proportion of retirees that engage in "active" leisure activities do so in an organized way and that this engagement forms an important part of their lifestyle.

TABLE 7.2 "Active" and "Passive Leisure" Activities: Participation Rates and Mean Time Spent on Each Activity Over Two Days by Participants Only

ACTIVITIES	MEN ($n = 696$)		WOMEN ($n = 919$)	
	% OF SAMPLE (COUNT)	MEAN TIME	% OF SAMPLE (COUNT)	MEAN TIME
Passive				
Television	96.1 (669)	3 h 34 min	96.8 (890)	3 h 4 min
Reading	80 (557)	1 h 18 min	75.4 (693)	1 h 17 min
Resting/time out	57 (394)	1 h 1 min	63.7 (586)	1 h 6 min
Radio	29 (202)	43 min	28.1 (259)	44 min
Games	24.1 (168)	52 min	28.1 (219)	53 min
Active				
Arts	4.8 (34)	1 h 3 min	3.5 (32)	45 min
Entertainment	8.3 (58)	1 h 17 min	5.4 (50)	1 h 21 min
Hobbies in nature	0.7 (5)	56 min	0.4 (4)	14 min
Physical exercise	12.2 (85)	1 h 14 min	8 (73)	53 min
Voluntary work	8.3 (58)	1 h 8 min	6.9 (70)	1 h 22 min
Use of computers	8.2 (57)	11 min	2.3 (22)	10 min
Studying	3.7 (26)	39 min	4.4 (40)	38 min

Note: Source: UK 2000 Time Use Survey; $n = 1615$; weighted.

However, the picture is very different for "passive" leisure activities that all have very high participation rates (Table 7.2). Almost all retirees (96% of men and 97% of women) report watching television and for relatively lengthy periods of more than 3 hours per day. Reading magazines, newspapers, and books is an activity also practiced by significant proportions of both sexes (80% of men and 75% of women) for more than 1 hour each day. It is also interesting that a large proportion of retirees reported lengthy periods when no specific activity was actually performed, as indicated by the "resting/time out" category. Overall, the information provided in Table 7.2 indicates that across a representative weekend day and a weekday, "active" leisure pursuits are practiced only by a small minority of British retirees in this cohort, while the majority of people engage extensively in "passive" indoor leisure activities.

Social Factors Influencing Participation in "Active" and "Passive" Leisure Activities

We now turn our attention to the relative influence of social factors on participation and/or duration of "active" and "passive" leisure pursuits. This is an important issue to explore given several Third Age theorists' recent propositions that active leisure emerges privately, independently of social divisions and that, overall, aging should be understood today as an agentic reflexive project (Featherstone & Hepworth, 1989). Table 7.3 provides information on the time spent daily on the two most prevalent and time-consuming passive leisure activities, watching television and reading newspapers and/or magazines, by different sociodemographic groups.

Health is strongly associated with television viewing, with both men and women who report bad health spending more time on this activity than respondents with good or fair health. The same strong negative correlation is found for educational level, with men with no qualifications watching almost daily 2 hours of television more than men of high educational level. The pattern is not as pronounced for women; only 1 hour difference is found between the same groups. Social class is also associated with the time spent on daily television viewing, with both men and women of lower social class spending more time on this "passive" activity than any other education group. Finally, we cannot discern a clear relationship between age and television viewing, since differences between age groups are almost negligible.

TABLE 7.3   Mean Time Spent Daily on Watching Television and Reading by Different Social Groups

	WATCHING TELEVISION		READING MAGAZINES/ NEWSPAPERS, ETC.	
	MEN ($n = 696$)	WOMEN ($n = 919$)	MEN ($n = 696$)	WOMEN ($n = 919$)
Variable				
Health (Self-assessed)				
Good	3 h 9 min	2 h 40 min	1 h 5 min	49 min
Fair	3 h 35 min	3 h 14 min	1 h 3 min	55 min
Bad	4 h 10 min	3 h 32 min	55 min	50 min
Education				
High	2 h 50 min	2 h 9 min	1 h 22 min	57 min
Low/trade	3 h 17 min	2 h 37 min	1 h 12 min	55 min
No qualification	4 h 41 min	3 h 9 min	53 min	50 min
Social class				
Managerial and professional	3 h 3 min	2 h 34 min	1 h 13 min	51 min
Intermediate	3 h 10 min	2 h 46 min	54 min	52 min
Routine and manual	3 h 58 min	3 h 10 min	54 min	52 min
Early retired/never worked	3 h 8 min	2 h 58 min	1 h 10 min	51 min
Age				
65–69	3 h 22 min	2 h 53 min	55 min	44 min
70–74	3 h 21 min	2 h 54 min	1 h 2 min	47 min
75–79	3 h 39 min	2 h 58 min	1 h 9 min	54 min
80–84	3 h 33 min	3 h 12 min	1 h 4 min	1 h 1 min
85–98	2 h 56 min	3 h 7 min	1 h 11 min	1 h 7 min

Note: Source: UK 2000 Time Use Survey. $n = 1615$; weighted.

However, socio-demographic characteristics are differently associated with time spent reading the newspaper, magazines, and/or books. For example, there is a positive relationship between educational level and time spent on reading. This is not a surprising finding given the traditional higher print media consumption of the more educated in society. Patterns are not as clear for other socio-demographic characteristics like health and social class. Finally, it is interesting that reading time increases somewhat in older ages, while this was not the case for television viewing.

Very different patterns are found for participation in "active" leisure pursuits as shown in Table 7.4, which shows the percentages of people of different social groups participating in at least one "active" leisure pursuit across the two diary days. Thirty nine percent of men and 28% of women engage in one "active" leisure activity during a typical week.

TABLE 7.4 Percentages Participating in "Active" Leisure
Pursuits in Different Social Groups

	MEN 39.3	WOMEN 27.5
Variable		
Health (Self-assessed)		
Good	48.7	34.9
Fair	25.6	21.8
Bad	17.4	11.7
Education		
High	57.7	50.9
Low/trade	37.4	35
No qualification	29.2	22.4
Social class		
Managerial and professional	48.6	38.8
Intermediate	41.6	35.1
Routine and manual	23.6	19.5
Early retired/never worked	41.1	28.6
Age		
65–69	42.7	34.3
70–74	37	25.7
75–79	31.4	26.9
80–84	30.3	24.1
85–98	31.6	13.4

Note: Source: UK Time Use Survey; $n = 1615$; weighted.

There is a strong positive association between participation in "active" leisure pursuits and health status. Among men reporting good health, 49% participate in one "Third Age" activity, while the proportion falls to 17% for retirees with bad health. The same pattern is found among women although differences are not as pronounced.

A positive relationship is also found for educational level and an active lifestyle. The pattern is linear. More men and women retirees of high educational background are more active compared to their less educated counterparts. Patterns are not as clear in the case of social class, except that men and women retirees from routine and manual working class occupational backgrounds consistently lead more passive lifestyles than all other social class groups. However, the proportions of "active" agers from higher professional and intermediate backgrounds are almost the same. It is also important to note that there are more "active agers" in the "Early retired/Never worked" group than in the lower social class, which may be an indicator of high-income assets of this category.

Finally, as might be expected, it is in the youngest age group (65–69) who are the most likely to be "active agers."

Overall, Tables 7.3 and 7.4 demonstrate a strong and complex association of structural and health factors with lifestyle practices. "Active" leisure pursuits, which have been linked with the theoretical concept of the Third Age in relevant literature, appear to be the province of those who are culturally and materially advantaged. It is the healthy, educated, upper-class, and middle-class men who more often engage in an active leisure lifestyle during a typical week while other groups extensively engage in indoor "low-demand" activities. This finding renders support to the claims of political economists of aging that the risks associated with aging significantly differ between social groups and "that this core message is as true today as it was nearly thirty years ago" (Walker, 2006, p. 69).

FUTURE STEPS: ISSUES TO CONSIDER

This chapter introduced the basic aspects of time-use research methodology to researchers in the field of social gerontology and discussed a few of the topics and analyses that can be conducted with time-use data sets to further explore the phenomenon of aging. An analysis of British time-use data from 2000 was also provided in the second part of the chapter in order to further elucidate the potential of the methodology.

It has often been argued over the last decades that the circumstances for a different leisured experience of mature age now exist (Laslett, 1987; Neugarten, 1974). However, despite this theoretical focus on the concept of the Third Age as a healthy period after retirement, social gerontology still lacks empirical knowledge on everyday life experiences during this new life phase. Time-use research constitutes a methodological tool that can provide important information regarding everyday life and leisure behavior of the "third-agers," complementing social gerontology's understanding of this new life-course structure.

The availability of harmonized cross-national data for the last decades permits researchers to test theoretical hypotheses regarding the increased level of leisure participation for recent cohorts of retirees and to reach an understanding of the changes and the continuities that have occurred in the everyday realities of older people through the years. Time-use analysis can also generate empirical input regarding the differences between the lifestyles of "third-agers" and that of older people in the "Fourth Age" of frailty and dependency. The most recent time-use surveys will also allow an examination of the experiences of aging by the baby boomer generation, which is now exiting the labor market and has constituted one of the most important pillars in articulations of theories regarding the "new aging" in Western societies. Finally, the intentions of research agencies to enrich complementary data-collection instruments with more information on subjective well-being and the intrinsic satisfaction of activities also open new avenues for scientific research on the concept and meaning of individual aging.

NOTE

1. For a detailed account on the history and the current state of national and international time-use research and available databases, the reader is referred to the website of the International Association for Time Use Research (IATUR) and the Multinational Time Use Study (MTUS) at www.iatur.org/ and www.timeuse.org/mtus/.

ACKNOWLEDGMENTS

The empirical part of this chapter was based on the United Kingdom Time Use Survey 2000, produced by the Office for National Statistics and IPSOS-RSL and supplied by the UK Data Archive, which bear no responsibility for any analysis and interpretation in this article. The data are Crown Copyright. The authors acknowledge funding from the European Union Marie Curie Research Training Network "The Biomedical and Sociological Effects of Sleep Restriction" (MCRTN-CT-2004-512362).

REFERENCES

Abraham, K., Maitland, A., & Bianchi, S. (2006). Nonresponse in the American time use survey: Who is missing from the data and how much does it matter? *Public Opinion Quarterly, 70*(5), 676–703.

Andorka, R. (1987). Time budgets and their uses. *Annual Review of Sociology, 13*, 149–164.

Bryson, V. (2007). *Gender and the politics of time. Feminist theory and contemporary debates*. Bristol: Policy Press.

Chase, D., & Godbey, G. (1983). The accuracy of self-reported participation rates: A research note. *Leisure Studies, 2*(2), 231-235.

Department for Work and Pensions. (2005). *Opportunity age: Opportunity and security throughout life.* Retrieved December 3, 2009, from http://www.dwp.gov.uk/policy/ageing-society/strategy-and-publications/opportunity-age-first-report/

European Commission. (2002). *Ageing policy.* Retrieved January 24, 2010, from http://ec.europa.eu/employment_social/soc-prot/ageing/index_en.htm

Fast, J., & Frederick, J. (2004). The transition to retirement: When every day is Saturday. *Days of our lives: Time use and transitions over the life course.* Statistics Canada (Catalogue no. 89-584-MIE).

Featherstone, M., & Hepworth, M. (1989). Ageing and old age: Reflections on the postmodern life course. In B. Bytheway, T. Keil, P. Allatt, & A. Bryman (Eds.), *Becoming and being old: Sociological approaches to later life* (pp. 143-157). London: Sage.

Frederick, J., & Fast, J. (2004). Living longer, living better. *Days of our lives: Time use and transitions over the life course.* Statistics Canada (Catalogue no. 89-584-MIE).

Gauthier, A. H., & Furstenberg, F. F. Jr. (2002). The transition to adulthood: A time use perspective. *The Annals of the American Academy of Political and Social Science, 580*(1), 153-171.

Gauthier, A. H., & Smeeding, T. M. (2003). Time use at older ages: Cross-national differences. *Research on Aging, 25*(3), 247.

Gershuny, J. (2002). Social leisure and home IT: A time diary approach. *IT and Society, 1*(1), 54-72.

Gershuny, J. (2005). *Stylised estimates, activity logs and diaries: Estimating paid and unpaid work time.* Paper presented at the XXVII International Association for Time-Use Research Conference November 2-4, Halifax, Canada.

Gilleard, C. J., & Higgs, P. (2000). *Cultures of ageing: Self, citizen and the body.* Harlow: Prentice-Hall.

Harvey, A. (2001). *Time use metadata.* Paper presented at the 2001 IATUR conference, October 3-5, Oslo, Norway.

Hill, M. S., Herzog, A. R., & Juster, F. T. (1999). *Time use by and for older adults.* Paper presented at the Workshop on Measurement of and Research on Time Use, May 27-28, Washington, DC.

Horrigan, M., Herz, D., Joyce, M., Robinson, E., Stewart, J., & Stinson, L. (1999). *A report on the feasibility of conducting a time use survey.* Paper presented at the Workshop on Measurement of and Research on Time Use, May 27-28, Washington, DC.

Laslett, P. (1987). The emergence of the third age. *Ageing and Society, 7*(2), 133-160.

Neugarten, B. (1974). Age groups in American society and the rise of the young-old. *The Annals of the American Academy of Political and Social Science, 415*(1), 187-198.

Office for National Statistics. (2003). The United Kingdom 2000 Time Use Survey Technical Report. Retrieved October 27, 2007, from http://www.statistics.gov.uk/downloads/theme_ social/UKTUS_TechReport.pdf

Osterberg, C. (2000). *Methodological guidelines of harmonised European time use surveys—With reference to experiences of the European Time Use Pilot Surveys.* United Nations meeting for conducting time-use surveys, October 23-27,

New York, USA. Retrieved February 5, 2010, from http://unstats.un.org/unsd/methods/timeuse/xptgrpmeet/eurostat.pdf

Robinson, J. P. (1985). The validity and reliability of diaries versus alternative time use measures. In F. T. Juster & F. P. Stafford (Eds.), *Time, goods, and wellbeing* (pp. 33–62). Ann Arbor, MI: The University of Michigan.

Robinson, J. P., Chenu, A., & Alvarez, A. S. (2002). Measuring the complexity of hours at work: The weekly work grid. *Monthly Labour Review, 125*(4), 44–54.

Robinson, J. P., & Godbey, G. (1997). *Time for life: The surprising ways Americans use their time.* University Park, PA: Pennsylvania State University Press.

Rowe, J. W., & Kahn, R. L. (1997). Successful aging. *The Gerontologist, 37*(4), 433–440.

Stinson, L. (1999). Measuring how people spend their time: A time-use survey design. *Monthly Labour Review, 122*, 12–19.

Sullivan, O. (2006). *Changing gender relations, changing families: Tracing the pace of change over time (Gender Lens).* Boulder, CO: Rowman and Littlefield.

Szalai, A. (Ed.). (1972). *The use of time.* The Hague: Mouton.

Ver Ploeg, M., Altonji, J., Bradburn, N., DaVanzo, J., Nordhaus, W., & Samaniego, F. (Eds.). (2000). *Time use measurement and research: Report of a workshop.* Washington, DC: National Academy Press.

Verbrugge, L., & Gruber-Baldini, D. (1993) *Baltimore study of activity patterns.* Ann Arbor, MI: Institute of Gerontology, University of Michigan.

Walker, A. (2006). Re-examining the political economy of ageing: Understanding the structure/agency tension. In J. Baars, D. Dannefer, C. Phillipson, & A. Walker (Eds.), *Aging, globalization and inequality: The new critical gerontology.* New York, NY: Baywood Publishing Company.

Wahl, H. W., Tesch-Römer, C., & Hoff, A. (Eds.). (2007). *New dynamics in old age: Individual, environmental, and societal perspectives.* New York, NY: Baywood Publishing Company, Inc.

Weiss, R. S., & Bass, S. A. (Eds.). (2002). *Challenges of the third age: Meaning and purpose in later life.* New York, NY: Oxford University Press.

Experiencing the Third Age:
The Perspective of Qualitative Inquiry

Graham D. Rowles and Lydia K. Manning

The genius of human aging transforms an inevitable physical decline into something new, a reinvention of the self, a portal that leads to a new freedom from the burdens of adulthood.
—WILLIAM H. THOMAS, 2004

QUALITATIVE INQUIRY IN THE ERA OF THE THIRD AGE

*T*he phenomenon of the Third Age, conceptualized as a period of healthy retirement, reflects 20th century demographic and social changes that transformed the very meaning of what it is to be old. Advances in health care and public health, improvement in standards of living, and the institutionalization of retirement have resulted in a larger, healthier older population (Carr, 2009). As has been noted in previous chapters, current generations of older adults are living longer and are wealthier and better educated than previous cohorts (Rubinstein, Moss, Kleban, & Lawton, 2000). The result has been the emergence of a new phase of life described as the Third Age. With a growing proportion of the US population realistically anticipating the ability to retire and yet remain active for a number of years, the Third Age has taken shape as an unprecedented opportunity to enrich the experience of growing old by providing a new and expanded model of old age to precede and, in many cases, supersede a traditional view of a period of inexorable decrement and decline (Carr, 2009; Thomas, 2004). Elders are themselves at the forefront of shaping a societal transition that is redefining the meaning of old age (Savishinsky, 2000). With increasing recognition of the Third Age, the need for deeper understanding of this emergent phase of life and for careful, sensitive, in-depth phenomenological exploration of its characteristics and nuances becomes ever more pressing. This provides an exciting new opportunity for gerontologists engaging in qualitative research because, consistent with one of the tenets of qualitative inquiry, the territory is largely uncharted.

In this chapter we offer a framework for conducting qualitative research that will enable us to move toward a deeper understanding of how people experience their Third Age. This framework is built on several interlocking themes. First, we situate the Third Age in historical context, suggesting that the intersection of demographic and societal changes has restructured the life course in a way that has redefined both the milieu in which we age and the essential experience of aging. There is a need to reveal and probe the lived experience and meaning of a lengthy period of healthy retirement. Second, we consider philosophical and methodological underpinnings of a qualitative approach to address this need. A third section of the chapter considers what is known about the experience of the Third Age and its potential meanings for older adults. What are the key substantive experiential questions that need to be asked about this phase of life? In order to frame such questions, we employ two ideal-type case studies to express diverse aspects of the older person's experience of their Third Age and illustrate how the critical questions to be asked relate to context, identity, and the opportunity provided to explore new dimensions of the self. Fourth, we consider the role of a critical qualitative perspective in explorations of the Third Age. The chapter concludes with the assessment of challenges and oppor-tunities inherent in inquiry into the experience and meaning of the Third Age and advocates the adoption of an expanded vision of qualitative inquiry as a methodology of engagement and responsible participatory action research.

SITUATING THE THIRD AGE

As the editors (Carr and Komp) discuss in the introduction, Laslett (1991) popularized the concept of the "Third Age" as way of describing the emerging group of older individuals who have the capacity to engage actively in society in later life. In recent years, the idea of a Third Age has gained widespread, although often implicit, acceptance as a mass phenomenon especially within Western societies. Yet, as Carr and Komp (Introduction, this book) note, there is ambiguity and a lack of consistency in scholarly definition and operationalization of the Third Age as a construct within gerontology, and the Third Age has been diversely described.

As people live longer in greater numbers, a new demographic imperative creates a social reality where older people have a stronger presence in the social structure of communities. In many parts of the world, the emergence of the Third Age is responsible for ongoing transitions in society and culture. As Weiss and Bass (2002) explain, the Third Age is not simply a prolonged middle age, nor a sustained and active old age, but rather a transition of institutions, norms, and opportunities for older individuals. This transformation involves not only older adults but also society at large. We are, in short, in the midst of a structural transition with consequences that will become increasingly apparent over the next decade (Weiss & Bass, 2002).

Qualitative researchers are uniquely positioned to uncover the deeper meanings of these transitions in the lives of individual older adults. But we can do more. Not only is there a rich potential to unveil the outcomes of structural changes with respect to the life experience of older individuals, but also we can explore and document the consequences of the presence of new generations of elders on society at large. We can begin to reveal and facilitate understanding of how this new life phase shapes organizations, businesses, government, the economy—the very identity of the societies in which we live. To best facilitate this understanding we must consider the philosophical and methodological underpinnings of a qualitative perspective on the Third Age.

PHILOSOPHICAL AND METHODOLOGICAL UNDERPINNINGS

Relatively little is known about how older adults experience their Third Age. We lack ethnographies of the Third Age. There are few systematic empirical studies of changing patterns of behavior during the Third Age. Much of what we know about emerging Third Age lifestyles is anecdotal or arises from portrayals of aspects of Third Age experience reported in popular literature (see, e.g., Goldman, 2006; Thomas, 2004). There is little grounded theory about this new phase of life. Perhaps most importantly, there has been limited discourse on the distinctive meanings of life during the Third Age, a period of life that currently lacks the clearly defined societal expectations of the preceding working and child-raising phase of life or the subsequent process of end-of-life physical decline and withdrawal from physically active engagement. It is almost as if we have stretched out the life course and simply inserted a new phase between working life and traditional old age without providing the recipients of this bounty with a roadmap as to how they should be living and what they are likely to experience. In the face of this void, older adults are themselves defining the experience through the lives they lead in the active early years of their retirement (Savishinsky, 2000).

This conceptual gap and differing perspectives on how older adults experience the Third Age provides an open invitation to phenomenological exploration. As a result of its methodological flexibility and potential for creativity in revealing key areas of meaning, value, and intentionality, qualitative inquiry is positioned to provide a strong foundation for understanding how older adults are reconceptualizing the early phase of later life and the extent to which they now view this period as a time of opportunity, growth, and positive change, rather than merely a period of psychological and social accommodation to future anticipated dependence and decline (Carr & Manning, 2010).

The key to successfully revealing and understanding the lived experience and meaning of the Third Age lies in embracing the philosophy, epistemology, and methodologies of qualitative inquiry. From a philosophical perspective there is need for humanistic exploration of the manner in which people frame their life and the way it is lived. Such an approach requires that we approach people's experience of the Third Age from the perspective of a questioning *concern with meaning* that we hypothesize becomes an increasingly pervasive motif during this phase of life (Frankl, 1946/2006; Rowles, 2008). For perhaps the first time in the history of Western industrial and postmodern culture, there is a phase of life in which for the masses, rather than solely the elite and affluent, there may be time to transcend the demands of obtaining the means for daily sustenance, child-raising, or accommodation to growing frailty. The Third Age provides an opportunity to actually live life in a manner that might facilitate true self actualization—for people to follow the admonition of Henry David Thoreau (1817–1862) to *"Live the life you have imagined."* To what extent can we best characterize the current era and the Third Age as a time when each person's being in the world comes to be viewed in these terms? Can it be legitimately argued that, beyond the potential for continued activity and societal participation, the Third Age now provides expanded opportunities for self-discovery, spiritual engagement, reflection, contemplation, and gerotranscendence—that it makes the journey of life experientially richer as well as potentially more productive (Harris, 2008; Scott-Maxwell, 1968; Sinnott, 2009; Tornstam, 2005)?

From the perspective of epistemology and methodology, understanding people's experience through the lens of liberated opportunity provided by the Third Age, will be facilitated by unleashing the full arsenal of qualitative methods that have achieved greater acceptance and prominence over the past few decades—participant observation, in-depth interviewing; focus groups; ethnography; interpretation of material culture; life histories; personal journals; art interpretation; photography; the content analysis of literature, poetry, and newspapers; and a plethora of additional data gathering and interpretation strategies—as well as new approaches yet to be discovered (Denzin & Lincoln, 2007).

Each of these approaches involves acceptance of a fundamental epistemological premise. Before attempting to manipulate variables to explain or predict human behavior, it is essential to ensure that the variables we use mean something in terms of actual lived experience rather than reflect ungrounded *a priori* assumptions of researchers unfamiliar with the life worlds of the people they study. It is also important to accept a rider to this premise; that it is necessary to continuously review and assess the ongoing experiential validity of the variables we use through post analysis return to the field to qualitatively assess the continuing viability of constructs. For, as "being" is actually a constantly evolving process of "becoming," it is essential in our methodologies to acknowledge the phenomenological dynamism of each situation we study (Groger & Straker, 2002).

Although this is a relatively new domain of inquiry, there are examples of qualitative researchers making theoretical and methodological contributions to an understanding of the Third Age. Cooper and Thomas (2002) adopt a qualitative lens in their exploration of the importance of dance as a way for older adults in the Third Age to claim visibility, generate "sub-cultural capital" and make meaning in later life. Rossen, Knafl, and Flood (2008), explore the various ways older women understand and express their views of successfully aging as they transition into a Third Age, concluding that successful aging is a deliberate decision having more to do with acceptance of circumstance rather than achievement. Leibing, through content analysis of Brazilian print media, concludes that older adults manifest relatively high levels of life satisfaction regardless of new ideologies concerning age and that they conceptualize themselves as third-agers or "not yet old" (2005, p. 28).

These models of research on the Third Age can be reinforced and complemented through recognition and further development of contemporary trends in qualitative scholarship. Schoenberg and Rowles (2002), for example, emphasize the need for *triangulation of methods*. Groger and Straker (2002) point out opportunities presented by *combining qualitative and quantitative methodologies*. There is increasing recognition of the critical *role of environmental context* and an understanding of place, including place viewed in temporal context, in effective qualitative research on old age (Rowles, 1983, 1993, 2008). For example, Groger (2002) discusses the importance of a nursing home setting in African-Americans' conceptualization of the portability of home. There is a need for models that incorporate the "increasing sophistication of our understanding of the roles of reactivity and reflexivity" (Schoenberg & Rowles, 2002, p. 16). For example, Reinharz (1997) emphasizes recognition of the multiple selves present in the researcher and how they shape the meaning and interpretation of data. We change and are changed in the process of inquiry. It is important to recognize this self-reflexivity in our scholarship and methods of exploration. Particularly important as we explore the meaning of a Third Age will be the need to *accept inconsistency* as a part of human experience. Our rage for order often precludes us from acknowledging that what people do does not necessarily make sense, even to them. Finally, there will be the need for the humility to accept that there may be *experiences beyond knowing* in a sense that can be effectively shared and realms of transcendent experience that are inaccessible to all but those who experience them.

THROUGH A QUALITATIVE LENS

Key questions and realms of context must be explored qualitatively before gerontologists can begin to adequately theorize the occurrences, events, and behaviors of individuals experiencing the Third Age. These initial questions are rooted in the existential and phenomenological realm of meaning. Settersten (2003) reminds us that the search for meaning has been ongoing since the start of recorded human history. Humans have long since grappled with existential questions about what it means to be aging, beginning at the dawn of human consciousness, progressing through an array of philosophers from the time of Cicero's *De Senectute* (1490) to the contemporary thinking of Achenbaum (1978), Cole (1992), and Moody (1997), and recent writing on the phenomenology of aging by Longino and Powell (2009). Questions stemming from this need to understand human existence and to make meaning of life are rooted in human nature: what does it mean to be alive and how do we make life purposeful and fulfilling? It is argued by some scholars that the period of later life is a time when processing these questions and coming to terms with the answers is crucial for older adults (Butler, 1963; Erikson, 1963; Moody, 1997; Settersten, 2003; Tornstam, 2005; Weiss & Bass, 2002). The Third Age as an emerging life phase, a part of the life course, is a time for older adults where these questions become salient, a time that may well be characterized by the potential for increased awareness and reflection on the meaning of life and reorientation toward attaining the fulfillment that can come from behaviors and lifestyles that manifest and actualize this search for meaning. Our responsibility as gerontologists is to ask third-agers themselves about their search for meaning and fulfillment and the degree to which this becomes an underlying motif of their lifestyle choices and everyday experience.

The collection, analysis, and interpretation of data are all co-constituted between ourselves as researchers and the people we study (Maykut & Morehouse, 1994). In attempting to understand human complexities and interpret their larger meaning, researchers become *human-as-instrument*, the "only instrument flexible enough to capture the complexity, subtlety, and constantly changing situation which is the human experience" (Maykut & Morehouse, 1994, p. 26). Essentially, using a qualitative lens in investigating the Third Age, we become human-as-instrument in probing the subtleties of older adults' *lived experience*. Below we use two ideal-type case studies to illustrate key aspects of how experiences of the Third Age are linked to meaning and context. We explore potentially positive aspects of the Third Age as well as potentially problematic characteristics as revealed in the lives of two individuals.

Living the Life You Have Imagined

I (first author) met John Klim early one Sunday morning while staying at the Regency Hotel. It was 6:00 a.m. and the dining room was sparsely populated. A short order cook with a particularly tall chef's hat was preparing eggs for another guest who like me had arisen early. I ordered an omelet. He flipped it fully eight feet into the air! As my breakfast nestled back into his frying pan, I asked him, "How often do you miss?" "Never! I'm Chef Klim," he replied, taking mock offense at my inquiry. We began to talk and, as his story unfolded, I was provided with a portal into the world of a man savoring his Third Age.

John had formally retired five years previously at 68 after working for several decades as head of the appliance department at a local Sears & Roebuck department store. He had looked forward to retirement and explained that he and his wife, Rita, made what they thought were elaborate plans for living out their "golden years." An avid gardener, he determined he would make his flowers the pride of the neighborhood and grow enough vegetables to move toward self-sufficiency. John was determined to cultivate not only his garden, but also the time and space to more fully experience the new openness and freedom of life that he felt accompanies retirement. In addition, Rita had been complaining for several years about a variety of repair and home modification tasks that needed to be completed in their home. The couple also decided they would travel, taking trips to places they had always wanted to visit, including the Holy Land.

As John explained it, all went well. The garden was restored to perfect order. With help from a friend who worked in construction, their home was appropriately modified, including the installation of a luxurious bath with air jets and a new walk-in shower adjacent to the master bedroom. Vacation trips were taken to Florida, to Israel and Jordan, and to Mexico, and a memorable cruise to Alaska resulted in several spectacular pictures now adorning the living room wall. But, as John phrased it, "After three years we had done just about everything. I began to get bored." He began to realize that his newfound freedom presented the opportunity to embark on a search for new opportunities. He also began to wonder about a deeper meaning and purpose in his life.

During one of his Florida trips, John took a short course on cooking. Upon his return home, he rejoined a group of his peers who convened every weekday morning to walk at the local mall, ending their exercise each day with extended coffee and conversation in the Food Court. One of his friends remarked that the Regency Hotel was looking for someone part-time to be a short order cook for Sunday breakfasts. John applied and obtained the job. Each Sunday morning he would rise at 4:00 a.m. and get to the hotel in time to prepare ingredients. He enjoyed the job and his friendly demeanor and easy conversational style soon endeared him to guests. After a few months he was asked to cover Saturday morning as well. And then, when the regular morning chef left, at 73, John found himself working six mornings a week. "Actually," he remarked, "It really isn't work." By the time I met him, his egg flipping and other culinary exploits had made him a celebrity and a large banner with his photograph announcing his status as "Chef Klim—the Omelet King" prominently adorned the entrance to the hotel restaurant.

John's transition from appliance salesman to part-time chef/hotel personality parallels the experience of hundreds of thousands of third-agers who have rediscovered themselves, pursued entirely new vocations and interests, and are living a lifestyle that previous generations could hardly have imagined. But as I probed deeper, I discovered more. Beyond being able to continue to engage with life in a manner that enabled him to feel purposeful and productive, John explained how his brief spell of formal retirement and his transition to a new part-time vocation had provided an opportunity to explore deeper aspects of his life and personhood, practicing self-reflexivity, and contemplative aging. He talked about how his work at the Regency had introduced him to an entirely new social network, about how he had been enabled to liberate the "showman" side of his personality, the satisfaction he derived from his increased level of volunteering at his church, his closer relationship with his grandchildren, and an intensification of his relationship with Rita. He relished the opportunity to read more biographies of great figures in history, something that had always been his passion. He talked about how the increased time he was able to spend in his garden enabled him to sit and simply enjoy being alive, how he would sometimes sit and savor the aroma of the flowers, marvel at the intricacy of the petals, the blending of colors, and the wonder of nature. It was, he said, as if he was now able to better appreciate his place in the universe and his relationship to past and future generations. In essence, John has exposed and expanded latent dimensions of his identity and is developing new meaning in his later life.[1]

For every John who has developed a new sense of identity in old age there are far too many for whom the Third Age, rather than being a time of renewal, fulfillment, and self-actualization, represents little more than an extension of, or even worse, movement into a lifestyle of disadvantage and challenge. Many third-agers are denied opportunities for fulfillment.

Being Denied a Third Age

If you want to have the time of your life at the end of your life, then you better be able to pay for it.
—Sophie Malounek, quoted in Savishinsky, 2000, *Breaking the Watch.*

Life's realities for Marshall Whitman illustrate Sophie Malounek's words. He continues to work a low-wage, now part-time, job at the factory in the conservative Midwestern Rust Bowl town where he spent 40 years of his working life. His plans for retirement at 65 with a secure pension and health benefits failed to materialize through no fault of his own. Marshall is not the fortunate product of cumulative advantage over the life course. Growing up poor in rural Appalachia and migrating to the city for employment proved beneficial, the ideal of rugged individualism woven into the fabric of the American Dream created an air of allure and enticement for Marshall. But the formulaic promise of working hard to secure a safe and solid retirement and old age did not go quite as planned. Marshall did retire at 65, but within two years he learned that health insurance was no longer covered in his limited pension plan. His only daughter lost her job and home. On his 67th birthday he returned to the factory on a part-time basis (although without benefits) "... to help make ends meet." Now 74, this African-American widower considers himself fortunate to be healthy enough to continue working not only for himself but also to supplement the meager income of his daughter and her three children, all of whom reside in his home. Although life is challenging and not lived exactly as planned, Marshall remains optimistic. "Living this way sure is better than the alternative," he wryly notes; he embodies the resilience of so many others in his situation.

Identifying as a third-ager is irrelevant for Mr. Whitman. His days are not spent contemplating the choice of attending yoga class or a workshop on spiritual transcendence. Rather, he remains immersed in the mundane activities associated with supporting an economically marginal household and providing for a late-life family. Yet, despite his inability to join his friends for their morning walk and coffee at the mall and his inability to share their pleasures during afternoons at the target range or tending their gardens, there is, nonetheless, an experiential deepening of his being in the world. Marshall enjoys partial benefits of a Third Age through his continuing ability to boisterously play with his grandchildren and intensify his connections and relationship with his daughter. He engages in lifelong learning, the learning that accompanies raising grandchildren. He attempts to meet women and date in the hopes that he may again one day discover love. And he relishes the free time that his semiretirement gives to sit on his porch, enjoy the warmth of the evening sun, quietly reminisce, and watch the occasional car pass by on the street below.

Marshall Whitman's partial Third Age is not the ideal described in the articles and texts of commentators touting active, postretirement, predisability, "successful aging." His Third Age reflects the paradoxical Janus-like ambiguity of postretirement life for many older adults. On the one hand, his partial Third Age is characterized by continuation of a work role and the financial strain and worry of supporting a family. But at the same time, he remains conscious of the fact that many of his former colleagues and age peers are enjoying days filled with leisure, volunteering, new opportunities for creative expression, and an existential freedom he can only wistfully observe from a distance.

Marshall Whitman's situation reflects socio-demographic predictors that make it difficult for many older adults to fully experience a Third Age; race, class, and socioeconomic status (Carr & Manning, 2010). His circumstances call into question pervasive assumptions about the benign characteristics of the Third Age and its implications for older adults. Existing scholarship lavishly explores the possibilities and opportunities associated with a Third Age. This is problematic in a number of ways, both for older adults and gerontology at large. The role of a qualitative perspective is essential in helping gerontologists to further uncover the myriad of ways older adults are experiencing a Third Age, and detecting barriers and obstacles for those experiencing something other than a new life stage permeated with time and opportunity and advantage.

A CRITICAL PERSPECTIVE

Critical gerontologists view the world from both individual and social contextual perspectives, recognizing that there is more to understanding the aging experience than is conventionally presented in mainstream gerontology. Minkler and Holstein (2008) explain that critical gerontology has developed over the last 30 years along parallel lines of political economy and the humanities resulting in its presence as a defined subfield of gerontology. The function of critical gerontology is to "cast a critical eye on society and the field of gerontology itself, critiquing structures, assumptions and practices of mainstream gerontology and the larger socio-political context in which they occur" (Ray, 2008, p. 97). Not only does this encourage mindful and informed critique within the context of broader societal economic and social structures and processes but it also advocates for gerontologists to be self-referential. This idea of reflexivity and being self-referential is an important aspect of qualitative inquiry, particularly as we explore the Third Age.

Arising in part from critique and opposition to narrowly defined perspectives on the "social problems of aging," critical gerontology is an alternative approach seeking to explore the potential opportunities and contributions associated with and experienced in late life (Moody, 2008). Critical gerontology asks us to explore the everydayness associated with meaning making in late life, in addition to encouraging us to find our own voice as we age and explore various realities associated with aging. These charges are useful in Third Age scholarship, as they encourage qualitative researchers to explore and discover how third-agers residing outside mainstream society and in the margins make meaning of their lives and identities in this emergent social role. Western society is criticized for creating dualisms regarding age; aging is viewed in either a positive or negative light (Biggs, 2001). Establishing and utilizing these binary constructs in our cultural conceptualization of age is dangerous, particularly when considering the Third Age as a new life stage. In this respect, our own characterization of John Klim and Marshall Whitman should be viewed as only two of a plethora of possible expressions and nuances of life experiences in the Third Age.

With an epistemological and methodological focus on acknowledging and cherishing the diversity and complexity of individual experience, qualitative researchers are well positioned to understand the myriad of ways older adults make meaning of their lives, and have a responsibility to delve deeply into the margins to explore not just the norm and the typical but also the rich anomalies and nuances of meaning making during the Third Age. Exploring the Third Age goes beyond recreating or expanding on the currently fashionable "successful aging" discourse to uncover the elements of a successful Third Age; it requires more than putting a new spin on positive aging. Rather, a critical perspective requires a focus on revealing and celebrating the diversity, complexity, and heterogeneity of the experience of the Third Age even as we explore the underlying societal processes and elements of political economy that shape the milieu in which this time of life is experienced.

In the United States and most western cultures, critical exploration of issues of gender, race, and class, and a quest for understanding grounded in full awareness of the role that power and privilege play in shaping people's lives are essential. This is especially important in view of the widening social gap and increasing resource disparity between the "haves" and the "have nots" in populations of baby boomers moving toward their Third Age (AARP, 1998; Frey, 1999). We must move beyond the crudity of most formal surveys and utilize the sophistication and subtlety of refined in-depth qualitative approaches to address penetrating questions that only such approaches can adequately address: Whose Third Age are we attempting to understand? What does it mean to be a third-ager? Does or can every person experience a Third Age or is the Third Age the preserve of a privileged few? How is experience of the Third Age manifested in different ethnic and cultural groups? Is a positive Third Age an entitlement? Do the disadvantaged even recognize the existence of such a possibility? Are third-agers any less or more "successful," "happy," or "fulfilled" in later life? Are opportunities to achieve gerotranscendence in any way enhanced through the gift of a Third Age? What is the appropriate societal response to the advent of the Third Age?

Challenges to the Third Age

A great deal of Third Age scholarship seemingly focuses on issues surrounding productive aging, as it is linked to economic productivity—productivity understood from a capitalist perspective. For example, Weiss and Bass (2002) organize their pioneering work on the Third Age on the premise of a tri-partitioned life course (childhood, adulthood, old age). As adults near completion of their working lives and start the journey into retirement they must reevaluate what it means to be old and how they will matter in the newly emergent first phase (postretirement and predisability) of a life-course stage traditionally pervaded by a motif of decline. Implicit in this conceptualization is the view that a tri-partitioned life course adequately reflects the normative life-course expectation of all older adults. There is also an assumption that if an individual so chooses they can with a high level of choice and autonomy create a Third Age experience of their own choosing within the early phase of their old age.

These two implicit assumptions in the conceptualization of a Third Age serve as challenges for critical gerontologists. A central obstacle in exploration of a new early late-life identity is beginning the complicated and difficult task of carving out whose Third Age it is about which we are talking. Dannefer's (2003) work on the life-course trajectories of child laborers and gang members is a useful model worth applying to Third Age scholarship. Dannefer concludes that a positive old age is the reward of those who have accumulated higher levels of material resources and cultural capital. Thus, the challenge is to uncover the verity of how and to what extent issues of power and privilege and other life-course factors shape which older adults get to experience a positive Third Age. An even bigger challenge is to reveal the circumstances of the marginal elderly in a manner that will cast light on the degree to which they are able to experience some elements of Third Age while being denied access to others.

Finally, we need to be aware of a paradox in the opportunities associated with the Third Age. Reconstructing the first phase of old age as a time of freedom when older adults are encouraged and expected to continue to contribute to society may be problematic for those who, for one reason or another (e.g., health or economic circumstances), are unable to give back according to societal expectations of volunteerism and civic engagement. The qualitative challenge is to explore the relationship between the evolution of life's meaning to people in their Third Age and their likely different definitions of productivity in relation to increasing societal expectations for some continuing manifestations of traditionally defined productivity.

FUTURE STEPS: ISSUES TO CONSIDER

As we look to the future, we contend that qualitative researchers have not only the opportunity, but also the responsibility to spearhead efforts to understand and act upon what it means to be an older adult in the era of the Third Age. We propose an integrative methodology of qualitative critique to attend to this important task. This approach entails the tricky and somewhat paradoxical task of trying to reconcile three interrelated and dynamic approaches to critical inquiry. First it will require pure description of the phenomenological experience, the essence of being an older person living a Third Age. Second, it will necessitate thoughtful interpretation of an evolving milieu—the changing medical, economic, social, political, and cultural environment which has spawned the opportunity for people to experience a Third Age, and at the same time, controls its manifestations. Third, a perceptive, holistic, and responsible interpretation of the Third Age as simultaneously an individually experienced and socially constructed phenomenon requires a focus on explicitly revealing and interpreting the disparities and injustices that result from the evolving engagement of personal experience and environmental context—the blending of person and place (Cutchin, 2004; Dickie, Cutchin, & Humphrey, 2006).

An array of qualitative approaches is available to explore the three dimensions of critical inquiry into the Third Age. The phenomenological method, reflexive in-depth interviewing, autobiographical writing, diaries and personal journals, focus groups, poetry, life histories, and other approaches designed to reveal the subtlety and richness of individual experience, all provide portals into the phenomenological world of the person experiencing the Third Age. In concert, through processes of triangulation, such methods facilitate a deeper understanding of what it means to experience a Third Age. Through the sensitive employment of such methods it will be possible to reveal the plethora of ways in which a Third Age consciousness is both implicitly and explicitly manifested by individuals: perhaps through increasingly mindful appreciation of mundane tasks (cooking, gardening, and caregiving); perhaps through a reframing of time and the evolution and focusing of relationships and connections, and new forms of intimacy (Carstensen, 1991, 2006; Carstensen, Isaacowitz, & Charles, 1999); perhaps through the discovery of new values and meaning in the redefinition of occupation and emergent forms of civic engagement (Martinson & Minkler, 2006); perhaps through lifelong learning (Williamson, 1997), expansion of leisure activities, or a flowering of creativity; perhaps through novel pathways of spiritual development and maturation; perhaps through the emergence of a more contemplative aging persona (Tornstam, 2005); perhaps through a more fierce internal grappling with the complexities and ambiguities of old age (Scott-Maxwell, 1968); and perhaps even through preconscious acceptance of status that simply allows the person to "be." It may well be that many people are content to let life simply flow over and around them and savor the richness of each moment in a spirit of unquestioning acceptance of their biography and place in the cosmos.

A comparable diverse array of qualitative approaches is also appropriate in probing and developing deeper understanding of the evolving milieu of the Third Age. Various levels of participant observation, photography, interpretation of historical records, content analysis of contemporary reports, and written materials, an arsenal of clever unobtrusive measures (Webb, Campbell, Schwartz, & Sechrest, 1966), ethnography, and the "thick description" of culture in context (Geertz, 1973), are complementary options for probing environmental context and tracking change in the milieu that nurtures the Third Age. In combination, these approaches can be used to develop a profile of the material environment, political economy, social and community structures, and historical processes that have generated societies that facilitate a Third Age.

But we suggest that it is from a third approach toward qualitative inquiry that the most powerful insights will arise. The most revealing and potentially useful window into the Third Age lies in embracing participatory research and the scholarship of engagement. While elements of such an approach are clearly implicit within research on individuals experiencing a Third Age and in studies of the environment of the Third Age, it is from participatory research, indeed, participatory action research that we are likely to reap the richest awards (Healy, 2001; Kidd & Kral, 2005; Ochocka, Janzen, & Nelson, 2002). This is because the Third Age is not a discrete, easily definable phenomenon but rather a cultural transformation in process. Only by fully participating in the Third Age experience and, in the process, acknowledging that through our work we are both mirroring and helping to shape the Third Age, can we fully tap the pulse of this evolving phase of life.

A participatory, action-oriented approach to research on the Third Age necessitates acknowledging the wholeness of experience. The person experiencing a Third Age, the environment of the Third Age, and the researcher of the Third Age are neither independent nor mutually exclusive entities. Rather, each is defined by and evolves in concert with the other in a dynamic person/environment/researcher transaction (Figure 8.1). The nexus of this transaction is the constantly evolving model of the Third Age to which we adhere.

Consistent with this perspective, older people experiencing their Third Age are critical contributors to shaping the phenomenon through the lifestyles they choose and the manner in which they find

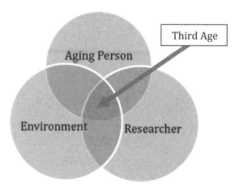

FIGURE 8.1   Participatory action model for qualitative inquiry into the Third Age.

meaning in new ways of being in the world. This lived experience of a shift in perspective about old age in which aging is no longer viewed as synonymous with decline and disengagement makes third-agers themselves the most appropriate people to define and interpret its characteristics. It is they who are in the best position to define the questions to be posed and identify agendas for intervention to address disjuncture and stresses generated by this new phase of life. In this context, gerontological researchers, functioning as tools for collecting and interpreting data, must seek to map a Third Age that adequately captures the way in which older adults understand the phenomenon and the language older adults use to describe their experiences (both positive and negative). As scholars, and as people who ourselves are part of the process of shaping the Third Age, it is also our responsibility to work with older adults to critique and to reveal injustices as they manifest themselves in the lives of persons experiencing a Third Age. There is a responsibility to use all of our methodological skills to reveal why for some older people like John Klim, a liberating Third Age exists as a pleasant outcome of privilege while for others, like Marshall Whitman, a partial Third Age affords more limited opportunities for growth and engagement during this new phase of life.

The implications of this holistic, integrative perspective on inquiry into the Third Age are many. We are not and cannot be bystanders observing from the sidelines. We must celebrate the relationship between knowledge and power. As scholars are fully engaged in the process of working with elders to reveal the experiential meaning of the Third Age, it becomes our moral obligation not only to interpret but also to act on the shared insight we gain with participants in our research. It is important to ensure that the character and experience of the Third Age we are mutually creating is one that liberates rather than constrains and is available in equal measure to all.

NOTE

1. For illustration of how some of these implicit Third Age developmental themes are becoming increasingly reflected in the literature, see Baltes and Carstensen (1996), Carstensen (2006), Thomas (2004), and Tornstam (2005).

REFERENCES

Achenbaum, W. A. (1978). *Old age in the new land: The American experience since 1790.* Baltimore, MD: The Johns Hopkins University Press.

AARP. (1998). *Boomers approaching midlife: How secure a future?* Washington, DC: AARP Public Policy Institute.

Baltes, M., & Carstensen, L. L. (1996). The process of successful ageing. *Ageing and Society, 16*, 397-422.

Biggs, S. (2001). Toward critical narrativity: Stories of aging in contemporary social policy. *Journal of Aging Studies, 15*(4), 303-316.

Butler, R. N. (1963). The life review: An interpretation of reminiscence in the aged. *Psychiatry, 26*, 65-76.

Carr, D. C. (2009). Aging in America: The link between productivity and resources in the Third Age. *Ageing International, 34*(3), 154-171.

Carr, D., & Manning, L. (2010). A new paradigm for qualitative research in the United States: The era of the third age. *Qualitative Sociology Review, 6*(1), 16-33.

Carstensen, L. L. (1991). Socioemotional selectivity theory: Social activity in life-span context. *Annual Review of Gerontology and Geriatrics, 17*, 195-217.

Carstensen, L. L. (2006). The influence of a sense of time on human development. *Science, 312*(5782), 1913-1915.

Carstensen, L. L., Isaacowitz, D. M., & Charles, S. T. (1999). Taking time seriously: A theory of socioemotional selectivity. *American Psychologist, 54*(3), 165-181.

Cicero, M. T. (44B.C/1490). *De senectute.* Colonie: H. Quentell.

Cole, T. R. (1992). *The journey of life: A cultural history of aging in America.* Cambridge: Cambridge University Press.

Cooper, L., & Thomas, H. (2002). Growing old gracefully: Social dance in the third age. *Ageing & Society, 22*(6), 689.

Cutchin, M. P. (2004). Using Deweyan philosophy to rename and reframe adaptation-to-environment. *American Journal of Occupational Therapy, 58*(3), 303-312.

Dannefer, D. (2003). Whose life course is it, anyway? Diversity and "linked lives" in the global perspective. In R. A. Settersten (Ed.), *Invitation to the life course: Toward new understandings of later life* (pp. 259-268). Amityville, NY: Baywood Publishing Company.

Denzin, N. K., & Lincoln, Y. S. (Eds.). (2007). *Handbook of qualitative research.* Thousand Oaks, CA: Sage Publications.

Dickie, V., Cutchin, M. P., & Humphrey, R. (2006). Occupation as transactional experience: A critique of individualism in occupational science. *Journal of Occupational Science, 13*(1), 83-93.

Erikson, E. H. (1963). *Childhood and society.* New York, NY: Norton.

Frankl, V. E. (1946/2006). *Man's search for meaning.* Boston, MA: Beacon Press (First published in German in 1946 under the title *Ein Psycholog erlebt das Konzentrationslager.* Original English title *From Death Camp to Existentialism*).

Frey, W. H. (1999). *Beyond social security: The local aspects of an aging America.* Washington, DC: The Brookings Institution.

Geertz, C. (1973). Thick description: Toward an interpretive theory of culture. In *The interpretation of culture* (Chapter 1). New York, NY: Basic Books.

Goldman, C. (2006). *Late-life love: Romance and new relationships in later years.* Minneapolis, MN: Fairview Press.

Groger, L. (2002). Coming to terms: African-Americans' complex ways of coping with life in a nursing home. *International Journal of Aging and Human Development, 55*(3), 181-203.

Groger, L., & Straker, J. K. (2002). Counting and recounting: Approaches to combining quantitative and qualitative data and methods. In G. D. Rowles & N. E. Schoenberg (Eds.), *Qualitative gerontology* (2nd ed.) (pp. 179-199). New York, NY: Springer Publishing Company.

Harris, H. (2008). Growing while going: Spiritual formation at the end of life. *Journal of Religion, Spirituality and Aging, 20*(3), 227-245.

Healy, K. (2001). Participatory action research and social work: A critical appraisal. *International Social Work, 44*(1), 93-105.

Kidd, S. A., & Kral, M. J. (2005). Practicing participatory action research. *Journal of Counseling Psychology, 52*(2), 187-195.

Laslett, P. (1991). *A fresh map of life: The emergence of the Third Age.* Cambridge, MA: Harvard University Press.

Leibing, A. (2005). The old lady from Ipanema: Changing notions of old age in Brazil. *Journal of Aging Studies, 19*(1), 15-31.

Longino, C. F., & Powell, J. L. (2009). Toward a phenomenology of aging. In V. L. Bengtson (Ed.), *Handbook of theories of aging.* New York, NY: Springer Publishing Company.

Martinson, M., & Minkler, M. (2006). Civic engagement and older adults: A critical perspective. *The Gerontologist, 46*(3), 318-324.

Maykut, P., & Morehouse, R. (1994). *Beginning qualitative research: A philosophical and practical guide.* New York, NY: Routledge Falmer.

Minkler, M., & Holstein, M. B. (2008). From civil rights to . . . civic engagement? Concerns of two older critical gerontologists about a "new social movement" and what it portends. *Journal of Aging Studies, 22*, 196-204.

Moody, H. R. (1997). *The five stages of the soul.* New York, NY: Anchor Books, Doubleday.

Moody, H. (2008). Aging America and the boomer wars. *The Gerontologist, 48*(6), 839-844.

Ochocka, J., Janzen, R., & Nelson, G. (2002). Sharing power and knowledge: Professional and mental health consumer/survivor researchers working together in a participatory action research project. *Psychiatric Rehabilitation Journal, 25*(4), 379-387.

Ray, R. E. (2008). Coming of age in critical gerontology. *Journal of Aging Studies, 22*(2), 97-100.

Reinharz, S. (1997). *Reflexivity and voice.* London: Sage.

Rossen, E. K., Knafl, K. A., & Flood, M. (2008). Older women's perceptions of successful aging. *Activities, Adaptation and Aging, 32*(2), 73-88.

Rowles, G. D. (1983). Place and personal identity in old age: Observations from Appalachia. *Journal of Environmental Psychology, 3*, 299-313.

Rowles, G. D. (1993). Evolving images of place in aging and "aging-in-place." *Generations, 17*(2), 65–70.

Rowles, G. D. (2008). Place in occupational science: A life course perspective on the role of environmental context in the quest for meaning. *Journal of Occupational Science, 15*(3), 127–135.

Rubinstein, R. L., Moss, M., Kleban, M. H., & Lawton, M. P. (2000). *The many dimensions of aging.* New York, NY: Springer Publications.

Savishinsky, J. (2000). *Breaking the watch: The meanings of retirement in America.* Ithaca, NY: Cornell University Press.

Schoenberg, N. E., & Rowles, G. D. (2002). Back to the future. In G. D. Rowles & N. E. Schoenberg (Eds.), *Qualitative gerontology: A contemporary perspective* (pp. 3–28). New York, NY: Springer Publishing Company.

Scott-Maxwell, F. (1968). *The measure of my days.* New York, NY: Knopf.

Settersten, R. A. (Ed.). (2003). *Invitation to the life course: Toward new understandings of later life.* Amityville, NY: Baywood Publication Company.

Sinnott, J. D. (2009). Complex thought and construction of the self in the face of aging and death. *Journal of Adult Development, 16*, 155–165.

Thomas, W. H. (2004). *What are old people for? How elders will save the world* (p. 61). Acton, MA: VanderWyk & Burnham.

Tornstam, L. (2005). *Gerontranscendence: A developmental theory of positive aging.* New York, NY: Springer Publishing Company.

Webb, E. J., Campbell, D. T., Schwartz, R. D., & Sechrest, L. (1966). *Unobtrusive measures: Nonreactive research in the social sciences.* Chicago: Rand McNally.

Weiss, R., & Bass, S. A. (Eds.). (2002). *Challenges of the Third Age: Meaning and purpose in later life.* New York, NY: Oxford University Press.

Williamson, A. (1997). "You're never too old to learn!": Third Age perspectives on lifelong education. *International Journal of Lifelong Education, 16*(3), 173–184.

Part III

Emerging Themes and Controversies in the Era of the Third Age

Chapter
9

From Retirement to "Productive Aging" and Back to Work Again

Scott Bass

THE PRODUCTIVE AGING SOCIETY IN THE ERA OF THE THIRD AGE

*F*or a segment of the population in the United States, aging is accompanied by a time period of an increasing number of years of relatively good health that is free from financial need and time obligations of work as well as child-rearing family responsibilities that may have occurred earlier in life. This time period, identified by Peter Laslett as the "Third Age" (Laslett, 1989), has afforded a variety of new challenges and opportunities for older Americans. Key to tapping the potential of these additional years is the way a nation and society creates financial and support structures that enable older people who choose to contribute back to society through continued work, new careers, mentoring others, creating new industries, or serving as meaningful volunteers. Over the past several decades gerontologists have studied and identified the activities in which older Americans are engaged and discussed this population as a potential national resource. This chapter examines the history of the productive aging movement in the United States and its relative success in fostering the kind of social and economic supports that give older people the range of options to choose new and meaningful activities for themselves and those around them later in life. The question posed, as to the way society provides opportunities to encourage and nurture this added resource of potentially productive and creative contributions from its citizenry, is paramount to the gift embodied with the development of the Third Age and reflective of the values of the prevailing society itself.

THE OVERRIDING ISSUES

Work and retirement behavior among those aged 55 and over has become increasingly variable in the United States due to unique individual circumstances surrounding health, available support systems, family circumstances, engagement in a career, and previous employment and savings/pension history (Ekerdt, 2010). The United States, compared to other Western economies, came late to the provision of a federal scheme to provide an assurance of an income stream for retirement in one's later years. In 1935, with the advent of the Social Security program, many Americans who previously might not have had the resources to retire were now able to exit from a lifetime career (Achenbaum, 1986). Leaving work by age 65 or earlier and entering a period of retirement was met with great popularity and the practice of retirement spread relatively quickly (Schulz, 1992). For the majority of older working Americans, it soon became the norm.

Over the years, Social Security has expanded its benefits to become a significant financial component in preparing for the option of retirement. For those with very low earnings and savings, Supplemental Security Income is also available to assist with basic needs for those unable to work (Schulz, 1992). However, Social Security was never designed to be the only source of income in retirement and was intended to be augmented with income from personal savings and employer-based pension plans (Bernstein & Bernstein, 1988). By 1986, 95% of the working population was covered by Social Security (Bernstein & Bernstein, 1988) and after World War II, if not before, retirement from lifelong work became a standard aspiration and expectation for most working individuals in the United States. Nevertheless, as this chapter highlights, while basic retirement income provisions have been established in the United States, these provisions continue to fall short of the economic needs of many, and in this context, there has been and continues to be a struggle for a vision or visions for the role of older Americans in contemporary society.

In a relatively short period of time in terms of societal change, 50 years, retirement went from an option available primarily for the wealthy to become the prevailing expectation, if not requirement, for older Americans. The time period associated with retirement would provide for a "golden age" where older people could enjoy family, travel, hobbies, leisure, and rest after a lifetime of toil (Moody, 1988). Further, the institution of retirement was seen favorably by most employers (Clark, Burkhauser, Moon, Quinn, & Smeeding, 2004). The system provided an orderly pathway for older workers, who after years of employment, would be replaced by eager younger workers often hired at a lower salary. From a macro perspective, it provided increased fluidity in organizations and made it possible for young people in need of employment to move into the workplace in slots vacated by the old.

The institution of retirement was welcomed in an industrialized America, but forced retirement based on age was soon brought into question. Protections for workers 40- to 65-years-old against age discrimination under the 1967 Age Discrimination and Employment Act (ADEA) made mandatory retirement illegal for this age group. In 1978, the law was amended such that mandatory retirement for those aged 70 and younger was prohibited. Mandatory retirement for most American workers was eliminated in the 1986 amendments to the ADEA, reflecting the prevailing view that it was unfair to force individuals to terminate employment solely based on age (Clark et al., 2004). Even though retirement is no longer required, the vast majority of older people opt out of the labor force by age 65.

It was in the context of the 1970s when civil rights were championed for women, minority groups, and the disabled that concerns were raised about the quality of life of older Americans (Butler, 1975). Through the control of infectious diseases and better health care, older Americans were now healthier and living longer than ever before. The span of time between retirement from work and eventual physical decline expanded from that enjoyed by previous generations (Laslett, 1989). And, as a consequence, older Americans began to explore the possibility of creating more options and flexibility for those who were expected to retire, but who under the ADEA were no longer obligated to retire. Questions about the role that able older people should play in contemporary American society came to the attention of the public and policy makers (Butler & Gleason, 1985). While many older adults were quite happy about the possibility of retiring and those who had were quite content in retirement, some of those who had retired already found the associated "roleless role" and loss of position and status in retirement as empty and without sufficient meaning and purpose. And, they spoke out about their circumstance.

A BRIEF HISTORICAL PERSPECTIVE

It was in 1982 when Pulitzer Prize winner Robert N. Butler first introduced the term "productive aging" (Butler, 2008), which became more widely known three years later when *Productive Aging: Enhancing Vitality in Later Life* (Butler & Gleason, 1985) was published. This edited volume was a summary of some of the topics discussed at a 1983 seminar held in Salzburg, Austria, devoted to health, productivity, and aging.

Butler's interest in the topic of work and role of older people was also evident earlier when he wrote the Pulitzer Prize winning book, *Why Survive? Being Old in America* (Butler, 1975). The book served as a stinging expose and critique of the circumstances older people find themselves in America. At the time, Butler was 48 years old and was the inaugural director of the National Institute on Aging at the National Institutes of Health. The penetrating analysis undertaken in the book served to significantly heighten public awareness of the experiences associated with growing old in one of the world's wealthiest nations.

In that work, Butler did not mince any words when he discussed the circumstances surrounding work and retirement for older people. In Chapter 4 he writes, "The right to work is basic to the right to survive. Work denied to older people by practice and by attitudes, is often needed to earn a living and provide personal satisfaction" (Butler, 1975, p. 64). He also points out that, "Each year as thousands of people are encouraged or forced to retire, their skills, knowledge, and wisdom are lost and their opportunities to instruct, teach, consult or advise, listen and reflect, as well as to work, are cut off" (Butler, 1975, p. 65).

Butler (Butler & Gleason, 1985, p. xi) notes nearly 10 years later that he was afraid that some of his views about older people and work might be viewed as too "radical" for the times and might affect the public's embracing the rest of his treatise in Why Survive? After considering the possibility of eliminating the entire chapter on work and aging, Butler decided to leave it in the book for the readership to reflect upon.

Now, years later after the pioneering work of Robert Butler and after many articles, essays, books, conferences, documentaries, testimonials, Congressional hearings, and public discussions, the United States is still at the crossroads of coming to an understanding of the role of older people in contemporary society. Historians, philosophers, political scientists, economists, theologians, lawyers, psychologists, social workers, anthropologists, physicians, public health experts, elected officials, business leaders, elder advocates, union officials, journalists, poets, family members, and many others have been engaged and have contributed to this topic. While there is now a substantive body of literature and policies that prohibit age discrimination in the workplace, we may not be much further along in our discourse about significant roles for the aged, which was an issue raised when Butler first hit the keystrokes of his typewriter or penned the text on paper several decades ago.

It was only a year after the appearance of *Productive Aging* when Robert Morris and Scott Bass published "The Elderly as Surplus People" in *The Gerontologist* (Morris & Bass, 1986). In that article, the question was advanced as to what extent the growing numbers of those 65 and older were, from an economic perspective, surplus or redundant, or could they be a vital untapped resource that could enable economic expansion or enhance the well-being of all? At the center of the question was the vexing issue of the appropriate role for older people given increasing life expectancy.

In a free market, if there is a need for selected goods or services, the marketplace will seek accommodation to ensure they are provided. The demand for selected services or goods will drive the provision and production with an associated labor force needed to produce, market, and distribute the product for consumption. If there is a shortage of skills or labor, new human resources that might not have been previously utilized are brought into the market to ensure that opportunity is not lost. These resources might include less traditional workers such as teenagers, older workers, displaced homemakers in need of training, or the disabled. Sometimes employers will look to importing workers from other countries to fulfill labor shortages. In any case, older workers who are interested and available to work become a possible labor force in times of high demand and low unemployment.

The belief here is that the market makes adjustments and if there is a need for additional workers because of demand, then those employers will find individuals willing to perform the needed services, even if it expands beyond traditional populations. If there is limited or no economic need, even a traditional labor force is at risk of steady employment. Older workers, viewed from this lens, serve as a swing labor force able to respond to market demands. The problem with this economic model of labor market expansion and contraction is that the engagement of an older nontraditional labor force is only operational in periods when traditional labor markets have been fully tapped and employers have few options other than exploring older worker laborers. These sorts of economic cycles and spurts only occur infrequently.

What the Morris and Bass article did, distinct from the moral argument put forward by Butler, was to consider the possibility of expanding opportunities for the older worker labor force through the development of a secondary labor market that performs useful tasks that were unlikely to be provided through the mainstream economy. That is, there may be services that are desired, but not provided as a result of the limitations of government budgets or the aggregate cost of service provision that older workers can perform.

For example, we could imagine a wide range of services and programs that would improve the quality of life of individuals throughout society, but are no longer available or have not previously been considered as viable within the current financial constraints. Without displacing primary sector workers, there are goods and services whose provision would both be enriching to society and would be found meaningful to older workers. These goods or services would be provided for modest compensation, well below traditional labor rates, but not for free. These "paid volunteers" could be engaged in part-time and full-time jobs that cut across the social and environmental service sectors and would respond to a specific need or problem area. While building on the concepts of several older worker programs such as Foster Grandparents and RSVP (the Retired Senior Volunteer Program), the paid volunteer model would be universally available to all income strata.

Unbeknownst to the authors Morris and Bass was a parallel conceptualization occurring in Japan (Schulz, Takada, & Hoshino, 1989). As early as 1973, Professor Kazuo Okochi, who had previously been president of Tokyo University, argued for the implementation of a community-based center that would provide the infrastructure to support a paid secondary labor market. The center would contract for goods and services that would not ordinarily be provided in the primary labor market. Such activity would not only benefit the community but would provide enhanced meaning and purpose to older Japanese who had recently retired from their previous lifetime careers. Initially known as the Corporation for the Aged, the first center in Edogawa Ward in Tokyo spurred an entire movement of centers nationwide (Campbell, 1992). These centers, called Silver Human Resource Centers (SHRC), now exceed 1600 throughout the country and enroll nearly 800,000 members.

In the SHRC model of a secondary labor market, leadership from the center goes out to the community and solicits contracts for services that can be performed by its older workforce. Examples of jobs include: proofreading, translation services, gardening, simple carpentry, basic clerical work, caretaking of facilities, delivery services, light manual jobs, and caretaking services for the homebound (Bass, 1994). An SHRC might obtain a contract from a film company needing extras to serve in a movie scene showing older people, it might help staff facilities with large numbers of parked bicycles or cars, it might distribute strollers at the local zoo, or it might be involved with fixing up a school playground. In each case, a contract is made with the SHRC and then the SHRC offers hourly paid jobs to its members. The jobs are part-time, designed to provide goods and services that might not be done otherwise and to give greater meaning and purpose in the lives of older retirees in Japan. (For additional information see Bass, 1994.)

The SHRCs are frequently compared with the National Service Corps programs such as the RSVP, Foster Grand Parent, or Senior Companion Program; however, they are fundamentally different when examined up close. The SHRCs are more like a private entrepreneurial business with an affiliated senior center. The SHRC has facilities, equipment, uniforms, vehicles, and the entire infrastructure of a successful small business. The members of the SHRC perform contracted work for the SHRC and are compensated on a paid hourly basis. If the SHRC fails to secure an adequate number of contracts with local public or private organizations, it will not have work opportunities for its members. SHRC members come from a variety of income groups; nevertheless, most have financial security and have retired with pensions sufficient to maintain their current standard of living. While the SHRC tasks may fulfill a community need, it is considerably different from a national volunteer program, such as the recent Edward M. Kennedy Service America Act of 2009, designed to encourage national service in areas of human need and targeted to the economically disadvantaged.

Clearly, the role of older people in society is a topic with salience among the developed nations facing a growing able older population. In 1989, British scholar Peter Laslett published *A Fresh Map of Life: The*

Emergence of the Third Age (Laslett, 1989). In the book, Laslett elaborated on the time period between retirement and eventual decrepitude. He describes a new stage of life beyond a period of striving, saving, and making a living to a special time period that is available for personal fulfillment. The Third Age is not defined as a point in chronological years, but as a time for individuals in wealthier developed nations where they have the choice to work, volunteer, travel, study, or contribute based on preferences rather than obligations. While these productive years will eventually slide into those of some combination of physical decline, dependence, decrepitude, and eventual death, which could be considered the Fourth Age, the Third Age reflects a canvas yet to be fully painted. The additional years of life afforded by preventive medicine and the medical advances have created a new template of life and a relatively long time period for many known as retirement. Yet retirement, as Laslett implies, may be a phenomenon reflective of a rather unique set of circumstances. He writes, "It is difficult to decide the extent to which retirement is a novelty in our time, a novelty as an established social status, and a novelty in experience, as a person event. Retirement as we know it is certainly responsible for situations without parallel in the past" (p. 122). To what extent is retirement a choice or a social expectation? Can nations afford a period of 20 years or more where able-bodied individuals disengaged from economic productivity and, in many cases, receive financial support from the state?

The literature of the later 1980s and early 1990s begins to question the role of older people in the Third Age in recognition of their obvious capability and vitality (see, e.g., *Abundance of Life*, by Harry R. Moody, 1988). In 1990, Butler, Oberlink, and Schechter (1990) published an edited volume, *The Promise of Productive Aging: From Biology to Social Policy*, that extended the discussion of the capacity of older people to include physicians, neuroscientists, cognitive psychologists, and biologists who examined the physical and mental capacity of older people and provided scientific evidence dismissing many of the myths associated with work potential among older people. While there were always older individuals in previous eras, never before in human history have so many lived so long and in such good health.

Following the scholarly work cited above, The Commonwealth Fund decided to fund a five-year research initiative that would help document current productive activities of older Americans. In 1991, the Commonwealth Fund retained Lewis Harris and Associates to conduct a nationwide survey to document the contributions and interests of older Americans.

The survey, involving 2999 participants aged 55 and over, provided a rich database identifying the allocation of time to productive activities including working, volunteering, caregiving, and participating in educational programs. Not only was a baseline of engagement established, but insights of those not engaged formally in productive activities and information about their willingness to become engaged if opportunities presented themselves were reported. The findings revealed significant levels of participation and surprising interest in returning to work for those who had retired (Bass, 1994).

With support from the MacArthur Foundation, John Rowe and Robert Kahn (1997) published their work on human capacity and pathways to successful aging in an article in 1997 and in a book, *Successful Aging* (Rowe & Kahn, 1998), the following year. Rowe and Kahn present a detailed discussion of the myths about the health of older Americans, their cognitive capacity, the ability at any age to change long-held habits and behavior, the significant contributions that older people provide to families and communities without financial remuneration, and the need for greater flexibility in the employment sector to allow older people to remain engaged well into later life. The book had a significant effect on what was the emerging consensus in the field of gerontology of the human potential and the role of older people in modern society.

Despite the growth of literature about the potential of older adults, little change was evidenced in policies and programs designed to fully engage older people, particularly in work. Aging advocacy organizations, policy makers, and the public in general expressed concern about an appropriate and constructive role of older people. Within the scholarly community, considerable discussion and debate continued about the role of older citizenry with concern among some that a productive aging mantra deemphasized the appropriate role for reflection, contemplation, and enjoyment. Concern was expressed whether productive aging in response to the ideology of a "roleless role" was an overinterpretation of the problem and whether the concept would create a new identity of what is valued and what is not as one ages. When considering what Holstein (1993) refers to as gender-based "differentials in power and prestige" (p. 237), a productive aging mantra can work against the range of roles enjoyed by older women and may too narrowly define the potential of a mature aging experience itself.

Nevertheless, advocates, program planners, and policy makers concerned about the roles for older Americans and the implications for the nation as the inevitable demographic shift unfolded continued unabated.

For example, innovators such as Marc Freedman, founder and president of Civic Ventures, sought funding to create programs that rewarded and engaged older people. In an effort to encourage older people with creative ideas, his company, Civic Ventures, established the Purpose Prize where Americans over age 60 are nominated to receive awards of up to $100,000 for innovative ways to solve social problems. His book, *Prime Time: How Baby Boomers will Revolutionize Retirement and Transform America* (Freedman, 1999), was published in 1999. This was followed in 2007 by his book, *Encore: Finding Work That Matters in the Second Half of Life* (Freedman, 2007).

William Zinke, the founding owner of Human Resource Services, Inc., a company that specializes in human resource consulting to some of the nation's leading corporations, became active regarding his own concern for the workforce for the future and the need for older workers. In 2000, Zinke organized a conference involving policy makers, academics, and employers in Washington, DC focused on meeting America's employment needs. The resulting edited book, *Working Through Demographic Change: How Older Americans Can Sustain the Nation's Prosperity*, was published in the same year (Zinke & Tattershall, 2000). Continuing his investment and energy on the topic of older workers, Zinke continued the dialog among influential leaders and intellectuals. In fact, he made a philanthropic gift to establish the Center for Productive Longevity and convened several working groups. In 2007, he organized another conference in Washington, DC that laid the foundation for *Utilizing Older Workers for Competitive Advantage* (Zinke, 2008), which was published in 2008.

Perhaps the definitive work on productive aging was published by Nancy Morrow-Howell, James Hinterlong, and Michael Sherraden in 2001. The book, *Productive Aging: Concepts and Challenges* (Morrow-Howell, Hinterlong, & Sherraden, 2001), was a result of a careful review of the literature, a conference with leading gerontologists from a wide array of disciplines, and a resulting series of summative chapters by each of the major conference participants.

Seizing on the changing intellectual landscape about the role of older people, two British authors, Chris Gilleard and Paul Higgs wrote two original works that reconsidered the context of aging in the modern postindustrial society. The first book, *Cultures of Ageing: Self, Citizen and Body* (Gilleard & Higgs, 2000), was followed by *Contexts of Ageing: Class, Cohort and Community* (Gilleard & Higgs, 2005). Through these two important books, Gilleard and Higgs identify a society in which older individuals are viewed in a new role as consumers with enormous choice and options. They argue that in industrialized societies, this life space of 20 or more years has evolved to a time period in which older people play an active role in purchasing goods and services and have choices in how they look, what they eat, and what they enjoy doing. Due to reduced obligations to work and family along with surpluses and affluence made available in a postindustrial society, cohorts of older people through accumulated capital and pensions are able to enjoy life and provide meaning through consumption and acquisition in a manner that has never been previously experienced by older adults. In the view of Gilleard and Higgs (2000, 2005), the Third Age is a time that is shaped by the individual's ability to purchase, consume, and reinvent as one chooses and can be subject to the fads, trends, and styles crafted by marketers, advertisers, image leaders, and fashion designers. Perhaps they spoke too soon.

PRODUCTIVE AGING VERSUS A PRODUCTIVE AGING SOCIETY

More than a quarter century after Butler first introduced the term productive aging, and hearing of its proponents and critics he notes that he would have preferred to have used the term productive engagement rather than productive aging (Butler, 2008). Clearly, the term conjures a concept, and for some this is not altogether what they have in mind for the ideal of Third Age. While the term productive aging has been embraced by many, some have questioned the definition and what activities are included in the definition of productive aging (Achenbaum, 2009). If paid work and volunteering are included as part of productive aging, what about house cleaning? What about listening to music? What about taking a lifelong learning course? In Europe, words such as active aging have been introduced to reflect a societal desire for the participation and engagement of older people (Walker, 2009). While disagreement remains among scholars with regard to exact definitions, most share the belief that society needs to find specific ways to embrace and offer options for meaningful engagement for the older individuals if they choose.

If we have productive aging as a goal for individuals, then are those who are not engaged in prescribed and identified activities then labeled "unproductive"? If so, then what is unproductive aging and who would be viewed as unproductive?

Productive aging, like many general terms that seek to point a direction, has been used to mean different things. The first formal definition was introduced in 1986 by the National Research Council as "activities that produce goods and services that otherwise would have been paid" (Morgan, 1986). Herzog, Kahn, Morgan, Jackson, and Antonucci (1989) refined the definition in 1989 citing "any activity that produces goods or services, whether paid or not, including activities such as housework, child care, volunteer work, and help to family or friends" (p. S130). Bass, Caro, and Chen (1993) wrote, "Productive aging is any activity by an older individual that produces goods or services, or develops the capacity to produce them, whether they are paid for or not" (p. 6). Productive aging is a term commonly used in Japan to discuss the aspirations for the aged.

If we are seeking to define what is included or excluded in the term productive aging and we are interested in the broader environment that provides the option for a meaningful and engaged experience in one's later years, then are we not really interested in what fosters a productive aging society? As early as 1993, Bass et al. (1993) titled their edited volume, *Achieving a Productive Aging Society*. The emphasis here is on the actions within society that enable the engagement of individuals.

A productive aging society is one in which older people are viewed as assets and contributors. In such a society, options for meaningful roles are available based on ability. Individuals would not be excluded based exclusively on chronological age. Programs sponsored by government, nonprofit agencies, or corporations would be available to provide opportunities for older people to participate in activities that are personally rewarding and designed to accommodate a flexible personal schedule. In a productive aging society, sufficient financial supports through income streams would be available to older adults allowing individuals to choose to work as personal preference rather than out of financial necessity. And, that work if preferred, can be scheduled on a part-time, seasonal, or full-time basis as desired. A productive aging society would be one where policy makers, government officials, and employers share the concept that the Third Age is a unique time in the life course where citizens have choices and options to consider that can lead to new and meaningful activities. These activities may be parallel or be different from the activities in one's previous career or life experience.

Think of a continuum of societies with aging populations. On one extreme is a productive aging society (p.a. society) and at the other end of the spectrum is a counter-productive aging society (counter-p.a. society); in the middle would be a society which is neutral toward

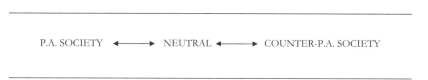

P.A. SOCIETY ◀──────▶ NEUTRAL ◀──────▶ COUNTER-P.A. SOCIETY

FIGURE 9.1 Productive Aging Society Continuum.

providing opportunities for the engagement of older people (see Figure 9.1). What would each of these societies look like and what would be the experience of growing old in each?

A productive aging society reflects the values of a community that seeks policies that enable all of its citizens to continue to live productive and rewarding lives as they choose. By engaging older people and expanding the availability and opportunity to participate in significant societal roles, their talent, experience, and insights would be retained or even maximized; the overall society would benefit from their participation and generations would appreciate the value of each other across age lines. In a productive aging society, the overall economy would benefit from the creativity unleashed as these experienced individuals could be a source of creating new industries and entrepreneurial activity. Mandatory retirement would not exist in this community. Pensions and health care would be portable and universal allowing job mobility. Support from the pension would allow those with health ailments to retire as needed and those who seek to retire by choice would have enough income to sustain a comfortable living well into the Fourth Age. Once retired for several years, individuals would have the option of returning to active part-time or full-time employment. Institutions like the Japanese SHRC would exist in local neighborhoods with minimal commute time required. Volunteer opportunities would be created that are both challenging and rewarding. Employers would establish positions that allow for seasoned employees to consider part-time and/or seasonal employment leaving time for family, travel, and recreation. Dedicated funds would be available from the government and private sector for older entrepreneurs to start new enterprises, either for-profit or nonprofit entities. For those working within industries, phased retirement would be an option. Every policy targeted at employers, workers, or the aged would be considered from the perspective of the outcomes they would pose on the constructive and sustained engagement of older individuals. In this way, overall society would benefit and be enriched.

At the other end of the spectrum is a counter-productive aging society. This may reflect Western societies prior to the establishment of effective pension systems wherein individuals were expected to work until they no longer could. Little distinction would be made among laborers by age. The quality of life for the aged who were no longer able to work and who might be feeble and incapacitated would be highly dependent on family financial circumstances. For most of these individuals, life would be unpleasant and uncomfortable. While this counter-productive aging society has the availability of continued labor, it would be a society that has too little age mobility and replacement in employment. It would be a community insensitive to the needs of older people, which is counter to the ideal of a productive environment.

A counter-productive aging society could also be a place where older people are forced to retire based on age and with no consideration of performance. Such a society would see older people, defined by a set chronological age, as less able, and as cognitively and physically less capable than their younger counterparts. This society would be one with distinct prejudices and clear evidence of age discrimination. Those who due to health conditions were unable to continue in their careers until the mandatory retirement age would be marginalized and treated as second-class citizens. And, once retired, individuals would be left entirely on their own to find activities that they find pertinent and enjoyable.

Finally, we have a third model: an aging society, which is more toward the middle of the spectrum. In this society, messages would be mixed and confusing. While retirement would be the cultural norm and most are expected to retire, it may not be mandatory. Those in poor health are the first to secure retirement and those with the health and stamina can continue to work longer. While the government may have a few programs for older retirees, these programs are targeted to serve the most vulnerable and lowest income. The majority of older citizenry are left to their own creativity with the burden of finding new opportunities left to individual resourcefulness. The role would immediately and abruptly shift from that of a producer of income in a job to someone dependent upon savings or pension. The demarcation between work and retirement is sharp and clear with little transition between full-time work and retirement. While not living in a world hostile or welcoming to older people, it would be a world in which little attention is given to the meaningful involvement of older people. The neutral world described more clearly reflects the state of the productive aging society in America and is one that many have criticized.

A PRODUCTIVE AGING SOCIETY: WHAT WENT WRONG

A fundamental principle for any movement toward a productive aging society is economic security in later life. Without a foundation of economic security provided through pensions and savings, older people will be obligated to work to maintain the lifestyle to which they have become accustomed. In America and virtually all Western societies, the citizenry has been acculturated to a certain level of goods and services. Gilleard and Higgs' (2000, 2005) description of a capitalist consuming society of choice and the wide availability of relatively affordable products has become a ubiquitous part of the landscape available to the public on a massive scale. After a lifetime of advertising and product positioning along with increasing normative social expectations, maintaining a level of comfort and ability to make selective purchases remains part of the American psyche. If working longer, even in a job that was unsatisfactory, meant that the quality of life enjoyed outside of work could be maintained, then working longer would be a very serious consideration. If, at the furthest extreme, leaving employment would mean inability to maintain the financial underpinnings of shelter, food, and basic amenities, then paid work will continue and be obligatory, forcing the individual to continue working even if chronic health conditions emerge.

A series of questions must be asked about the institution of retirement in America:

- Has America reached the high water mark in terms of the affordability of a "good" Third Age?
- Will the financial security enjoyed by the previous retired generation exist as we look to the future?
- Is the United States regressing, holding ground, or moving forward on the continuum of becoming a productive aging society?

The answers to these questions are rooted deeper than in a cursory examination of the state of the economy. Unemployment rates will rise and fall and employment opportunities and early retirement incentives will be influenced by these cycles. The same is true with the stock market and investments; they will run in cycles based on the overall strength of the economy.

Fundamental to the economic security that leverages an individual's ability to contribute to a productive aging society is a foundation based on the assurance of sufficient income later in life after many decades of labor. In the United States, this is contingent on amassing sufficient resources through Social Security, individual savings and assets, and an employer-based pension scheme. While there are important policy issues to resolve in fully stabilizing Social Security and considerable discussion as to the level of benefits derived, there is and will be a basic federal retirement insurance system for the foreseeable future. It is one component necessary for a secure Third Age, but not the exclusive source.

While considerable attention has been given to Social Security, a critical issue involving employer-based pensions has gone through significant change and one that may seriously threaten the promise of a productive aging society. Three types of pension plans dominate the marketplace: (1) defined benefit programs, (2) defined contribution programs, and (3) hybrid programs. They differ in:

- The mechanisms used to determine eventual benefits;
- The sources of revenue used to support an income stream in retirement;
- Where the risk is placed (on the individual or on the employer);
- The portability of the pension should the individual change employer; and
- The regulations applicable to the two types of plans (Clark et al., 2004).

Throughout the 1990s, employers began to shift from defined benefit programs to defined contribution programs. The drop in the number of employers maintaining defined benefit programs has been dramatic and has shifted the burden of investment of pension funds from the employer to the employee (Schulz & Binstock, 2006). A variant of this shift has been the hybrid plans that has elements of both plans, but still begins the process of shifting investment decisions to the employee. The vast majority of those employees with an employer-sponsored pension now have defined contribution plans and, while this gives the employee far greater choice in investment and retirement planning, the consequences for retirement security need to be questioned.

The advantage of the defined benefit plan is that the employee would theoretically be assured a guaranteed income after retirement if the employee remained with the firm for most of his or her career. The limitation of the scheme is that benefits accrue with longevity and the benefits are often nonexistent for employees who serve less than five years in a single firm. After 20 or 30 years with a single firm, the benefits can be substantial, replacing a large portion of the workers' income in retirement. Another limitation of the defined benefit plan in today's mobile society is that it is not portable should an employee leave one employer and start with another firm. This is a serious limitation. The defined contribution plan, on the other hand, can follow the worker wherever one works. In principle, this shift from defined benefit to defined contribution seems to be one that was viewed quite favorably by both employer and employee and, for the most part, workers accepted the change with many eagerly signing up for the most popular version, the 401(k) plan, which was first introduced to the tax code in 1978 (Hacker, 2006).

Only about half of the workforce is covered by any employer-sponsored pension, and for the other half, there is only Social Security and their personal savings and assets, which are often quite modest (Munnell & Sunden, 2004). For the fortunate half of the working population eligible for an employer-based pension program, many of those participating in defined contribution plans have the choice to take a portion of their pretax earnings and place them in a 401(k) plan. Participation is optional, and the amount invested is under the discretion of the employee up to a specified amount set by the Federal government.

Given the choice of contributing to a defined contribution plan, data reveal that 20 percent of those eligible for the plan do not participate at all (from the Current Population Survey in Munnell & Perun, 2006). This means that far more than half of the current working population in the United States will only have Social Security and whatever savings they might accrue to support them should they stop working. With a low savings rate within the United States, one should question the viability of retirement as we know it, let alone the engagement of a productive aging society.

FUTURE STEPS: ISSUES TO CONSIDER

The development of a productive aging society remains a vision for an engaged society; it has only matured in its definition, its dialogue among interested individuals, its policies and programs identified, and its potential considered over the past several decades. However, underpinning a productive aging society necessitates basic income security. For a myriad of reasons, many quite understandable, the underlying foundation that provided so many individuals access to a robust Third Age is facing challenges. As cited above, very few Americans have pensions at all and 20% of those eligible for defined contribution plans have declined to participate at any one point in time. The consequence is clear as noted by Munnell and Perun (2006), "These developments, coupled with declining levels of earnings replacement under Social Security, mean that future retirees will have to work longer if they want to maintain their preretirement standard of living in retirement" (p. 1).

With this structural backdrop, imagine the consequence of declining equity in home values, low interest rates, a volatile stock market, and a lackluster economy with increased unemployment. Such a scenario places further constraints on the options available for a productive Third Age society. It affects the retirement savings and pensions of the underemployed, unemployed, and the salaried employees differently with cumulative negative effects for all, but particularly for the lower-income individuals who are disproportionately minorities and women (Weller & Wenger, 2009). Yet, this is what has happened near the end of the first decade of the 21st century and it raises the question as to the availability of retirement as we have come to know it (and secondarily the promise of the Third Age) with the current assets invested in a defined contribution plan, a struggling economy, many without pensions, and comparatively high unemployment, particularly among older workers.

The economy will run its cycle and the future will bring greater stability. However, there are fundamental structural issues in the United States that need to be addressed in order to move the bar more toward a productive aging society. Even should policy makers devise a better underlying pension scheme providing greater economic security, the exploration of new structures to help tap this underused national treasure of human potential needs clear focus and leadership. The establishment of a national commission for this purpose would be an important initial step. The National Commission on a Productive Aging Society could be created by executive order or by Congress, but it is desperately needed to begin shaping a national dialogue about America's full potential. While the economic circumstances have changed, the goal is not significantly different from what was first articulated by Robert Butler in 1982. The task ahead remains to build policies, programs, and practices for a society that values its older people by providing the choice to participate in meaningful opportunities in the Third Age.

REFERENCES

Achenbaum, W. A. (1986). *Social security: Visions and revisions.* Cambridge, UK: Cambridge University Press.

Achenbaum, W. A. (2009). A history of productive aging and the boomers. In Robert B. Hudson (Ed.), *Boomer bust? Economic and political issues of the graying society* (pp. 47–60). Westport, CT: Praeger Publishers.

Bass, S. A. (1994). *Productive aging and the role of older people in Japan: New approaches for the United States.* New York, NY: Japan Society, Inc.

Bass, S. A., Caro, F. G., & Chen, Y. (1993). *Achieving a productive aging society.* Westport, CT: Auburn House.

Bernstein, M. C., & Bernstein, J. B. (1988). *Social security: The system that works.* New York, NY: Basic Books, Inc., Publishers.

Butler, R. N. (1975). *Why survive? Being old in America.* New York, NY: Harper & Row, Publishers.

Butler, R. N. (2008). *The longevity revolution: The benefits and challenges of living a long life.* New York, NY: Public Affairs.

Butler, R. N., & Gleason, H. P. (1985). *Productive aging: Enhancing vitality in later life.* New York, NY: Springer Publishing Company.

Butler, R. N., Oberlink, M. R., & Schechter, M. (1990). *The promise of productive aging: From biology to social policy.* New York, NY: Springer Publishing Company.

Campbell, J. C. (1992). *How policies change: The Japanese government and the aging society.* Princeton, NJ: Princeton University Press.

Clark, R. L., Burkhauser, R. V., Moon, M., Quinn, J. F., & Smeeding, T. M. (2004). *The economics of an aging society.* Malden, MA: Blackwell Publishing Ltd.

Ekerdt, D. J. (2010). Frontiers of research on work and retirement. *The Journals of Gerontology, 65B*(1), 69–80.

Freedman, M. (1999). *Prime time: How baby boomers will revolutionize retirement and transform America (First.).* New York, NY: Public Affairs.

Freedman, M. (2007). *Encore: Finding work that matters in the second half of life.* New York, NY: Public Affairs.

Gilleard, C., & Higgs, P. (2000). *Cultures of ageing: Self, citizen and the body.* Essex, England: Pearson Education Limited.

Gilleard, C., & Higgs, P. (2005). *Contexts of ageing: Class, cohort and community.* Cambridge, UK: Polity Press.

Hacker, J. S. (2006). *The great risk shift.* Oxford: Oxford University Press.

Herzog, A. R., Kahn, R. L., Morgan, J. L., Jackson, J. S., & Antonucci, T. C. (1989). Age differences in productive activity. *Journal of Gerontology: Social Sciences, 44*(4), S129–S138.

Holstein, M. (1993). Women's lives, women's work: Productivity, gender, and aging. In S. A. Bass, F. G. Caro, & Y.-P. Chen (Eds.), *Achieving a productive aging society* (pp. 235–248). Boston: Auburn House.

Laslett, P. (1989). *A fresh map of life: The emergence of the third age.* Cambridge, MA: Harvard University Press.

Moody, H. R. (1988). *Abundance of life: Human development policies for an aging society.* New York, NY: Columbia University Press.

Morgan, J. N. (1986). *Unpaid productive activity over the life course. In productive roles in an older society.* Washington, DC: National Academy Press.

Morris, R., & Bass, S. A. (1986). The elderly as surplus people: Is there a role for higher education? *The Gerontologist, 26*(1), 12-18.

Morrow-Howell, N., Hinterlong, J., & Sherraden, M. (2001). *Productive aging: Concepts and challenges.* Baltimore & London: The John Hopkins University Press.

Munnell, A. H., & Perun, P. (2006). *An update on private pensions.* Issue Brief, Center for Retirement Research, Boston College. Retrieved from http://crr.bc.edu/images/stories/Briefs/ib_50.

Munnell, A. H., & Sunden, A. (2004). *Coming up short: The challenge of 401 (k) plans.* Washington, DC: Brookings Institution.

Rowe, J. W., & Kahn, R. L. (1997). Successful aging. *The Gerontologist, 37*(4), 433-440.

Rowe, J. W., & Kahn, R. L. (1998). *Successful aging.* New York, NY: Pantheon.

Schulz, J. H. (1992). *The economics of aging.* New York, NY: Auburn House.

Schulz, J. H., & Binstock, R. H. (2006). *Aging nation: The economics and politics of growing older in America.* Westport, CT: Praeger Publishers.

Schulz, J. H., Takada, K., & Hoshino, S. (1989). *When "Lifetime Employment" ends: Older worker programs in Japan.* Waltham, MA: Brandeis University.

Walker, A. (2009). Commentary: The emergence and application of active aging in Europe. *Journal of Aging & Social Policy, 21*(1), 75-93.

Weller, C. E., & Wenger, J. B. (2009). What happens to defined contribution accounts when labor markets and financial markets move together? *Journal of Aging & Social Policy, 21*(3), 256-276.

Zinke, W. K. (2008). *Utilizing older workers for competitive advantage: The new human resources frontier.* Boulder, CO: Center for Productive Longevity.

Zinke, W. K., & Tattershall, S. (2000). *Working through demographic change: How older America can sustain the nation's prosperity.* Boulder, CO: Human Resource Services, Inc.

Chapter
10

Challenges and Opportunities for Relationships in the Era of the Third Age

Denise Brothers and Jenny de Jong Gierveld

RELATIONSHIPS IN THE ERA OF THE THIRD AGE

A social network is the collection of relationships and a site for the exchange of social support throughout the life course. Later life is no different in that regard when compared with earlier life stages. However, older adults in the "Third Age" face unique opportunities and challenges for relationships. Conceptually, the Third Age is the time in later life characterized by relatively good health and lessening family and work obligations (Laslett, 1989). In theory, it is a time when older adults have the freedom to pursue personally meaningful activities less scripted by the societal expectations present in earlier life stages. We use terms such as "conceptually" and "in theory" because the idea of Third Age is highly (and rightfully so) critiqued by scholars (see Chapters 1 and 4, this book) as a privileged life stage, not possible for or necessarily desired by everyone, a time period determined by the culmination of a lifetime of advantage and disadvantage based on social location, a contemporary life phase based on both the patterned work history more typical for men than for women as well as a partnering trajectory characterized by traditional and heterosexual ways of partnering (e.g., marriage, divorce, remarriage, widowhood). At the same time, however, never before have so many older men and older women entered a life stage characterized by the Third Age, and this emerging life phase presents some unique challenges to and opportunities for relationships of the individuals who are fortunate enough to experience it.

This chapter describes the demographic changes that have taken place and brought about a Third Age, and explores ways in which these changes have altered personal relationships. Specifically, we describe how demographic changes have brought about improved life chances for women, and how the simultaneous sociostructural and cultural changes (including individualization) have altered the composition of family and households as well as the nature of gender relations. In particular, changing gender relations, smaller family sizes, increasing levels of childlessness, living alone, remarriage, and cohabitation are all presenting opportunities and challenges to personal relationships, and are permanently altering the landscape by which we examine and understand relationships in later life. We complete our discussion on relationships in this emerging life stage by describing the practice of repartnering, a relationship phenomenon which is becoming more common in the Third Age.

THE DEMOGRAPHIC TRANSITION AND CHANGING LIFE BIOGRAPHIES

The Third Age emerged at the societal level essentially in response to the macrolevel changes described by Demographic Transition Theory (see Chapter 5, this book). The demographic transition describes how modernization of a country moves a population with high mortality and fertility to low mortality and fertility. While in premodern or traditional societies, the high mortality rates necessitate high fertility rates (i.e., women have more children in order to guarantee the survival of a few offspring who can provide them with care and support in old age), in many demographic-transitioning countries, once improvements in mortality are "felt" by the population, fertility rates start to decline (Coale, 1973).

However, the structure and roles of women's lives are at the root of the societal conditions that must be present in order to have fertility rates decline (Coale, 1973). These conditions, which contribute to women's life chances, are the ability of women to control their own fertility decisions, their access to ways of controlling fertility, and other options for women to participate in their economic and social worlds in ways previously inaccessible, such as education and labor force participation. For most industrialized countries, these societal changes were well under way in the 1960s and 1970s. Since then, new behavioral patterns, norms, and attitudes concerning fertility, and the formation and dissolution of unions have affected society as a whole. These changes are caused and supported by in-depth cultural and sociostructural changes. Cultural changes have altered norms and values of the population. Most salient among these changes is a decline in normative control shaping the behavior of young adults brought on by the weakening authority of parents and religious institutions, which reinforces fulfilment of individual desires and preferences to a much greater extent when compared with previous cohorts. These cultural changes, linked to processes such as secularization and individualization, support and reaffirm opportunities of individuals to create their own life biographies, or, in other words, to decide for themselves how they wish to organize their lives.

Important sociostructural changes associated with the demographic transition include a general increase in the wealth and health of the overall population. Educational advancement has improved substantially; more than ever before, young men and women are continuing full-time education up to and beyond high-school and postsecondary levels. Women are participating in the labor market at record levels, and their ambition to combine work and family is a broadly accepted way of life. This has been made possible by the emerging availability of reliable contraceptives (such as "the pill"), allowing women (and couples) to control the size of their families. As a result, women have fewer children.

The sociostructural and cultural changes of the second half of the 20th century—also known as an integral part of the "second demographic transition" (Van de Kaa, 1987)—have deeply affected the ways in which family and household structures are designed, and help to explain how the improvement in women's life chances have created new opportunities and expectations for partner relationships, including union formation, divorce, and repartnering during their adult life. Partner relationship trends include the postponement of union formation and the practice of starting intimate relationships via cohabitation before or as an alternative to marriage. The percentage of young adults following the traditional biography of leaving the parental home to marry, followed by the birth of children and parents living together until death, has decreased significantly, and has been replaced by what is called a "choice biography." Within a "choice biography" is a broader variety of options and transitions (e.g., leaving the parental home to live alone, to start cohabitation, separating, returning to the parental home, marrying, divorcing, and repartnering). Postponing union formation can also delay child bearing, which increases the chances for childlessness and smaller families. Moreover, the increasing acceptance of divorce has changed household compositions. The adoption of new norms concerning divorce has altered the traditional long-term bond between parents and children. For example, a large proportion of divorced mothers are confronted with managing—in the absence of a partner—the household with dependent children, and many divorced fathers have irregular contact with their biological offspring.

Individualization and Dependency in Family Relationships

Individualization has not only contributed to more varied life biographies, but has also brought about great changes in the ways in which people rely on one another. These changes are illustrated by descriptions of the ways individuals organize their lives in preindustrial societies and industrialized (or modern) societies. These descriptive efforts, while simplistic, help to illustrate how different societal contexts contain prescribed expectations about the role (including availability) of family members in the lives of individuals, and show the increasing complexity of modern-day life relationships.

In general, families in preindustrial societies are formed and function around the common good of its members. The economic livelihood of the family depends on mutual dependence, requiring clearly defined roles and expectations of its members. These qualities function in a way to create standard life biographies for men, women, and children. The functions of relationships, such as social support, are relatively straightforward to coordinate, given the continuity and stability of roles and social institutions.

Where the context for relationships in preindustrial societies can be characterized by continuity and stability, the modern societal context for families is characterized by one word: dynamic. Instead of relying on clearly delineated roles and expectations of family form and function, to a certain extent individuals have more freedom to decide how best to design and behave in their relationships, leading to multiple life biographies because the standard biography no longer holds true for many. This deinstitutionalization, or the "weakening of the social norms that define people's behavior in a social institution" (Cherlin, 2004, p. 848), is apparent in the practice of intimate relationships, such as marriage. Partnering, in general, is less ruled by normative expectations, as "pure relationship," or the formation and continuation of intimate relationships based on the extent to which physical and emotional needs are mutually met, becomes a stronger litmus test for relationship satisfaction and continuation (Giddens, 1991, 1992) than simply deriving satisfaction from the ideals of the "companionate marriage" or the performance of the highly differentiated gendered roles of husband and wife and father and mother inherent in a traditional nuclear family (Cherlin, 2004).

Jamieson (1999), however, warns us not to overemphasize the ideals of the "pure relationship," since "[p]ersonal relationships are not typically shaped in whatever way gives pleasure without the taint of practical, economic and other material circumstances" (p. 482). In other words, while qualities of a "pure relationship" may be at work in some relationships, few would be considered unaffected by the realities of human circumstance. At the same time, though, if the Third Age is characterized by lessening family and work demands (or circumstances), this life stage could be where we are more apt to find examples of a "pure relationship."

Modernization has significant implications for families. The role of marriage and gender specialization inherent in preindustrial societies loses strength in its power to organize the lives of individuals in industrial and postindustrial societies (Coontz, 2000). There is no longer one standard family biography, but many family biographies. Divorce and remarriage have increased and diversified the size of social networks, but without guaranteeing the reliability of members of the social support network (Beck & Beck-Gernsheim, 2002). In addition to increasing rates of divorce and remarriage, other ways of partnering and repartnering, such as cohabitation and "living apart together" or LAT (described below) further adds to the complexity of family relationships. The geographic mobility that comes along with modernization also provides challenges to relationships; family members tend to be less tied to one geographic area, and thus, can end up living apart from one another. These dynamic and less stable qualities of modernization can make forming and maintaining relationships more challenging.

Another way in which modernization has altered family responsibilities and reinforced individuality is through the rise of the welfare state. Instead of recognizing the family as the unit in need, individuals are recipients of services. Shifting caregiving responsibilities to the state and the market has further eroded the importance of marriage (Coontz, 2000). In addition, in many countries, such as Northern and Western European countries, the formal care provided by the state complements the informal intergenerational family care, changing the role of family members (Haberkern & Szudlik, 2010).

Despite the dynamic nature of contemporary family life, there are common challenges facing modern families. Increasing human longevity has placed "unprecedented ... responsibility ... [on] adult children ... for their parents, who in previous generations were unlikely to live long enough to require substantial and prolonged assistance" (Coontz, 2000, p. 289). Not only is responsibility to longer-living parents a new family phenomenon, but many adults have dependent family members from multiple generations, such as when young adult children move back into the parental home, an aging parent is caring for an adult child with a disability, or grandparents become parents to their grandchildren.

Although the need for care work (e.g., childrearing, caring for sick or disabled family members) is present in and performed predominantly by women in all types of societies, women in modern societies have more complex life biographies, creating more demands on their time, helping to give rise to a care-work industry. The standard female biography of women as caregivers, being primarily homemakers, wives, and mothers, present just decades ago, has become just one of many ways women can organize their lives. Women have more varied options in which to structure their lives, including combining work and family roles. In an effort to balance the demands from these roles, caring for a family member, such as an aging parent or a young child, is often outsourced, such as hiring personal care workers or child care services.

Women's education and employment opportunities have also allowed a growing number of women to be more financially independent, no longer relying on parental support until marriage, when the husband would then take on the material responsibility for a wife and family. Despite more fragmented work histories and earning less than men, many women are entering later life having had a lifetime of employment earnings and a certain level of income security in later life, optimizing their opportunity for a certain level of financial independence in the Third Age.

THE IMPROVEMENT IN WOMEN'S LIFE CHANCES AND CHANGING GENDER IDEOLOGY

The improvement in women's life chances has no doubt brought with it challenges to and alteration of gender ideology. Studies show that changing roles for women (i.e., not only moving into the workforce but into historically male-dominated occupations) are bringing about changes in characteristics attributed to women (Diekman & Eagly, 1999; Diekman

& Goodfriend, 2006). Women over time are perceived as possessing slightly decreasing feminine traits and more masculine characteristics. Comparatively, the perception of men over time shows maintenance of masculine qualities, but lacking a similar increase in feminine characteristics since men's roles in the domestic sphere and female-dominated occupations have not changed to the same degree as women's roles have (Diekman & Eagly, 1999).

However, this is not to say that men's roles are remaining stagnant. Movements are underway in many countries to recognize and support men's increasing domestic roles in families. For example, in the early 1990s, the United States passed a federal law allowing women and men to take up to 12 weeks of job-protected time off for the birth or adoption of a child, or to care for a sick family member. Likewise, in other culturally modern countries, such as Sweden, Norway, and the Netherlands, a growing number of men are taking on caring tasks for family members with support from state welfare regimes. For example, in the Netherlands an increasing portion of men "invest" one day per week to care for their young children.

Other studies of gender ideology show that conforming to gender stereotypes appears to have more to do with the performance of family and work/education roles than with growing older (Lynott & McCandless, 2000; Roberts, Helson, & Klohnen, 2002). While there is some evidence of gender attitudes becoming less traditional with age for older cohorts of women, life experiences, such as years of education and employment, marital status, and the number of children, are stronger predictors of gender attitudes among women. In general, more years of education and/or employment are correlated with less traditional gender attitudes of women, while being married and the number of children (especially young children) are positively correlated with more traditional gender attitudes.

Gutmann (1987) provides evidence of how couples' performance of gender roles is strongly tied to their respective parenting roles. The parental imperative model explains how, in order to effectively parent children, fathers and mothers take on gender-linked qualities (i.e., women become affiliative/communalistic and men become aggressive). Once parental responsibilities lessen (i.e., with the "launching" of children), women and men reclaim aspects of their personality they were required to suppress in order to parent successfully (i.e., women become more agentic and men become more communal). Fathers who no longer have young-adult children in their homes are more likely to describe themselves in feminine terms, and report moving from a patriarchal marital style to more collaborative or conceding styles. On the other hand, mothers in these "empty nests" report asserting themselves more in their marriages (Huyck, 1996; Huyck & Gutmann, 1992).

FAMILY AND MARITAL STATUS IN LATER LIFE: IMPLICATIONS FOR HOUSEHOLD COMPOSITION

The demographic transition and its accompanying sociostructural and cultural changes impacting the population as a whole have resulted in specific conditions for later-life families and households. Many potential third-agers reach this stage of life with few or no children, with varying contact intensity with their children, all of them in small-sized families, many living alone, and others in long-term partner relationships due to the increasing longevity of both men and women.

Older adults in the Third Age have typically reached a phase during which their children (if any) have left the parental home. Given the culturally accepted possibilities related to "choice biographies," many older couples without children in the household, opt to continue the couple-only household, while many of their peers without a partner opt for living alone in a one-person household. In most industrialized countries, the generations of older adults characterized by a small number of children and high risk for divorce and repartnering do not favor coresidence with adult children, but instead choose to live independently for as long as possible. Consequently, an increasing percentage of older adults live in one-person households. However, shared cultural preferences do orient them to appreciate regular and close contacts with children (and grandchildren): intimacy, but at a distance (Rosenmayr & Köckeis, 1963).

Third-agers living alone do not necessarily need regular assistance; third-agers by definition are in good health. However, some of those living alone may, currently or in the future, need regular assistance with temporary health challenges or more permanent disabilities. This will likely require them to draw on support from members of their social network, all of whom live outside their household. To successfully live independently in a one-person household and maintain a satisfying support network of kin and nonkin requires substantial social capacities, time, energy, and a good health situation.

Ideally, the support network functions as a convoy (Kahn & Antonucci, 1980): as a person ages, he/she is surrounded by a set of people who reciprocally provide and receive social support. Accordingly, maintaining good contacts with members of the convoy is a minimum requirement to guarantee optimal embedment in later life. Given that families and households are becoming smaller, policy makers are concerned that older adults are at a risk of losing social support. However, research has shown that children, including children living at longer distances, are willing and prepared to provide help although the amount of support is not independent from the partner history of parents and children (De Jong Gierveld & Dykstra, 2006, 2008). In this context, ever-divorced fathers and older adults without children are at risk for a lack of support and for loneliness. On the other hand, research has shown that many older adults without children succeed in forming and maintaining a personal network of family members and friends who are able to provide mutual support when needed (Dykstra & Hagestad, 2007).

Current trends and future projections show that countries will be confronted with significant changes in the marital and household composition of the older segment of their populations. Some of the trends are quite clear: more adults than in the past will be confronted with the dissolution of their marriage via divorce. Of those who divorce, many pursue a new partner relationship that may lead to remarriage or cohabitation, while others, especially divorced women, become heads of a one-parent household and after the children leave home, end up living in a one-person household. Therefore, the increase in divorce affects the percentage of adults in the Third Age who live alone as well as in reconstituted households.

Another significant but contrasting trend due to increasing life expectancy is the postponement of widowhood. Life expectancy is sharply increasing for both women and men, and consequently, the portion of the life span spent in marriage increases for the couples who are still together in later life, the so-called "ageing-together" phenomenon (Gaymu, Ekamper, & Beets, 2008). Other emerging phenomena affecting men and women in the Third Age are the increasing number of people who never married, but instead are in long-term cohabiting unions, and the growing proportion of divorced or widowed men and women who start a new partner relationship without remarrying and without sharing the household.

Living alone in later life after divorce or widowhood is a reality for many third-agers, especially those living in Northern and Western European countries and also in the United States, and increases the risks for loneliness. Finding a new partner may be an attractive option for older adults to alleviate the risk of loneliness. Others, particularly widows, might hesitate to give up the freedom and independence they enjoyed after coming to terms with bereavement (Lopata, 1996). In opting for either living alone or sharing a household with a new partner, one has to weigh the benefits and drawbacks of both options. Sharing a household—that is to say, living as a couple—may provide people with personal care, reciprocal attention and support, companionship, and the division of household tasks. Possible negative aspects include frustrations when one partner invests less time, money, and effort in the cooperative undertaking than the other, or when a partner invests less than what was initially negotiated at the onset of cohabitation. In weighing the options, some may conclude that remarriage requires too great a sacrifice. Instead, some opt for a consensual union because it is characterized by less strict rules, and others prefer to continue living alone. Finally, some older men and women opt to start a partner relationship without living together. These men and women in a "living-apart-together" relationship continue to live in a one-person household, intermittently (e.g., several days per week or on weekends) sharing a household with their partner (De Jong Gierveld, 2004).

OPPORTUNITIES FOR NEW TYPES OF PARTNER RELATIONSHIPS IN THE THIRD AGE

Third-agers today are involved in a variety of partner relationships and household types—in first marriages, remarriages, consensual unions, one-parent families, or living alone—and many older adults without a partner relationship, living with good health and freedom from family and work responsibilities present earlier in life, may be pursuing new romantic relationships in the Third Age. Repartnering in later life can result in marriage (or remarriage), cohabitation, or living apart together (LAT). LAT is an exclusive partner relationship in which the individuals maintain separate residences, intermittently sharing households during the weekends or at other times. Essentially, LAT is an alternative to cohabitation and marriage. Later-life repartnering in general and LAT specifically reflect some of the sociostructural and cultural characteristics that have helped to bring about the Third Age, including the relatively good financial health of the older adults, qualities of individualization (especially those of the "pure relationship"), as well as the improvement in women's life chances which provide them with the opportunity and means to maintain autonomy in later-life stages and subsequently alter traditional gender relations.

Alternative living arrangements such as consensual unions and LAT became realistic alternatives to remarriage in the late second half of the 20th century. Sociocultural changes in the second half of the 20th century led people to move away from traditional patterns of behavior, resulting in a reduction in behavioral conformation (Inglehart, 1997). The pace of accepting new attitudes and behavioral patterns differs significantly among countries and regions, but began in earnest in Western Europe after 1970 (Gaymu et al., 2006). Specifically, older adults repartnering in the 1970s opted for a consensual union, and in the beginning of 1980s LAT became a more common way to repartner for older adults (De Jong Gierveld, 2009). In addition, age at last partner dissolution also influences repartnering practice. Men and women aged 55 years or over at last partner dissolution are less likely to remarry, but are three times more likely to begin an LAT relationship than those who are younger than 55 years of age at last partner dissolution (De Jong Gierveld, 2004).

Repartnering is significantly associated with educational level and income status of older men, while the relationship of these qualities to the repartnering practices of older women remains inconclusive. Men with fewer years of education are less likely to start a new partner relationship than men with more years of education. Being employed at the time of the dissolution and thus having more opportunities to meet a new partner hastens repartnering for men but not for women. All of these illustrate the overall attractiveness of potential male partners with socioeconomic prospects (Sweeney, 1997).

Older men and women may hesitate to begin a new couple household facing difficulties discussed earlier related to starting a new cooperative undertaking. Moreover, people are afraid of losing contact with their children and friends, particularly if the repartnering involves leaving the family home, moving, or merging households. In contrast, LAT enables them to easily combine the continuation of kin and nonkin social relationships of the past with a new partner relationship (De Jong Gierveld, 2004).

LAT: A Unique Relationship for Third-Agers

There are clear gender differences in older adults' interest in repartnering following the death of a spouse. Despite the argument that the demographic imbalance in the number of men and women of older ages prevents women from repartnering, studies from Great Britain and the Netherlands show that many older women who have lost husbands report the newly found autonomy and freedom (including freedom from having to take care of another spouse) they had gained since becoming a widow, and higher satisfaction with the single life (compared to older men who have lost wives) as reasons for not wanting to repartner (Davidson, 2001, 2002; Stevens, 2002). Women especially appear reluctant to remarry in order to avoid gendered expectations of care and household labor for a spouse (Davidson, 2001).

Advancing age also appears to influence the desire to repartner. The older a man or woman is, the less likely they are to want to repartner, especially those over 70 years (Stevens, 2002). Research in the United States also shows that older adults are less likely to date or to report wanting to marry or cohabit when compared with younger adults, and that men of all ages report an interest in marriage and cohabiting more so than women (Bulcroft & Bulcroft, 1991; Moorman, Booth, & Fingerman, 2006). Widows interested in remarriage tend to be younger than widows not interested in remarriage (Moorman et al., 2006).

In addition to gender and age differences related to interest in repartnering, the actual practice of repartnering shows similar patterns. Dutch men are more likely than Dutch women to report repartnering at all ages, and to repartner more quickly than women following marital dissolution (De Jong Gierveld, 2002). In addition, when it comes to different repartnering outcomes (marriage, cohabitation, or LAT) age and gender also seem to be influential. LAT arrangements tend to be favored over marriage or cohabitation by both older men and women (over 70 years old), and women are more likely to be in LAT relationships than remarrying or cohabiting (De Jong Gierveld, 2002).

The reasons women give for their reluctance to repartner are similar to those given by women for being in an LAT relationship. Swedish women in LAT relationships report valuing the autonomy of living alone and freedom from duties they performed in previous marriages as reasons for maintaining this type of a relationship (Karlsson & Borell, 2002, 2005). Further, women note that their homes represent a way of establishing boundaries in LAT relationships. Maintaining boundaries include negotiating the possession of house keys, controlling one's schedule, and establishing different degrees of social integration of one's partner with friends and family (Karlsson & Borell, 2005). Findings from these studies suggest that a woman's own home not only represents a site for boundary work in LAT relationships, but also a site where they can circumvent or avoid some of the trappings of earlier domestic life.

It is not surprising, therefore, that "older women play a vital role in establishing and upholding LAT-relationships" (Karlsson & Borell, 2002, p. 11). However, this is not to say that gender roles in later life are totally transformed through dating or LAT relationships. In fact, a traditional gender role ideology still prevails in some instances. For example, one study in the United States found that older women expect men to initiate dating and pay for meals (Dickson, Hughes, & Walker, 2005). In addition, Swedish LAT couples report a traditional division of gender roles when spending time together at each other's homes, with women cooking meals and men performing home repairs (Karlsson & Borell, 2002).

These studies provide evidence that the practice of repartnering in the era of the Third Age is highly gendered, and reflect some of the changes in gender relations that have occurred since the improvement of women's life chances, especially women's preference to preserve autonomy and independence. In general, older men tend to repartner more quickly and more often than women, preferring shared residential ways of partnering, while older women are less likely to repartner at all, and when they do repartner, they are more apt to enter into an LAT relationship than a shared residential partnership. While traditional gender roles may be preserved when LAT couples spend time together, women's desire to maintain independence appears to be at the root of this type of later-life relationship.

FUTURE STEPS: ISSUES TO CONSIDER

There is a novelty to the Third Age; it is a stage and way of life which we have never witnessed before in human history, a stage which has developed because of the demographic transition and the associated sociocultural changes in the Western industrialized world. Examining the topic of opportunities for and challenges to relationships in the Third Age, we find it useful to take into account how the *context* for relationships has changed substantially, given these sociocultural changes. Future research should continue to address the implications of these relatively rapid changes (e.g., changing gender relations, smaller family sizes, childlessness, living alone, and repartnering) on the lives of older men and women, of which third-agers are simply an advantaged subgroup.

The concept of linked lives (see Chapter 1, this book), or the idea that our lives are interconnected with the lives of others in our social network, be it kin or nonkin relations, describes the ways in which our lives remain tied to others throughout the life course, including into the life stage characterized by the Third Age. The degree to which lives are linked, and the essence of this interconnectedness, may alter across the life course whereby responsibility to or for others remains a reality in *all* stages of life. The definition of the Third Age gives the false impression that individuals in this life stage are "free" from family obligations present in earlier life stages; further, it fails to define how the social support inherent in relationships evolves over the life course. Throughout life, new relationships emerge, and demands and support from existing relationships continually change, including sometimes ceasing all together. It could be argued that third-agers who are retired and still healthy could have a *greater* demand placed on them to care for people in their social networks. In other words, while they may be retired and relatively healthy, their lives are linked to others who may not be in good health, or for other reasons, may be dependent on a third-ager. For example, many third-agers may be caring for a sick spouse, or previously launched children may move back home and financially rely on their third-ager parents. It is important for researchers to examine and understand how the reality of linked lives in the modern cultural context colors or impacts the experience of the Third Age. Specifically, future research should continue to address the realization of these responsibilities to and for others for repartnered third-agers, especially for those older adults who are in LAT relationships or in blended families. For example, to what extent will partners who do not share living quarters on a 24-hour basis take on responsibility to care for their partner who is confronted with long-term health problems? What is the pattern of support that flows between stepparents and stepchildren in this life stage?

In addition to the changing context and assumptions guiding relationship research in later life, there are several other topics that require further examination. Maintenance (and even formation) of relationships no longer requires a physical presence. What do we know about the effects of new technologies on the embedment of older adults in their social networks? Since emailing, "chatting," and video conferencing have become easily accessible to the general public, third-agers have the opportunity for more regular contact with the people in their social networks, including children, grandchildren, and siblings than previous generations of older adults. To what extent are these new ways of communicating in use among third-agers, and how does the use of technology to stay connected to family members contribute to their life satisfaction? Future research should address the effects of improving opportunities to be in contact with family members through the use of technology, especially in light of the trend of more parents and children living long distances from one another due to an increase in work migration, especially among the highest-educated children (Vullnetari & King, 2008).

Finally, relationship research agendas (including those concerned with the Third Age) must continue to evolve beyond the contextual assumptions inherent in heteronormativity that gives primacy to heterosexual intimate relationships and parent–child relations. With the increase in the number of individuals who remain single, and couples who do not have children, as well as the growing acceptance of gay and lesbian unions, an increasing number of older adults will reach the Third Age having life-course experiences well outside or beyond the life-course trajectory of heterosexual unions for the purpose of family formation. How does a lifetime of being single, or never having children, or being in a gay or lesbian union impact the experience of the Third Age, a contemporary life phase defined more by the patterned work history more typical for men than for women, as well as a partnering trajectory characterized by traditional and heterosexual ways of partnering?

REFERENCES

Beck, U., & Beck-Gernsheim, E. (2002). *Individualization*. London: Sage Publications Ltd.

Bulcroft, R. A., & Bulcroft, K. A. (1991). The nature and functions of dating in later life. *Research on Aging, 13*(2), 244–260.

Cherlin, A. J. (2004). The deinstitutionalization of American marriage. *Journal of Marriage and Family, 66,* 848–861.

Coale, A. (1973). The demographic transition. *International Population Conference,* Vol. I. Belgium: IUSSP.

Coontz, S. (2000). Historical perspectives on family studies. *Journal of Marriage and the Family, 62,* 283–297.

Davidson, K. (2001). Late life widowhood, selfishness and new partnership choices: A gendered perspective. *Ageing and Society, 21*(3), 297–317.

Davidson, K. (2002). Gender differences in new partnership choices and constraints for older widows and widowers. *Ageing International, 27*(4), 43–60.

De Jong Gierveld, J. (2002). The dilemma of repartnering: Considerations of older men and women entering new intimate relationships in later life. *Ageing International, 27*(4), 61–78.

De Jong Gierveld, J. (2004). Remarriage, unmarried cohabitation, living apart together: Partner relationships following bereavement or divorce. *Journal of Marriage and Family, 66*, 236–243.

De Jong Gierveld, J., & Dykstra, P. A. (2006). Impact of longer life on care giving from children. In Z. Yi, E. M. Crimmins, Y. Carrière, & J.-M. Robine (Eds.), *Longer life and healthy aging* (pp. 239–259). Dordrecht, the Netherlands: Springer.

De Jong Gierveld, J., & Dykstra, P. A. (2008). Virtue is its own reward? Support giving in the family and loneliness in middle and old age. *Ageing and Society, 28*, 271–287.

De Jong Gierveld, J. (2009). *Living apart together after widowhood or divorce; intimacy and social integration.* Paper presented at the 62nd Annual Scientific Meeting of the Gerontological Society of America, Atlanta, GA, USA. November 18–22, 2009, .

Dickson, F. C., Hughes, P. C., & Walker, K. L. (2005). An exploratory investigation into dating among later-life women. *Western Journal of Communication, 69*(1), 67–82.

Diekman, A. B., & Eagly, A. H. (1999). Stereotypes as dynamic constructs: Women and men of the past, present, and future. *Personality and Social Psychology Bulletin, 26*(10), 1171–1188.

Diekman, A. B., & Goodfriend, W. (2006). Rolling with the changes: A role congruity perspective on gender norms. *Psychology of Women Quarterly, 30*(4), 369–383.

Dykstra, P. A., & Hagestad, G. N. (2007). Roads less taken: Developing a nuanced view of older adults without children. *Journal of Family Issues, 28*(10), 1275–1310.

Gaymu, J., Delbès, C., Springer, S., Binet, A., Desquelles, A., Kalogirou, S. et al. (2006). Determinants of the living arrangements of older people in Europe. [Déterminants des modes de vie des personnes âgées en Europe.] *European Journal of Population, 22*, 241–262.

Gaymu, J., Ekamper, P., & Beets, G. (2008). Future trends in health and marital status: Effects on the structure of living arrangements of older Europeans in 2030. *European Journal of Ageing, 5*, 5–17.

Giddens, A. (1991). *Modernity and self identity.* Standford, CA: Stanford University Press.

Giddens, A. (1992). *The transformation of intimacy.* Stanford, CA: Stanford University Press.

Gutmann, D. L. (1987). *Reclaimed powers: Toward a new psychology of men and women in later life.* New York, NY: Basic Books, Inc.

Haberkern, K., & Szudlik, M. (2010). State care provision, societal opinion and children's care of older parents in 11 European countries. *Ageing and Society, 30*, 299–323.

Huyck, M. H. (1996). Continuities and discontinuities in gender identity. In V. Bengston (Ed.), *Adulthood and aging: Research on continuities and discontinuities.* New York, NY: Springer Publishing Company, Inc.

Huyck, M. H., & Gutmann, D. L. (1992). Thirtysomething years of marriage: Understanding husbands and wives in enduring relationships. *Family Perspective, 26*(2), 249–265.

Inglehart, R. (1997). *Modernization and postmodernization. Cultural, economic and political change in 43 societies.* Princeton, NJ: Princeton University Press.

Jamieson, L. (1999). Intimacy transformed? A critical look at the "pure relationship". *Sociology, 33*(3), 477–494.

Kahn, R. L., & Antonucci, T. C. (1980). Convoys over the life course: Attachment, roles and social support. In P. B. Baltes & O. Brim (Eds.), *Life-span development and behaviour* (Vol. 3, pp. 253–286). New York, NY: Academic Press.

Karlsson, S. G., & Borell, K. (2002). Intimacy and autonomy, gender and ageing: Living apart together. *Ageing International, 27*(4), 11–26.

Karlsson, S. G., & Borell, K. (2005). A home of their own: Women's boundary work in LAT-relationships. *Journal of Aging Studies, 19*, 73–84.

Laslett, P. (1989). *A fresh map of life: The emergence of the third age.* Cambridge, MA: Harvard University Press.

Lopata, H. Z. (1996). *Current widowhood: Myths and realities.* Thousand Oaks, CA: Sage Publications.

Lynott, P. P., & McCandless, N. J. (2000). The impact of age vs. life experience on the gender role attitudes of women in different cohorts. *Journal of Women & Aging, 12*(1/2), 5–21.

Moorman, S. M., Booth, A., & Fingerman, K. L. (2006). Women's romantic relationship after widowhood. *Journal of Family Issues, 27*(9), 1281–1304.

Roberts, B. W., Helson, R., & Klohnen, E. C. (2002). Personality development and growth in women across 30 years: Three perspectives. *Journal of Personality, 70*(1), 79–102.

Rosenmayr, L., & Köckeis, E. (1963). Propositions for a sociological theory of ageing and the family. *International Social Science Journal, XV*, 410–426.

Stevens, N. (2002). Re-engaging: New partnerships in late-life widowhood. *Ageing International, 27*(4), 27–42.

Sweeney, M. M. (1997). Remarriage of women and men after divorce; the role of socio-economic prospects. *Journal of Family Issues, 18*(5), 479–502.

Van de Kaa, D. J. (1987). Europe's second demographic transition. *Population Bulletin, 42*(1), 1–47.

Vullnetari, J., & King, R. (2008). Does your granny eat grass? On mass migration, care drain and the fate of older people in rural Albania. *Global Networks, 8*(2), 139–171.

Chapter 11

Relevance of Social Capital and Lifestyle for the Third Age

Dawn C. Carr and Jon Hendricks

SOCIAL CAPITAL IN THE ERA OF THE THIRD AGE

*W*ithin postindustrialized societies, the growing age of individuals in which they can expect to be healthy and retired has transformed the structure and makeup of social roles associated with later life. In conjunction with the introduction of retirement programs, improved health practices have led scholars to consider the unique opportunities associated with a newly recognized period of life in which individuals have the time and the capacity to remain actively involved. Termed the Third Age, this period of extended vitality has recast old age and retirement more generally, as a time of involvement rather than stigmatized superannuation. For retired people, it is being seen as a period of continued growth and development. In any number of contexts older adults are being encouraged to engage in civic roles as a way to help meet communal needs and contribute to societal well-being. In short, retirement is no longer perceived simply as a marker of marginalization but as a positive feature for society and individuals alike, promoting social integration and personal well-being, and more specifically, a time in which older adults are perceived as having the potential to contribute social capital.

Although discussions on the implications of the Third Age have largely been positive among social scientists, policy makers, governmental, and nonprofit leaders with regard to individual opportunities and civic engagement, there is no consensus, and others have expressed qualms about the potential costs to society of the growing number of older adults. In particular, social programs that support the health and well-being of older adults, a pillar of welfare states, are now underwriting a much larger proportion of the population, many of whom are less "needy" than they were when the programs were implemented. Questions are being raised about whether such entitlements should be granted to those who have the wherewithal to go without. Furthermore, there are proportionally fewer people paying into these programs through participation in the labor force. The reasons for the latter are complex; not only have decreased fertility rates and increased longevity transformed the population structure, but the nature of labor force participation is shifting as unemployment or underemployment become more common and an ever larger portion of the labor force is involved in service industries with their lower wage structures and less stable career trajectories. Despite the potential upside of the Third Age, costs and benefits of population aging have surfaced in discussions on the Third Age as the sacred cows of a generation ago are sometimes cast as greedy geezers now.

It is fair to characterize the tenor of discussions on the Third Age as a time for personal fulfillment, with considerable merit as a potential solution to problems related to population aging tinged with concerns about ever-greater demands on welfare entitlements accompanying old age. Ironically, third-agers are often described as individuals who are financially secure enough to afford to retire and healthy enough to continue contributing through various forms of civic engagement. As a result, third-agers are increasingly expected to be a factor in society in socially and economically valuable ways outside of the work force, while offsetting some of the onus associated with population aging. In other words, the era of the Third Age is emerging as a time in which older adults are being reconceived as a resource, rather than merely as a drain on society's munificence.

The perception that older adults and third-agers in particular are not only capable of contributing to society but also possess a "drive to engage" (Weiss & Bass, 2002, p. 191) has facilitated a paradigm shift in the social roles associated with later life. A growing focus on the responsibility of older adults to help compensate for the challenges associated with population aging has led to assumptions that third-agers can and should engage in unpaid, productive ways. Adler and Goggin (2005) maintain that a civic engagement movement is gaining momentum and they are joined by Reilly (2006), among others, who propose that there is a potential for transformative changes in society as a result of the functional capacities associated with Third Age volunteers. As the tradition of Third Age engagement becomes even more established, there is every reason to assert that third-agers as a group might be described as having the capacity to produce a substantial amount of social capital, which may increase the status, opportunities, and value of older adults, while society as a whole benefits (Carr, 2005).

Contributions of Third-Agers to Social Capital

Social capital, conceived of as a type of resource, is often used to describe the ways in which a shared investment of individuals can have a positive effect on those involved, on those who are part of their social networks and on society. The proffering of social capital has become a popular means of discussing the kind of contributions made by those in the Third Age. Specifically, with the concept of social capital being utilized to capture contributions to the social good, the benefits deriving from enhancing social capital justify initiatives encouraging third-agers to engage productively in society. Both concepts, the Third Age and social capital, highlight a refocusing of efforts to promote civic responsibility to society through engagement in socially and economically valuable social roles during later life. It would seem that third-agers who are engaged are motivated by a desire to feel useful, productive, to give something back, and by opportunities for interaction (Grano, Lucidi, Zelli, & Violani, 2008).

Many discussions on social capital have emphasized the positive aspects of social capital for individuals (Bourdieu, 1985) and social groups (Putnam, 2000), as well as the positive correlates associated with the Third Age. Nonetheless, some scholars have criticized the extent to which writings about the Third Age, social capital, and their intersection, have largely overlooked one major issue—the extent to which some older individuals lack access to opportunities to engage in such activities and have different incentives for participation (Ekerdt, 1986; Holstein, 2006; Martinson & Minkler, 2006). In our way of thinking, the implications of both the research and the criticism are that social capital research in the context of the Third Age cannot progress without a meaningful framework with which to understand benefits and barriers to engagement in activities that contribute to social capital. This chapter proposes a framework with which to guide future research seeking to advance discussions on social capital and the Third Age.

Specifically, we review key literature about social capital and the Third Age describing how social structural forces interact with individual behaviors to produce socially beneficial outcomes. We propose a framework that seeks to fully capture the interaction of the individual and societal benefits in the accumulation of social capital through an adaptation of Hendricks and Hatch's (2006, 2009; Hatch & Hendricks, 2010) lifestyle framework. We conclude with a description of future steps for Third Age research utilizing the proposed framework to begin uncovering the barriers to engagement in activities that promote the accumulation of social capital, and factors that may intervene to diminish inequality issues preventing such engagement.

FROM AN INDIVIDUAL TO A SOCIETAL RESOURCE: THE RECONCEPTUALIZATION OF SOCIAL CAPITAL

The construct of social capital was introduced in contemporary social science as a resource available to individuals through interactions with others within their community. It was championed as an important resource for individuals with access to rich social networks and who, therefore, are connected to particular opportunities that facilitate mutually beneficial exchanges with others. In recent years, however, social capital has been reconceptualized as a societal resource created by individuals who choose to engage in activities that benefit greater society. In other words, social capital has been adapted to describe ways in which society accumulates a stock of resources when individuals engage in ways that are economically and/or socially valued. Although a useful orientation for promoting agenda which seek to increase the participation of capable citizens in socially valued activities, this reconceptualization overlooks a key factor in the production of social capital—the fact that some individuals have more opportunities, capabilities, and incentives than others to contribute in this way.

Social Capital as an Individual Resource

Subsequent to the insights of Bourdieu (1985) in France and Coleman (1988) in the United States, social scientists have begun to speak of social capital that comes of such network dynamics as key factors affecting the roles we play in later life and how we age. For social gerontologists, the heritage is that old age does not occur *ex nihilio* any more than it is merely the expression of biological destiny. How we age reflects the places in which we are ensconced and the social resources that come from our social relationships. The seminal contributions of Bourdieu and Coleman, building on earlier contributions by Weber and others suggest that access to social capital for individuals is strongly related to their position within social hierarchies. For example, Bourdieu indicates that social structures influence the amount and variety of social capital, which in turn creates and reflects social inequalities. He describes the benefits reaped by individuals based on participation in social networks and groups, indicating that the combinations of the actual or potential benefits of resources to individuals are related to institutionalized social relationships. In a nutshell, Coleman and Bourdieu suggest that although individuals reap important benefits from social capital, by virtue of the social structural arrangements within a particular society, some individuals have greater access to the acquisition of social capital than others. As a result, the utilization of social-network connections to ensure access to opportunities and other forms of social capital is not equally distributed. Those inequalities play out in the coloring of experience and the way life unfolds. Those who are advantaged in terms of social capital, generally reap those advantages in the later years as well. Conversely, those who cannot access the resources implied by social capital experience less than optimal circumstances throughout life.

From a more explicitly economic perspective, Lin (2001) suggests that social capital is the investment in social relations with expected returns in the marketplace, with the "marketplace" including something of value either economically, politically, as a form of labor, or as a value to the community. The value is provided by individuals in particular networks working together and functioning as resources for one another. Specifically, he suggests that social capital includes the quantity and/or quality of resources that an actor can access or use, and the location of these resources within a particular social network influence the context and value of these resources (Lin, 2001). Through this conceptualization, Lin describes the way in which social capital enhances the likelihood of instrumental returns for some individuals but not others, which supports Coleman and Bourdeiu's claims that social capital inevitably contributes to, and is the product of embedded forms of inequality. Lin argues that social capital has a substantial effect on individual differences such as socioeconomic attainment. Consequently, not all individuals or social groups can uniformly acquire social capital or receive returns from social capital.

Social Capital as a Societal Resource

Expanding these traditional interpretations, more recent conceptualization of social capital as a societal resource generally overlooks issues related to inequality. This contemporary perspective has reoriented discussions on social capital to align with rhetoric about individual opportunities to contribute to the social good, with implications about individual responsibility. Putnam (1995, 2000) introduced a representation of social capital in which the benefit of social capital is described as primarily societal. Putnam claims that societies can create and benefit from a "stock" of social capital, and that the structure of whole nations shapes individual and collective contributions made to this stock of resources. Although this conceptualization is compelling in that it raises awareness of benefits of individual behavior to the broader society, unlike that of Coleman, Bourdieu, and Lin, it does not explicitly consider the extent to which individuals' access to social-capital resources vary such that some individuals accrue lesser benefit and are, therefore, capable of contributing less to society. One of the consequences of this paradigm shift is refocused attention on the responsibility of individuals to contribute to the accumulation of social resources, with little consideration of the differences in individual capability, opportunity, or incentive. This more simplistic orientation has become particularly popular in gerontological writings because the concept of social capital can be easily utilized to justify the reasons older adults should contribute to society through social participation and volunteerism. In fact, this description of social capital has been subsumed by other concepts like "civic engagement" (Holstein & Minkler, 2003), a phrase Putnam uses interchangeably with social capital to support initiatives seeking to promote efforts to increase awareness about civic responsibility, operationalized as participation in social groups and engagement in unpaid contributions to organizations.

Consequences of New Conceptualizations of Social Capital

The orientation of social capital for explorations of ways that society, not just individuals, benefit from social network connections and engagement in socially valuable roles has created new assumptions about the interaction between individual behaviors and social structural arrangements. Some discussions on social capital maintain that individuals invest in and safeguard relationships and associations they feel will provide a return on their investments and give them access to interpersonal resources (Baum & Ziersch, 2003). The implication is that individuals will be active in and contribute to activities where their return on investment is self-evident, meaning that it provides fodder buttressing their self-concepts and sense of identity. What Bronfenbrenner (1979) terms the "ecology of human development" applies throughout life, including during the Third Age when individuals are embedded in various social milieux and from which they derive feedback, be it positive or negative. In the event of negative feedback, which Rosenberg (1986) terms "contextual dissonance," participation rates will plummet as more self-relevant opportunities are accentuated. However, individual initiative and incentive are not the only factors shaping to what degree individuals contribute social capital.

Network research suggests that relational networks that have been called "webs of significance" (Geertz, 1973), help actors gain not only a sense of themselves but access to critical information that may provide opportunities, power, and solidarity. In this way, the consequences of lower social status positions may be diminished through the pursuit of social capital. However, as Adler and Kwon (2002) note, most research highlights these positive outcomes of social ties and relational network connections to the exclusion of the potentially negative consequences of social capital. Similarly, Portes (1998) claims that such simplistic depictions of social capital as social network connections facilitating individual participation in socially valuable roles have led to it being misused and misunderstood and further development is required. As Portes and Landolt (1996) clarify, an actor's capacity to obtain resources through connections and from consociates does not guarantee positive outcomes in all instances. They suggest that recent research on social capital confuses the ability to secure resources with resources themselves. The fact that wealth and resources are unequally distributed means actors may have valuable social ties and still have limited access to quality resources. They suggest that the more positive aspects of social capital have been adapted by different researchers to conveniently demonstrate how aging actors shape societal outcomes which is a product of growing concerns about declines in overall economic productivity. The consequences of population aging and thus lower participation rates in the labor force have provided an impetus for explorations into ways to facilitate reasonable solutions to the management of the growing number of older adults by encouraging healthy retirees to contribute to the greater good.

PRODUCTIVE AGING AND SOCIAL CAPITAL IN THE THIRD AGE

The emergence of a recognized Third Age has helped to redefine and refurbish assumptions about older adults' social roles, opportunities, and capabilities to engage in society. The introduction and expansion of welfare policies and programs for older adults was initially built on the assumption that individuals and societies benefited from the retirement of older adults from the labor force and improved health in later life. However, societal consequences of increased longevity, adding years to life, have led to concerns about the sustainability of social programs designed to support older individuals who are no longer in the labor force. In addition to living longer, retired workers are receiving transfer payments from a smaller labor force and from a lower wage structure than earlier. Concerns about the appropriateness of these transfer programs have contributed to explorations into ways in which healthy older adults can counterbalance the burden population aging has placed on the broader society, with third-agers described as uniquely capable of offsetting the costs of population aging by engaging in unpaid, productive activities (i.e., contributing social capital). Butler, among others, points out that healthy, retired individuals, or third-agers, harbor the greatest discretionary funds in most modern societies, direct intergenerational transfers to younger people, possess ample resources of a number of types, are active consumers within the so-called "silver industries" or the gray market as well as in other ways, require relatively fewer health services, and remain productively engaged through work or volunteerism (Butler, 2005, p. 547).

Discussions on productive aging typically describe the extent to which older adults "produce goods and services that otherwise would have to be paid for," or activities that can be quantified into some type of economic value (Caro, Bass, & Chen, 1993, p. 6). A commonly cited form of productive aging is volunteering, with an array of research demonstrating that volunteering benefits individuals and society through social interactions and improvements in the health and well-being of older adults and by providing much needed services within communities (e.g., Bukov, Maas, & Lampert, 2002; Burr, Choi, Mutchler, & Caro, 2005; Greenfield & Marks, 2004; Morrow-Howell, Hinterlong, Rozario, & Tang, 2003; Van Willigen, 2000). Utilizing a standard economic metric, approximately 17 billion US$ was contributed by the estimated 8.75 million older Americans who, in 2008, volunteered an average of 96 hours each (US Bureau of Labor Statistics, 2009, Table 2). Clearly, contributions of this magnitude do indeed offset some of the declines in public and private spending as well as provide a return on investments in various entitlement programs intended for older people. Depictions of productive aging typically cast third-agers as those adults most likely to contribute (Cutler, Hendricks, & O'Neill, 2011); however, the expectation that third-agers are uniquely capable of participating in such activities by virtue of the fact that they are retired and healthy overlooks two important issues: choice and capability.

Some scholars suggest that the construct of productive aging is not just descriptive of what older adults can, should, and do provide society, but is also proscriptive in that continued engagement in productive roles may be perceived as necessary for the well-being of society. Holstein and Minkler (2003), among others, have raised important questions about the extent to which the language of productive aging and a close cousin of both productive aging and social capital—civic engagement—is promoting potentially unrealistic expectations regarding what people can and should do in later life, and thus, is inadvertently creating a normative discourse about what makes a "good" old age. Productive aging initiatives like volunteerism or civic engagement more generally, demonstrate a growing divergence between the promotion of positive opportunities and choice in later life as the benefits of increased longevity, improved health, and the institutionalization of retirement interface with the rights of citizens and their cultural values. One further complication is the fact that the increased length and quality of later life that occurred in conjunction with population aging have not been equitably distributed such that some individuals and social groups have reaped the benefits of these societal improvements more than others. In other words, not all third-agers are endowed with the same unique capabilities to engage in productive activities and therefore, do not experience the same benefits of such participation (i.e., accumulation of social capital).

These frameworks for thinking about contributions of third-agers reveal core values and ideological perspectives shaping the way later life is defined in postindustrial societies, early in the 21st century. In particular, these include: (1) the tension between the significance of personally meaningful versus socially valued opportunities in later life; and (2) the tension between individual responsibility (including choice) to contribute to society and the opportunities and capabilities to do so. The notion of social capital is predicated on social relationships that allow individuals to have access to the resources of others and also determines the amount and quality of those resources ("actual or potential resources that inhere within social networks or groups for personal benefit"; Carpiano, 2005, p. 83). Third-agers' chances to contribute to a society's "stock" of social capital through engagement in productive activities like volunteerism, is shaped by individual variation in the capability, opportunity, and incentive to participate.

Having access to resources should not be confused with actual resources themselves (Portes, 1998). Merely having discretionary time outside the work force and being relatively healthy does not necessarily provide an individual with the opportunity or capability to contribute to the social good. Certainly, some third-agers are well positioned to participate in socially beneficial activities and benefit individually from doing so. However, what is potentially more important is understanding what factors allow some individuals to benefit from contributing and what inhibits others from engaging in a Third Age lifestyle altogether. In order to explore the factors that influence whether and how much older individuals contribute to the social good, it is necessary to understand the factors that influence the accumulation of social capital at the individual and societal levels.

UNDERSTANDING ACCESS TO A THIRD AGE LIFESTYLE: A FRAMEWORK FOR SOCIAL CAPITAL

As described above, the initial adaptation of social capital frameworks to social science brought together complex ideas about the consequences of social interactions in the procurement of resources. Although connections with social networks have the potential to produce positive outcomes for individuals within a given group, the ability to acquire social capital resources is shaped by more than just the nature and quality of social relationships. An actor's actions are shaped by individual characteristics, traditionally characterized as human capital, and the benefits of social engagements characterized as social capital that are shaped in turn by social structural arrangements. Although social capital has the potential to contribute to the well-being of broader groups, the extent to which individuals within a given society have the opportunity and/or capability to contribute to a society's stock of social capital varies. There are intricate mechanisms that shape both microlevel and macrolevel aspects of social capital, and without accounting for these interactions, those in lower-status populations, like older people, may be at risk of being exploited through the advancement of potentially unrealistic expectations regarding how they can and should engage in society. Furthermore, social capital may continue to be unrealistically portrayed as a "cure-all" for all maladies affecting society at home and abroad (Portes, 1998). A more comprehensive elucidation of social capital should recognize the limitations of what social capital provides to individuals and societies.

Part of the attention to the Third Age with regard to discussions on social capital can be attributed to the long debate among gerontologists as to the optimal levels of engagement after retirement. Whether it is better to maintain maximal levels of activity and engagement or to relinquish such patterns and go gently into old age serves to typify the two positions. As should be apparent, proponents of the Third Age generally assert that given the salutary effects of virtually all forms of engagement and social interaction, a person moving into the later years would be well advised to make the most of interaction and involvement, surrendering as little as possible as late as possible (Musick, Herzog, & House, 1999; Rotolo, 1999; Rowe & Kahn, 1998). As we pointed out above, some commentators even assert that there is a "drive to engage" that remains viable well into old age, promoting productive involvements long past the point previously thought to be the beginning of the decline (Weiss & Bass, 2002). Taking volunteering and other forms of civic engagement as illustrative of the way social capital is generated by Third Age activity, it is usually conceded that volunteering bolsters an individual's sense of well-being. It is proposed to provide positive effects in terms of both physical and mental health, help individuals feel as though they are paying something back, and provide a source of compensation for role loss through the substitution of volunteer activities for others that may have fallen away even while maintaining a sense of being part of an on-going agenda (Cutler & Hendricks, 2000; Hendricks & Cutler, 2004).

On the societal side of the equation, contributions to the communal good and the offsetting of budgetary rescissions not only provide needed goods and services but help maintain a sense of solidarity and integration. Active third-agers counter some of the negative perceptions of retirement as a time of passivity. The evidence suggests that patterns of greater involvement will likely continue and grow even further among those who will retire in the coming decades. The contributions made by third-agers have a salutatory effect on the economy and on governmental outlays (Cutler et al., 2011).

If the agenda of productive aging advocates (including those promoting civic engagement and volunteerism) to increase the amount of social capital produced by third-agers, then it is especially important that social scientists recognize that it is neither the presence of inequality within a particular society nor the perception of individual benefits alone that determine whether and how much third-agers participate in the production of social capital. Rather, contributions to the "stock" of social capital in a particular society by a particular social group is influenced by incentives, values, and choices, all of which are contextualized by individuals within a given social environment.

According to Stebbins (1997), lifestyle can be characterized as a collection of distinctive attributes or recognizable patterns of behaviors reflecting shared interests and life situations integrating related values, attitudes, and orientations that create characteristic identities among those who share those attributes and attitudes by virtue of being members of one or another collectivity. In terms of the topic of interest here, Gilleard and Higgs (2005, 2007), describe a Third Age lifestyle as distinctive in the proposed role of agency and responsiveness to the culture of consumption that has been articulated by expectations of economically valuable contributions to society. Although Stebbins as well as Gilleard and Higgs recognize the importance of lifestyle in shaping social interactions, lifestyle has not been directly examined as a mechanism by which older individuals reap benefits from society or as a series of pathways leading to contributions to the collective good. We contend that a lifestyle framework is useful for exploring the ways in which the intersection between social capital and the Third Age is defined by multifaceted interactions between individual and societal characteristics that shape the accumulation of social resources and the subsequent individual and societal consequences.

The lifestyle framework introduced by Hendricks and Hatch (2006) can be applied to social capital discussions in the Third Age to more adequately illuminate how relational bonds between individual and societal factors interconnect to shape the amount and quality of social capital resources third-agers both benefit from and contribute to (see Figure 11.1). This framework describes the mechanisms that intersect to shape what people do and how meaning is ascribed to these activities. With some scholars suggesting that engagement in a Third Age lifestyle implies allegiance to activities perceived to be socially valuable, it is critically important that greater attention is paid to the complex pathways that lead some people to take on voluntary activities while others are inclined not to engage in such activities. Hendricks and Hatch's framework suggests that if scholars want to examine the relationship between

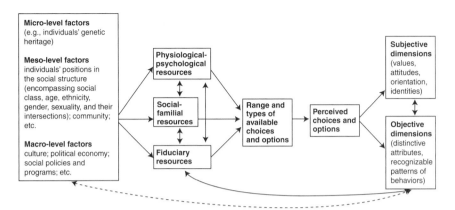

FIGURE 11.1   Hendricks and Hatch's Lifestyle Framework. *Source*: Hendricks, J., & Hatch, L. R. (2006). Lifestyle and aging. In R. Binstock & L. George (Eds.), *Handbook of aging and the social sciences 6/E*. San Diego, CA: Academic Press. Reprinted by permission.

personal resources and social capital outcomes, it is necessary to consider the extent to which individuals perceive that the availability of particular resources produces a sense of choice about what activities are accessible, and furthermore, whether engagement in such activities aligns with one's values. Underlying that assertion is a concern with agency, choice, and the construction of meaning. Implicit in the model and to dialectical approaches to the aging process is the belief that old-age lifestyles are a result of opportunities, choices, and interaction along the way.

With the language of current social capital discussions attributing higher value to those older adults who are perceived to choose to contribute in economically valuable ways, a new form of ageism is percolating that is centered in discussions on social capital and the Third Age. The increasing perception is that third-agers who engage in socially (i.e., economically) valuable activities are conforming to their social roles, whereas those who do not, are in a sense, being deviant. Social gerontologists need to be cautious about perpetuating the segregation and valuation of older adults by participation in particular activities, and should explore ways of promoting choice and opportunities to engage in ways that are simultaneously socially and personally fulfilling in later life. Consideration of the lifestyle framework within discussions on social capital certainly provides a start. The challenge, of course, remains that with a greater proportion of the life course spent in later life, there is now, more than ever, a need for older adults to remain integrated and invested in the issues facing the larger society. With the passage of the Edward M. Kennedy Serve

America Act of 2009, including incentives included under provisions specifically targeted at third-agers under the Encore Fellowship program, there is every reason to assume that rates of engagement in volunteerism will increase over current patterns and perhaps amount to what Freedman (2006–2007) terms "social-purpose encore careers." Of course, the question is whether such roles will become normative or coercive.

FUTURE STEPS: ISSUES TO CONSIDER

With the burgeoning of the population living well beyond normative retirement age, there is significant potential for Third Age engagement. With the shifting compositional characteristics of baby boomers just now approaching retirement, their higher educational levels, skills, and wealth being cases in point, patterns of participation are all the more likely to increase. Among the numerous other questions yet to be addressed is whether shifts in the economy will alter the willingness, indeed the ability of third-agers to take up civic engagement and contribute to a stock of social capital. Also, the role of gender differences is yet to receive significant attention despite widespread recognition that not only do women and men experience retirement differently, but also how they do so reflects relational impacts of public policies not necessarily designed with both genders in mind. As more and more women are engaged in life-long labor force involvement, will their willingness to volunteer or take up other forms of civic engagement be altered? Comparable questions hold for minority populations; will patterns of participation be different than among the majority? As well intentioned as Third Age researchers are, they have barely begun to scratch the surface of these and other abiding questions. Calasanti and King (see Chapter 4) provide a clear perspective on the types of research that is apropos if Third Age researchers are to pay appropriate attention to issues such as gender.

Not to be overlooked are the types of opportunities available to third-agers who might wish to be involved. Without meaningful roles, engagement in socially valuable roles is not automatic. The opportunities must match the educational level, skill sets, and interest levels of those entering the Third Age both from positions of advantage and from the full array of social economic statuses and ethnicities. Forging appropriate policies and removing potential barriers to full participation is essential. Yet neither is likely without a firm foundation of scholarly research into various facets of the Third Age.

Finally, in light of what we have said of social capital, it is incumbent on researchers to develop an encompassing framework. Our nominee is one that considers social capital as a benefit for both community and individuals —a lifestyle framework that can be used to consider the societal and individual factors that shape what people do and how engagement in particular activities are valued. Social capital is a resource upon which individuals can draw and which they provide to their social groups. As researchers explicate the role of the Third Age as a socially meaningful and recognized one, we must be mindful of the value of organizing conceptual frameworks. By approaching issues of the Third Age with such frameworks in mind, we are more likely to provide insight into this new phase of the life course.

REFERENCES

Adler, R. P., & Goggin, J. (2005). What do we mean by "civic engagement"? *Journal of Transformative Education, 3*, 236-253.

Adler, P. S., & Kwon, S. (2002). Social capital: Prospects for a new concept. *The Academy of Management Review, 27*(1), 17-40.

Baum, F. E., & Ziersch, A. M. (2003). Social capital. *Journal of Epidemiology and Community Health, 57*, 320-323.

Bourdieu, P. (1985). The forms of capital. In J. G. Richardson (Ed.), *Handbook of theory and research for the sociology of education* (pp. 241-248). New York, NY: Greenwood.

Bronfenbrenner, U. (1979). *The ecology of human development: Experiments by nature and design.* Cambridge, MA: Harvard University Press.

Bukov, A., Maas, I., & Lampert, T. (2002). Social participation in very old age: Cross-sectional and longitudinal findings from BASE. *Journals of Gerontology: Psychological Sciences, 57B*(6), P510-P517.

Burr, J. A., Choi, N. G., Mutchler, J. E., & Caro, F. G. (2005). Caregiving and volunteering: Are private and public helping behaviors linked? *Journal of Gerontology: Social Sciences, 60B*, S247-S256.

Butler, R. (2005). Do longevity and health generate wealth? In M. L. Johnson (Ed.), *The Cambridge handbook of age and ageing* (pp. 546-551). Cambridge: Cambridge University Press.

Caro, F. G., Bass, S. A., & Chen, Y. P. (1993). Introduction: Achieving a productive aging society. In S. A. Bass, F. G. Caro, & P. Y. Chen (Eds.), *Achieving a productive aging society* (pp. 1-25). Westport, CT: Auburn House.

Carpiano, R. M. (2005). Toward a neighborhood resource-based theory of social capital for health: Can Bourdieu and sociology help? *Social Science & Medicine, 62*(1), 165-175.

Carr, D. C. (2005). Changing the culture of aging: A social capital framework for gerontology. *Hallym International Journal of Aging, 7*(2), 103-115.

Coleman, J. (1988). Social capital in the creation of human capital. *The American Journal of Sociology, Organizations and Institutions: Sociological and Economic Approaches to the Analysis of Social Structure*, 94(Suppl.), S95–S120.

Cutler, S. J., & Hendricks, J. (2000). Age differences in voluntary association memberships: Fact or artifact. *Journal of Gerontology: Social Sciences, 55B*, S98–S107.

Cutler, S. J., Hendricks, J., & O'Neill, (2011). Civic engagement and aging. In R. Binstock, & L. K. George (Eds.), *Handbook of aging and the social sciences*. San Diego, CA: Academic Press.

Ekerdt, D. (1986). The busy ethic: Moral continuity between work and retirement. *The Gerontologist, 26*, 239–244.

Freedman, M. (2006–2007). The social-purpose career: Baby boomers, civic engagement and the next stage of work. *Generations, 30*(4), 43–46.

Geertz, C. (1973). *The interpretation of cultures*. New York, NY: Basic Books.

Gilleard, C., & Higgs, P. (2005). *Contexts of ageing: Class, cohort and community*. Cambridge: Polity Press.

Gilleard, C., & Higgs, P. (2007). The third age and the baby boomers: Two approaches to the social structuring of later life. *International Journal of Ageing and Later Life, 2*(2), 13–30.

Grano, C., Lucidi, F., Zelli, A., & Violani, C. (2008). Motives and determinants of volunteering in older adults: An integrated model. *The International Journal of Aging and Human Development, 67*, 305–326.

Greenfield, E. A., & Marks, N. F. (2004). Formal volunteering as a protective factor for older adults' psychological well-being. *Journal of Gerontology: Social Science, 59B*, S258–S264.

Hatch, L. R., & Hendricks, J. (2010). The concept of lifestyle: Adapting to old age. In J. Cavanaugh & C. Cavanaugh (Eds.), *Aging in America: Psychological, physical and social issues* (Vol. 3, pp. 106–128). Westport, CT: Greenwood.

Hendricks, J., & Cutler, S. J. (2004). Volunteerism and socioemotional selectivity in later life. *Journal of Gerontology: Social Science, 59B*, S251–S257.

Hendricks, J., & Hatch, L. R. (2006). Lifestyle and aging. In R. Binstock & L. K. George (Eds.), *Handbook of aging and the social sciences* (pp. 301–319). San Diego, CA: Academic Press.

Hendricks, J., & Hatch, L. R. (2009). Theorizing lifestyle: Exploring agency and structure in the life course. In V. Bengtson, M. Silverstein, N. Putney, & D. Gans (Eds.), *Handbook of theories of aging* (pp. 435–454) New York, NY: Springer.

Holstein, M. (2006). A critical reflection on civic engagement. *Public Policy & Aging Report, 16* (4), 21–26.

Holstein, M., & Minkler, M. (2003). Self, society and the "new gerontology." *The Gerontologist, 43*, 787–796.

Lin, N. (2001). *Social capital: A theory of social structure and action*. New York, NY: Cambridge University Press.

Martinson, M., & Minkler, M. (2006). Civic engagement and older adults: A critical perspective. *The Gerontologist, 46*, 318–324.

Morrow-Howell, N., Hinterlong, J., Rozario, P. A., & Tang, F. (2003). Effects of volunteering on the well-being of older adults. *Journal of Gerontology: Social Sciences, 58B,* S137–S145.

Musick, M. A., Herzog, A. R., & House, J. S. (1999). Volunteering and mortality among older adults: Findings from a national sample. *Journal of Gerontology: Social Sciences, 54B,* S73–S180.

Portes, A. (1998). Social capital: Its origins and applications in modern sociology. *Annual Review of Sociology, 24,* 1–24.

Portes, A., & Landolt, P. (1996). The downside of social capital. *American Prospect, 26,* 18–22.

Putnam, R. (2000). *Bowling alone.* New York, NY: Simon & Schuster.

Putnam, R. D. (1995). Bowling alone: America's declining social capital. *Journal of Democracy, 6(1),* 65–77.

Reilly, S. L. (2006). Transforming aging: The civic engagement of adults 55+. *Public Policy & Aging Report, 16,* 3–7.

Rosenberg, M. (1986). *Conceiving the self* (2nd ed.). New York, NY: Basic Books.

Rotolo, T. (1999). Trends in voluntary association participation. *Nonprofit and Voluntary Sector Quarterly, 23,* 199–212.

Rowe, J., & Kahn, R. (1998). *Successful aging.* New York, NY: Pantheon.

Stebbins, R. A. (1997). Casual leisure: A conceptual statement. *Sociological Review, 25,* 251–272.

U.S. Bureau of Labor Statistics. (2009). *Volunteering in the United States, 2008.* Retrieved July 27, 2009, from http://www.bls.gov/news.release/volun.nr0.htm.

Van Willigen, M. (2000). Differential benefits of volunteering across the life course. *Journal of Gerontology: Social Sciences, 55B,* S308–S318.

Weiss, R. S., & Bass, S. A. (2002). Epilogue. In R. S. Weiss & S. A. Bass (Eds.), *Challenges of the third age: Meaning and purpose in later life* (pp. 189–197). New York, NY: Oxford University Press.

Cultural Ideals, Ethics, and Agelessness: A Critical Perspective on the Third Age

Martha Holstein

NORMS AND EXPECTATIONS IN THE ERA OF THE THIRD AGE

O ur sense of self-worth largely depends on a belief that we are leading good and decent lives and that people we respect in turn respect us. Yet, the task of defining a worthy self, especially in old age, is made more difficult by current societal conditions in which the self has become detached from communal meanings and roles that once governed every part of human life (Cole, 1992). While not arguing for a return to such overarching communal meanings, the need for what Charles Taylor (1984) calls "horizons of meaning" goes on. This horizon offers a strong notion that certain ways of life are infinitely better than others. Culture, which reflects the "values, beliefs, orientations, and underlying assumptions prevalent among people in a society" (Harrison & Huntington, 2000, p. xv), provides many of the resources we need for developing that notion and a self-worthy of respect. At the same time, we need to be watchful about how cultural figurations, tropes, and narratives can lead to the internalization of values and expectations that may conflict with important elements of our biographical selves, elements that include our socioeconomic status, gender, race, as well as our self-conceptions.

In the popular press and in many academic circles, discourses on older ages—the period before major disabilities set in, now often referred to as the "Third Age"—offer newer ideals for what it means to live a "good" old age. These ideals are premised on continued good health and relative affluence. These discourses move in two major directions: one emphasizes continued productivity (see Chapter 9, this book) and the other postmodern consumerism where status derives from consumption rather than production (Blaikie, 1999; see also Chapter 3, this book). With the further assumptions that the demands of paid work and family responsibilities have been mitigated, these discourses suggest that as "age" itself loses its place as a meaningful category, ageism, lacking an anchor, will disappear.

These emerging discourses, built upon several disparate parts—successful aging, productive aging, civic engagement, and posttraditional or postmodern aging—assume that one *can* and *should* maintain good health in advanced old age. These norms are meant to replace the stereotypical "decline and loss" paradigm that once served as the dominant motif in discussions on old age. They share several recognizable components: they are, at once, both descriptive and normative establishing one way of life as the norm against which all are measured; they see the world of old age from a privileged perspective; they aim to demonstrate that the old are not burdens on society but rather contributors as producers or consumers; they strive to open opportunities and change images of aging but often fail to consider the structural inequalities that shape what is possible and probable for individuals. In these ways the "productive" stream is deeply traditional—it affirms voluntarism and the creation of certain forms of social capital, and is built on the American ideals of productivity and "success." In its postmodern form, it glorifies the voice of freedom and self-fulfillment, certainly another voice in this country's cultural repertoire.

Introduced by social historian Peter Laslett (1991) to account for expanding time between the end of traditional paid work and family responsibilities and the onset of debilitating illnesses, the Third Age, for Laslett, in his aptly titled book, *A Fresh Map of Life: The Emergence of the Third Age*, ought to be a time for personal fulfillment on an individual and collective level, since older people are "trustees for the future" of society (p. 196). In the years since the publication of his book, the protean concept of the "Third Age" has evolved and has been, at least in the United States, filled in with more explicit ideas of how the time ought to be used. In this chapter, I describe what I see as the now-dominant expressions of what one ought to do and be as one gets older.

I then describe what I call the "particular circumstances" that mark older ages. While understandings of "age" might be socially constructed, they rest on material and existential foundations that are not eliminable. These circumstances are keys to one's ability to realize the aims these discourses promote, and they also suggest the possibilities that open up if we consider old age as a unique time in human lifespan development to be honored for itself, neither split into two periods nor erased in favor of "agelessness" (Andrews, 1999). Because age itself is a relational category, there will always be "younger" and "older." The problem is not to eliminate age but to infuse it with cultural meanings that do not denigrate gray hair or slower steps.

With these background conditions clarified I critique these new "oughts" with two assumptions in mind—that we all care about how our lives go over the long term and that it is particularly important toward the end of life that we are able to see ourselves as living moral lives. I will thus ask whether images, ideals, or norms that are upheld as worthy or good and desirable are oppressive, possible for individuals to do, and reflect a view of the moral life that fits for most, if not all, of the people at whom it is directed. I argue that the prevalent normative images of a "good" old age do a disservice to large numbers of older people today, especially nonaffluent women and people of color.

I conclude with tentative proposals for how older people can claim their voices in the context of these emergent cultural messages. Because systems of meaning are social in nature and personal identity requires social recognition (Lindemann-Nelson, 2001), I look toward communicative processes—narratives of varied sorts—that ordinarily take place in the microcommunities of which we are a part. There one can challenge identities that others impose on us and redefine what it means to live a good and worthy life.

DOMINANT NORMATIVE IDEALS FOR THE "NEW" OLD AGE

Over the past 20 years or so, four different ways of changing how we think about old age have emerged—"productive aging," "successful aging," "civic engagement," and "postmodern or posttraditional aging." In a direct challenge to the view that old age burdens society, the reverse has been promoted—older individuals ease the demands on social resources by engaging in socially valued activities. They work, volunteer, respond to communal needs, consume, and are productive—all culturally resonant attributes. These discourses serve as counterweights to long-held views that old age is primarily about individual decrements or losses to which elders and societies needed to adapt (Phillipson, 1998). In a culture where youth is venerated and old age is devalued, calling attention to relative good health, continued contributions, and freedom challenges prevailing imagery.

In a bid for total freedom, postmodern (or posttraditional) geronto-logy upholds an image of older individuals, who are free to reinvent themselves in whatever ways they choose. Essentially playful, this image has a certain seductiveness—sexy grandma (perhaps with purple hair), running on the beach or returning to school at 85—as if we do not have to age at all. These views attest to the power of agency as individuals nego-tiate their "multiple selves in an ongoing, open-ended, and meaningful fashion" (Chapman, 2004, p. 13). For postmodernists, self-creation, self-invention, consumerism, and change are the new hallmarks of aging well (see Gergen & Gergen, 2000; Gilleard & Higgs, 2000).

These oddly contradictory views—productivity and civic engagement do not fit well with playful postmodernism—nonetheless share the under-lying idea that "old" applies only to those in the Fourth Age. The message is that we are only as old as we feel, that 60 is the new 40, and that one-by-one, biomedicine and the new genetics will chip away at the dis-eases that we cannot prevent by good and healthful living (Friedan, 1993; Post & Binstock, 2004). The young body is projected on the old body as a norm (Harper, 1997, p. 167). Underscored by research into successful aging (Rowe & Kahn, 1987) what has emerged as a vision for the "new" Third Age (no longer old age) seems to be the contemporary evocation of the "golden years."

I take a closer look at these ideas. Introduced in the late 1980s, pro-ductive aging or, as some prefer, a "productive aging society" (see Chapter 9) emerged, in part, as a response to the "greedy geezer" image of older people propounded by Americans for Generational Equity (AGE). AGE accused these older individuals of busily and happily spending their chil-dren's inheritance and impoverishing society along the way. To counteract AGE's campaign against entitlement programs and the societal burden of the old, gerontologists demonstrated that older people contribute to their families and their communities (Bass, Caro, & Chen, 1993) in significant ways. The generally unexamined implication of this attack and response is that human value is linked to those who live independently, contribut-ing rather than "burdening" society with their needs. While not silencing AGE's attack on entitlement programs, since ideologies are not easily silenced by "facts," the notion of productive aging helped to launch what has become a major theme in gerontology—"positive aging."

While the concept of productive aging has not disappeared, it has largely been supplanted by discussions related to civic engagement. Government, foundations, and private organizations have directed considerable resources and attention toward promoting significant voluntarism among older people to fulfill community needs. Not surprisingly, civic engagement caught on. It captures this country's self-image—individual initiative, private action as opposed to government intervention, neighbors helping neighbors, and transforming these actions into national priorities. It also challenges the "bowling alone" phenomenon that Putnam (1995) describes by seeing voluntarism as a renewed commitment to creating social capital. It does not, however, typically emphasize political organizing. Encouraging such political action would broaden the reach of civic engagement and make it less a symbol of privilege than a symbol of the ongoing struggle for justice (Martinson & Minkler, 2006). Instead, essentially conservative, it emphasizes what Walker (1999) describes as the "career self in which life plans, built upon a solid economic foundation and internalized self-control, unfold with a certain continuity" (p. 104). Oddly Victorian in its emphasis on control, civic engagement universalizes a way of life that lacks universal resonance.

What, however, is particularly troubling is a subtle subtext in both "productive aging" and "civic engagement"—a belief that *could* implies *should*. If one is capable of doing so, there is an assumption that individuals have an obligation to keep on contributing. In direct contrast to the playful postmodern self, the self that the "movement" for civic engagement praises is the responsible self who must pay civic "rent" for the space he/she occupies. Comparing it with the civil rights movement, its advocates describe it as "the creation of a national vision for aging that fosters productive engagement *as an expectation* of later life..." (Reilly, 2006, p. 1 emphasis added). By fulfilling this obligation, older people can serve their communities while relieving the pressure on public dollars.

THE "PARTICULAR CIRCUMSTANCES" OF BEING OLD

When Betty Friedan (1993) set out to write *The Fountain of Age*, she did not know that she was "deeply embedded in an ageist ideology." She soon realized that "the fountain of age didn't mean, *can't* mean, the absence of physiological, emotional, or situational change" (Friedan, 1993, p. xxviii, cited in Andrews, 1999, p. 309). As 79-year-old Connie Goldman, a writer and producer, notes (pers. comm., March 16, 2010), we come to recognize that what we are now is not what we once were; thus, we should not try to hold on to whom we used to be. If we deny age, we deny the importance of what has happened to us over our lifetime. We see that "people in their seventies *typically* and *predictably* have a different relation than people in midlife to illness, death, and decline" (Ruddick, 1999, p. 49).

To begin, I consider one of the most fundamental differences, which starts in early life and deepens in later life: the effects of social and economic location. To be born with the proverbial silver spoon in one's mouth, unless one has been a profligate spender, leads to quite a different range of opportunities in old age than being born in a low-income housing project or even into a working class family that is marginally making ends meet. Race, class, and gender matter. Who hears rats in the walls at night and who relocates to lush retirement communities? Who takes care of whom? Who faces a rich array of choices and who does not? Income insecurity is a particularly serious problem for many older people, especially women (Wider Opportunities for Women). Our health status also varies with our economic status (Minkler, Fuller-Thomson, & Guralnik, 2006). Advantages and disadvantages accumulate (Dannefer, 2003).

But there are also some important commonalties, each of which raises additional questions about norms that elevate a particular vision of the good life in old age. First, by 65, life passed is far longer than life left. Losses have already started to accumulate for elders, their families, and friends; hence, "facts and fears of decline and loss are central to the lives of the elderly" (Ruddick, 1999, p. 49). Yet, what should be a truism becomes something to resist acknowledging. Perhaps this resistance occurs because it is too hard to associate this fact with the possibilities for continued joy and growth. Second, no matter how well older people have cared for themselves, with rare exceptions, one's physical capacities change as the years go by. Bodies do not perform as well as they once did even if one remains able to manage day-to-day life with relative ease. Older people are more vulnerable—to the icy streets, steep bus steps, and long climbs into subway stations. There may be a fear of falling as balance becomes less reliable. Third, family relationships change. For women, widowhood is likely since women live longer than men and tend to marry men who are older than they are. Relationships with children may change. They are forming their own nuclear families and are busy with career building. Fourth, older people often experience a cultural disjuncture. They grew up in a very different time and so can easily feel disconnected from contemporary culture. Yet, given the importance of culture in providing important resources for constructing and maintaining identity, individuals need to find their authentic voices amidst the cultural clamor. As they straddle past and present, they need to make decisions about how to live when many of their former anchors have disappeared.

When individuals leave the "Third Age" of relative well-being and enter the "fourth age" when the possibilities for "agelessness" are no longer possible, the major goal becomes staying out of an institution (Cohen, 1988; Minkler, 1990). The fact of embodiment becomes even more important since physical changes alter relationships with the world and inform the choices that are possible. Hence, 80-year-olds might stop doing certain things. Perhaps there will be some memory loss or other cognitive difficulties even in the absence of dementia. Perhaps getting on and off airplanes will be harder and so travel will not seem as enticing as it once did. More friends may die or become ill; and if not already widowed, widowhood becomes more likely. These changes require individuals to reinterpret their lives as some identities disappear and others appear. It becomes as Furman (1997) astutely observed, "a struggle of the soul to affirm what is possible, to let go what is not" (p. 102).

In sum, heightened awareness that our bodies are no longer reliable, a sense that life is foreshortened and that the end is nearer than the beginning, and a belief that others cannot see us as we see ourselves are important markers as we age. From the "Third" to the "Fourth" Age these changes subtly evolve, often without a radical departure although at times it is one event, a fall and a broken hip, cognitive changes, or serious illness that catapults us into the "fourth age." And these changes are all occurring during a time of deep global shifts that have weakened the social safety net and strengthened the individualistic strain in this country.

THE CRITIQUE

I begin by raising concerns about norms that value a certain kind of subjectivity. First, because the new or emerging discourses about the "Third Age" emanate from a position of relative privilege, they can marginalize alternative ways of life, threaten the well-being of the less well-off or less healthy, and flatten the vast differences among people who are old. When older people may need a rich array of cultural ideals and norms, they are greeted with mutually reinforcing ideals of agelessness. These norms may then be experienced as oppressive, irrelevant, or frustrating. While all may benefit from narratives that see older people as full and competent adults, they may be morally problematic if such recognition depends on one meeting already powerful cultural expectations such as productivity, control, and mastery, a form of life most often associated with masculine ideals (Walker, 1999).

Second, by not acknowledging contingency and ambiguity, these narratives deny the developmental possibilities that can emerge from these seemingly negative features of old age. To integrate change with continuity as we age means acknowledging what one has been and what one is becoming—both the good and the problematic (Atchley, 1987; Baltes & Baltes, 1990). We are not what we once were. Third, in the effort to eliminate negative stereotypes of old age, these narratives bring a new form of ageism now directed at the less vigorous and less healthy. Fourth, the emphasis on good health and relative affluence can serve to undercut public policies that are essential for the late-life well-being of many older people, especially women and people of color. These narratives are peculiarly apolitical—while urging the creation of opportunities they are silent about the structural origins of inequalities that only worsen in old age.

Finally, because we cannot be expected to do what we are unable to do, I believe we must challenge the presuppositions that each of these related ideals set forth—that people will have the health, and the material, emotional, and social supports, necessary to live up to the expectations these norms create. Yet, empirical evidence makes it stunningly clear that even this basic expectation cannot be assumed. Recent research (McLaughlin, Connell, Heerings, Li, & Roberts, 2009), for example, demonstrates that few older people (11.9%) age "successfully" by the "successful aging" (Rowe & Kahn, 1987) standards. Not surprisingly, advanced age, gender, and lower socioeconomic status were key factors in predicting who could not meet these standards. Aging well is thus heavily dependent on socio-structural factors.

We find these problematic elements of the "Third Age" discourse to be morally significant because they are the backdrop against which older people define themselves and test their identities as changes take place. As Lindemann-Nelson (2001) observed, "personal identity, understood as a complicated interaction of one's own sense of self and others' understandings of who one is, functions as a lever that expands or contracts one's ability to exercise moral agency" (p. xi).

On the basis of these observations, I highlight three key concerns that need to be carefully considered in future research and discussions regarding the Third Age. First, I argue that "Third Age" is a term that promotes the ideals of the privileged. Second, the implicit messages about the Third Age are creating a foundation for a new kind of ageism in which only those older adults who contribute to society or are healthy and active in retirement are perceived to be valuable. In contrast, those in the Fourth Age, or who are disabled, are viewed as a drain on social resources and are thus not valuable. Finally, I am concerned about the extent to which the promotion of a Third Age culture advances a "new gerontology" that has no substantive political agenda. In general, organizing efforts in the pursuit of social justice remain sidelined in these discourses, and gerontologists seem strangely unconcerned with how their agendas build upon a lifetime of relative advantage.

The View of Privilege

The individualistic and privileged standpoint from which the "new gerontology" originates cannot account for the people unable to meet day-to-day expenses. The postmodern and the productive self are both totalizing narratives that speak from and to the center and not the margins. Successful aging shares this problem. To age "successfully" demands much of us throughout our lives, much of which is beyond our control. We can stop smoking but we cannot easily escape poverty. Proponents who see aging through a lens of privilege thus falsely assume that living these versions of a good old age is available to all by dint of our private efforts.

Simply then, to be civically engaged or productive is a choice primarily available to the privileged. There is a vast difference between starting a new housing service in one's community using one's life experiences and contacts or returning to work as a white collar part-time consultant and having to work at a minimum wage job just to make ends meet. Further, for the privileged, work and civic activities have been and may continue to be sources of respect and often substantial earnings that also leave time for self-care and nurture. For those who are privileged, continuation of such activities may be ongoing sources of self-esteem. For women and people lower down on the income scale, however, work is often arduous and not a source of respect. For these workers, time or resources for self-care and nurturance are limited. A lifetime of "women's work" like caring for older people at home or a nursing home or flipping burgers at McDonalds will most likely make her a failure rather than a successful aged person. This blindness to the interlocking system of inequalities marginalizes those who, through no fault of their own cannot, or will not, meet expectations. In this way, civic engagement and productivity, which are foundational to the ideals of the Third Age, seen through the eyes of a woman who has struggled to make ends meet all her life might make it seem more like a burden than a privilege, one more expectation or necessity no different than what she experienced during her earlier years. This observation does not overlook the fact that many people, who have worked very hard for a living and have little in the way of income or assets, do not want to keep on giving. Many do, especially in the role of caregivers to other family members. The point, however, is that this perspective can place them in a position of being negatively judged if they want to rest—even if they still have the good health to continue. That is the difference between opening opportunities and creating new expectations. So a major problem these prevailing ideas for the "Third Age" presents is its appropriateness for only a small percent of the American population. This means that "blaming the victim" for not fulfilling the new requirements for a good old age will further devalue an already devalued group. Banishing the negative fears of old age from public discourse does not eliminate them.

Persistence of Ageism

Productive aging rhetoric holds that once the public becomes aware of all the contributions that older people make, ageism will disappear. Proponents also seek to make ageism disappear by arguing for "agelessness." Neither approach has eliminated ageism; they have merely postponed it. As long as one conforms to midlife norms, ageism might be contained. This elevation of the Third Age transferred age-related prejudices to people in the Fourth Age or even more broadly, to anyone who fails to live up to expectations regarding social contributions and vigorous good health (Holstein & Minkler, 2003), that is, anyone who is not "young."

To claim that the now-dominant images of aging reinforce rather than challenge ageism may, at first glance, seem counterintuitive. Is it not better, one might ask, to see images of busy, apparently happy, fit-looking, even sexy, older people in film and TV, in magazine ads, and foundation reports than seeing the caricatures that now are marketed as humorous birthday cards or in ads for walkers or wheelchairs? Admittedly, this is a dilemma. The dilemma is, in part, created by this country's inability to overcome its historical patterns of dichotomous thinking in which there is a "good" and "bad" old age (Cole, 1992). "Elevating the Third [Age] . . . is only done by treading down the fourth. The labeling problem is wished on to even older and more defenseless older people" (Blaikie, 1999, citing Young and Schuller, p. 181). The unintentional devaluing of people who no longer meet the norms of midlife can result in behaviors that are self-defeating such as not asking for help even when it is urgently needed. The societal goal for fourth-agers, often internalized by these elders (Cohen, 1988) compared to the active engagement expected from third-agers is rarely about a full life, albeit constrained by physical or cognitive changes, but more about preserving independence, which seems to mean little more than staying in the community (Cohen, 1988; Minkler, 1990). It is also about offering choices even if those choices have little or no meaning to them (Agich, 1990). Deep old age becomes even more frightening. The inability to measure up to the emergent norms of the Third Age reinforces an already existing problem and deepens the possibilities for negatively appraising one's life situation.

The Nonpolitical Agenda

Ethics provides a means to expose hidden values and call attention to their differential impact on people based on the particular features of their lives. The background conditions and messages that shape public attitudes and public policy influence the contextually based choices that we make. Of grave concern is that the "new gerontology" has no substantive political agenda or commitments to organizing in the pursuit of social justice. Nor is there a concern for how these agendas build upon a lifetime of relative advantage. Yet, personal choices are structured by public factors. By sidelining a social justice agenda, which seems so apt for a program of civic engagement, little is done to alter the conditions' possibility for many older people. In a clear synergy between social science and moral philosophy, Meyers (1997) notes that "unless some people see injustice and oppression that others deny, there will be no impetus for change" (p. 198). To see from the perspective of the marginalized is a critical political task.

For these reasons, we argue that it is essential for advocates of civic engagement to refocus their efforts to support projects that build a movement for improved social conditions for elders (and for people of all ages). The "greedy geezer" is back in the news. Without organized effort, the drive to portray positive images of aging, based on health and financial well-being, may inadvertently fuel efforts to change programs essential to the well-being of far too many older people.

Thus, we find it peculiarly ironic that the senior employment program that develops low-wage work opportunities for low-income older people is often considered a form of civic engagement. For people so engaged, work is a necessity rather than an opportunity for joining self-fulfillment to social good as is so often portrayed by Third-Age rhetoric. We wonder what choices these men and women would make if asked to consider what self-fulfillment would mean for their lives. Without an organized political movement to call attention to these important issues, perceptions that those who "choose" to engage in activities deemed economically valuable will reify inappropriate perceptions of what connotes a "good" old age and thus harm the moral standing of the most vulnerable older adults.

A TENTATIVE PROPOSAL: THE MEANING OF OLD AGE FOR INDIVIDUALS AND SOCIETIES

While I have sought to probe and challenge emerging discourses about a "good" old age, I know that the cultural environment, whether explicitly normative or not, will influence us as we try to make sense of our own lives. It is in our interest that this environment is not limited to images that are both unrecognizable and unrealizable by large numbers of people. In this last phase of our lives, we need the greatest freedom possible to flourish in whatever way makes the most sense to us. As Meyers (2002) asks: how can we get in touch with ourselves and speak in our own voices when culture bombards us with its messages? That the normative impact of civic engagement, productive aging, or postmodern aging is unintentional does not lessen its possibilities for harm.

What then would it take to create social conditions that "permit and encourage us to critically assess and influence the social ideals that in turn shape our lives?" (Clement, 1996, p. 25).

Since social groups are identity confirming (Lindemann-Nelson, 2001) and since we are encumbered selves that are influenced by culture, we can use dialogue or conversation with others, as a way to sort through what is valuable for us and what is not. The affirmation that we are leading valuable lives can gain strength in microcommunities and provide a foundation by which to form more realistic assessments about what being a "third-ager" implies. Many older individuals find biography, autobiography, fiction, and poetry as both resources for multiple ideas about growing old and also as a means to grapple with inevitable changes (see Holstein, Parks, & Waymack, 2011). Building on the communicative-dialogic model, there is much potential for identity work achieved through narrative and "re-stroying" (Ray, 2007). These are ideal ways to examine meaning and purpose in later life. These various sources—written and participatory—are ways to develop what Hilde Lindeman-Nelson (2001) calls counterstories that repair damaged identities or return to us our own voice so that we can retell our own story in the company of others. Such stories are flexible and adaptable to changes we experience. They do not demand a universal theme or a master story, especially one that demands that we become certain ideal types—namely sexual, productive, busy, and self-reliant (Cole, 1992). Nor do they demand that we be slim, graceful, and energetic.

If communities of meaning—formal and informal—are critical elements in helping us to explore and struggle with what we fear, hope for, or find meaningful as we age, there is a further way that living well in old age takes more than individual effort. Collective assurance that the foundation for a decent life is in place for all is essential. While the efforts of elder volunteers are praiseworthy, they cannot replace public guarantees of a social safety net. Certainly creating opportunities for work and for voluntarism are important as well, but opportunities are different than expectations.

As people turn to such communities of meaning, created or already existing, often hidden resources can be brought out to facilitate claiming one's own voice. People want to be accountable and want to confirm their sense of agency, but do so in nonoppressive ways. We further support recent commitments to focus on changing the environment to meet the evolving needs of individuals as they age rather than focusing on the individual's need to adapt as his/her physical or cognitive capacities change. This view affirms Ruddick's (1999) effort to describe the virtues of age as something we do not ever achieve but rather we work toward *ongoing efforts of virtue* (p. 52, italics in the original) in relation to other people. Virtue is something that people make together through networks of "social relations and policies."

Facing Contradictions and Making Meaning

Old age is a bundle of contradictions but not an unhappy time if basic needs are met. Hence, we reaffirm the heterogeneity of the category "old" and argue for a "bottom-up" development of stories about "my old age." These stories can capture the varied ways people make sense of aging and old age without first denying that it actually exists. Such stories grow naturally in microcommunities such as the beauty shop studied by Frida Furman (1997) where women supported one another in their resistance to the dominant ideals that prevailed outside the beauty shop. These ideals derogated their thinning hair and "turkey necks." We can hear these stories at any place where people feel free to talk about their experiences of aging and old age. Relying on an approach to seeing, hearing, and reading about how people actually make sense of old age provides a more authentic understanding of later life than the relentlessly positive view advanced by the "new gerontology." These formulations tend to impose inappropriate expectations about later life that ultimately do a disservice to the many older people who are hurt both physically and psychologically. Bodies are real and our identities are inevitably influenced by our experiences as embodied selves.

Thus, we cannot evade what is considered the dark side of aging. Instead, we need a model of resistance that allows older people to integrate the changes that are taking place despite their best efforts at control. The "Third Age" is "lived against a background of realization of what comes next. The meaning of any activity . . . is colored by awareness of a powerfully ambiguous future" (Rubenstein, 2002, p. 39). Although emphasizing the negative features of old age, or negatively viewed by current cultural standards, further separates the old from everyone else by acknowledging illness and death, it is equally risky to highlight ideas about old age that focus almost entirely on "positive" aging. This effort interferes with older adults' ability to realistically assess what it means to them to live a life of meaning despite, and maybe even because of, changes. It is time to regain a balance between the positive and negative poles of aging so that we do not marginalize people whose physical or cognitive capacities make them dependent on others, or elevate those who are fortunate enough to retain vigor and good health into their 80s or 90s.

FUTURE STEPS: ISSUES TO CONSIDER

Throughout this chapter, I have noted the critical importance of context in making later life a place of reasonable contentment and acceptance. I have also called for a political agenda since, in its absence, too many older people will have little of that leisure to do anything with their lives but work and fear falling off the edge. If later life is to be truly a time of freedom (for women especially, given that this may be the only time they are free to pursue their own dreams and goals), they need the resources to enjoy this freedom. A mere right to choose, to be left alone, does not offer many older persons the opportunity to experience the freedom they might otherwise enjoy.

Conceptually, this chapter has built upon the view that "norms matter because we [individuals] are situated selves, embedded in society and culture ... [we] resonate with what is valued in the environment" (Holstein & Minkler, 2003, p. 791). Hence, as philosopher Owen Flanagan (1991) suggests our identities, self-respect, agency and even or contentment need complex social systems in order to flouish. While these social systems often impose constraints on what is possible, as does our health status, income and so on, they contain the images and ideals that help us to make sense of our lives, to decide how to live, and to gain (or not) self-respect. This view of the relational self (see Mackenzie & Stoljar, 2000) reminds us that our environments give us the materials that help us determine what we value; without those environments, autonomy would be impossible. The social or relational self is a "biographically anchored and reflexive project" realized in conversations with others and with "oneself" (Dannefer, 2003, p. 272) in particular cultural contexts.

From small groups, whether in living rooms or public places, conferences or virtual communities, much like the consciousness raising groups of the 1970s, older people can work to claim their own voices. From there, ideas may travel "upwards" so that they can begin to transform cultural attitudes and reflect the facts of aging and the multiple voices of people from the margins as well as from the center. The starting place for a denser, more democratic sense of the potential for both the Third and the Fourth Ages is "the embodied, socially situated, and divided self" who is able to develop a "rich understanding of what one is like" and is also able to make adjustments as one's capacities change (Meyers, 2002, p. 22). What is seen as a valued life in old age must be open to more than the relatively few.

Yet, culture remains important and thus the now-dominant norms for the "Third Age" require continued scrutiny and challenge. This task will not be easy. While gerontologists might not have social power, the media and other cultural vehicles that pick up the new discourses do. That is why media giants like Helen Mirren or Meryl Streep are so important. While most older people recognize that these images are not them, the norms that this chapter have discussed encode meanings of aging that we have argued are not reflective of or suitable for many, if not most, older people in this country. They create social and personal expectations that can damage a self already trying to make sense of changes that are not culturally favored. Acts of resistance are difficult, in part because these "Third Age" ideals are so attractive, but they are necessary lest these emergent norms become even further entrenched. We propose microcommunities as places of support and meaning-making that can confront figurations that do not fit one's self-conception. In such communities, one can tell the truth about oneself, and the communities can correct one's story or redirect one's thinking in ways that are helpful and enlightening. We have also suggested that for such communities to flourish, basic security is critical. One is apt to worry less about meaning and identity than getting food on the table.

In conclusion, we suggest that challenges to these norms must also occur in the professional circles in which they have taken hold. The excitement that these new norms generate is palpable. Using ethics as a source of critical consciousness, we can raise questions about the unexamined commitment to norms that are potentially damaging to so many. We must take advantage of every opportunity (and create opportunities) to offer more emancipatory imagery.

ACKNOWLEDGMENTS

I would like to thank my colleagues Jennifer Parks and Mark Waymack for their comments on an earlier draft of this chapter. I also thank Dawn C. Carr, this volume's editor, who did wonders in her efforts to pare the chapter down to an appropriate size.

Portions of this text are reprinted with permission from Springer Publishing Company, 2010.

REFERENCES

Agich, G. 1990. Reassessing autonomy in long-term care. *Hastings Center Report,* *20*(6), 12–17.

Atchley, R. (1987). *Aging: Continuity and change.* Belmont, CA: Wadsworth.

Andrews, M. (1999). The seductiveness of agelessness. *Ageing and Society, 19,* 301–318.

Baltes, P., & Baltes, M. 1990. *Successful aging: Perspectives from the behavioral sciences.* Cambridge, UK: Cambridge University Press.

Bass, S., Caro, F., & Chen, Y.-P. (Eds.). 1993. *Achieving a productive aging society.* Westport, CT: Auburn Press.

Blaikie, A. (1999). *Aging and popular culture.* Cambridge, UK: Cambridge University Press.

Chapman, A. (2004). Ethical implications of prolonged lives. *Theology Today, 60*(4), 479–496.

Clement, G. (1996). *Care, autonomy, and justice: Feminism and the ethic of care.* Boulder, CO: Westview Press.

Cohen, E. (1988). The elderly mystique: Constraints on the autonomy on the elderly with disabilities. *The Gerontologist, 28*(Suppl.), 24–31.

Cole, T. (1992). *The journey of life: A cultural history of aging in America.* New York, NY: Oxford University Press.

Dannefer, D. (2003). Cumulative advantage/disadvantage and the life course: Cross fertilizing age and social science theory. *Journal of Gerontology: Social Sciences, 58B*(6), S327–S337.

Flanagan, O. (1991). *Varieties of moral personality: Ethics and psychological realism.* Cambridge, MA: Harvard University Press.

Friedan, B. (1993). *The fountain of age.* New York, NY: Simon & Schuster.

Furman, F. (1997). There are no older Venuses: Women's responses to their aging bodies. In M. U. Walker (Ed.), *Mother time: Women, aging, and ethics.* Lanham, MD: Rowman & Littlefield.

Gergen, K., & Gergen, M. (2000). The new aging: Self-construction and social values. In K. W. Schaie, & J. Hendricks (Eds.), *The evolution of the aging self: The social impact on the aging process* (pp. 281–306). New York, NY: Springer Publishing.

Gilleard, C., & Higgs, P. (2000). *Cultures of aging: Self, aging and the body.* New York, NY: Prentice-Hall.

Harper, S. (1997). Constructing later life/constructing the body: Some reflections from feminist theory. In A. Jamieson, S. Harper & S. Victor (Eds.), *Critical approaches to aging and later life* (pp. 160–172). Buckingham, UK: Open University Press.

Harrison, L., & Huntington, S. (Eds.). (2000). *Culture matters: How values shape human progress.* New York, NY: Basic Books.

Holstein, M., & Minkler, M. (2003). Self, society and the "new gerontology." *The Gerontologist, 43*(6), 787–796.

Holstein, M., Parks, J., & Waymack, M. (2011). *Ethics, aging, and society: The critical
turn.* New York, NY: Springer.

Laslett, P. (1991). *A fresh map of life: The emergence of the third age.* Cambridge,
MA: Harvard University Press.

Lindemann-Nelson, H. (2001). *Damaged identities, narrative repair.* Ithaca, NY:
Cornell University Press.

Mackenzie, C., & Stoljar, N. (Eds.). (2000). *Relational autonomy: Feminist perspectives on autonomy, agency and the social order.* New York, NY: Oxford University
Press.

Martinson, M., & Minkler, M. (2006). Civic engagement and older adults: A critical
perspective. *The Gerontologist, 46*(3), 318–324.

McLaughlin, S., Connell, C., Heerings, S., Li, L., & Roberts, J. S. (2009). Successful aging
in the United States: Prevalence estimates from a national sample of older adults.
Journal of Gerontology: Social Sciences, 65B(2), 216–226.

Meyers, D. (1997). Emotion and heterodox moral perception: An essay in moral social
psychology. In D. Meyers (Ed.), *Feminists re-think the self* (pp. 197–218). Boulder,
CO: Westview Press.

Meyers, D. (2002). *Gender in the mirror. Cultural imagery and women's agency.*
New York, NY: Oxford University Press.

Minkler, M. (1990). Aging and disability: Behind and beyond the stereotypes. *Journal
of Aging Studies, 4*(3), 245–260.

Minkler, M., Fuller-Thomson, E., & Guralnik, J. (2006). *New England Journal of
Medicine, 355*(7), 695–703.

Phillipson, C. (1998). *Reconstructing old age: New agendas in social theory and
practice.* London: Sage.

Post, S., & Binstock, R. (2004). *The fountain of youth: Cultural, scientific, and ethical
perspectives on a biomedical goal.* New York, NY: Oxford University Press.

Putnam, R. (1995). Bowling alone: America's declining social capital. *Journal of
Democracy, 6*(1), 65–78.

Ray, R. (2007). Narratives as agents of social change: A new direction for narrative
gerontologists. In M. Barnard, & T. Scharf (Eds.), *Critical perspectives on ageing
societies.* Bristol, UK: Policy Press.

Reilly, S. F. (2006). Transforming aging: The civic engagement of adults 55+. *Public
Policy and Aging Report, 16*(4), 1, 3–7.

Rowe, J. W., & Kahn, R. L. (1987). Human aging: Usual and successful. *Science, 237,*
263–271.

Rubenstein, R. (2002). The third age. In R. Weiss & S. Bass (Eds.), *Challenges of the third
age: Meaning and purpose in later life.* New York, NY: Oxford University Press.

Ruddick, S. (1999). Virtues and age. In M. W. Walker (Ed.), *Mother time: Women,
aging, and ethics* (pp. 45–60). Lanham, MD: Rowman & Littlefield.

Russell, L. H., Bruce, E., Conahan, J., & Wider Opportunties for Women. (2006).
The WOW-GI National Elder Economic Security Standard: A methodology for

determining economic security for elders. Washington, DC: Wider Opportunities for Women.

Taylor, C. (1984). *Sources of the self*. Cambridge, MA: Harvard University Press.

Walker, M. (1999). Getting out of line: Alternatives to life as a career. In M. Walker (Ed.), *Mother time: Women, aging, and ethics*. Lanham, MD: Rowman & Littlefield.

Young, M., & Schuller, T. (1991). *Life after work: The arrival of the ageless society*. London: HarperCollins, cited in Blaikie, A. (1999). *Aging and popular culture*. Cambridge, UK: Cambridge University Press.

The Third Age: Fact or Fiction— and Does It Matter?

Linda K. George

O ne of the advantages of being asked to write the afterword for a book is that one is required to read everything that comes before it. In this case, that was pure pleasure. This is a path-breaking volume. As a set, the chapters in this book successfully achieve several things: They provide timely information about the conceptualization of and research about the Third Age, they are written by a superb cadre of authors from both the United States and Europe, they address a broad range of issues regarding the Third Age from a variety of scholarly viewpoints, and, most important for me, each chapter is remarkably thoughtful and thought provoking.

I took copious notes while reading all the chapters. Each chapter provided me with nuggets of insight—issues that I had never considered or about which I had not recognized their significance. Obviously, I cannot do justice to all of the issues that intrigued me in this brief addendum. Nor will I attempt to summarize the major themes of the book as is often offered in an edited volume. Instead, my comments will focus on the notion of a Third Age *per se*. Specifically, I will address three issues: Is the Third Age a discernable life stage (i.e., does it really exist)? Does it matter if there is a Third Age—and if so, why? And, what are the implications of the Third Age for social gerontology?

IS THE THIRD AGE A DISCERNABLE LIFE STAGE?

Given the exponentially increasing attention in science, public policy, and public discourse, can there be any doubt that the Third Age is a new and very real stage of life? After reading the chapters in this book, I must conclude that there are several reasons to doubt that the Third Age exists.

To establish whether there is a Third Age, it is necessary to define it. As pointed out in numerous chapters herein, however, a consensual definition of the Third Age remains elusive. The simplest—and, arguably, lowest common denominator—definition appears to be that the Third Age is the stage of life that occurs after the termination of paid work (i.e., retirement) and before the onset of health problems sufficiently disabling to restrict activities. A variety of approximate age ranges characterizing the Third Age, and anticipated lengths of its duration have been proposed, but this heterogeneity is irrelevant to the defining characteristics of departure from the labor force and the maintenance of good health. Authors also vary with regard to what they view as the defining lifestyle of the Third Age with some focusing on unpaid productive activities (e.g., Freedman, 1999), others emphasizing leisure and self-actualization (e.g., Sinnot, 2009), and still others focusing on consumerism (Gilleard, Higgs, Hyde, Wiggins, & Blane, 2005). Regardless of lifestyle issues, however, the basic definition of the Third Age remains the period of life in which individuals are retired from work, and yet remain healthy.

An advantage of this definition is that it makes it relatively easy to empirically identify third-agers. One would assume, then, that high-quality estimates of the number of third-agers in the United States and other countries would be readily available. Apparently this is not the case—authors in this volume did not provide estimates of the percentage of people in a given age range who meet the definition of third-agers. Using standard single decrement life tables, Carr (2009) provides the most detailed projections to date of age at entry to the Third Age and of duration and proportion of life spent in the Third Age in the U.S. population. Although these results are interesting, they fail to clarify the proportion of the total population, or of a specified age range of the population, who are third-agers. Moreover, and as noted by Brown and Lynch (Chapter 5), life tables provide *averages* for the population being studied. They cannot tell us the *proportion of individuals* who meet the definition of third-agers. Midwinter (2005) estimates that in the 1990s, 21% of the British population was third-agers. This estimate was based on projections of labor force participation and disability rates, however, rather than on a representative sample of individuals. These efforts are noteworthy, but an estimate of the number or proportion of third-agers based on a representative sample of individuals remains unavailable.

Thus, my first concern with the notion that the Third Age is a new life stage rests on the fact that we do not know how many people enter and leave the Third Age or how long they live in it. Setting aside the issue of the proportion of the population needed for justifying the claim of a life stage (a complex, unanswered issue), it seems premature to declare a new life stage in the absence of information about its prevalence. Confidence that the Third Age is a new life stage would differ substantially, presumably, depending on whether 20% or 80% of the population meet the criteria for membership in it at some point in the adult life course.

Related to the issue of prevalence, but even more theoretically and practically important, is the issue of inequalities and heterogeneity within the age range typically associated with the Third Age. I was pleased to see the extent to which chapter authors identified inequality as a significant problem with the concept of the Third Age. Authors raising this issue include both advocates of "critical gerontology," that is, Komp, Calasanti, and King, Rowles and Manning, and Holstein—and those whose work rests on other perspectives—that is, Moen, Brown, and Lynch, and Carr and Hendricks. The crux of this issue is whether the definition of the Third Age applies only to the most privileged members of society.

By definition, third-agers are sufficiently healthy to maintain active lifestyles. They also must be sufficiently affluent that their pensions, Social Security benefits, and other assets provide adequate income in the absence of paid work. It seems obvious that many individuals who are in the age ranges viewed as typical of the Third Age lack sufficient health, income, or both to qualify as third-agers. It is well established that a substantial proportion of adults in their 50s, 60s, and 70s have health-related limitations in their activities (e.g., U.S. Census Bureau, 1997). And, although the average age at retirement has decreased during the past four decades, large proportions of adults in their 50s and 60s continue to work full time either because they want to work or because they cannot afford to retire (Flippen & Tienda, 2000). Just as we lack information about the specific number and/or proportion of individuals who meet the criteria for membership as a third-ager, we lack information about the number and proportion of people who do not meet those criteria. Nonetheless, it is safe to conclude that a substantial proportion of adults who are chronologically eligible for membership do not qualify. Thus, paying attention to inequalities also leads to the question of what the threshold is for declaring a new life stage. I cannot provide a consensual or empirically valid definition of that threshold, but my strong sense is that the proportion who do cross the threshold for the Third Age is not large enough to claim a new life stage.

An issue that received relatively little attention in the chapters, but which is highly relevant to whether or not the Third Age exists are the macro-level and historical dynamics concerning the institutionalization and deinstitutionalization of the life course. Most scholars agree that since the 1950s there have been strong signs that the life course is deinstitutionalizing (see, e.g., Chapter 1 by Moen). Age norms have not been eradicated, but they are taken much less seriously and there are a few sanctions applied when they are violated. The chapter in this volume by Brothers and Gurvald superbly demonstrates the erosion of traditional norms governing marriage and family formation. Compared to 50 years ago, smaller proportions of the population are marrying, rates of divorce increased greatly although they leveled off during the past two decades, remarriage is very common, fewer people are having children, childbirth is less closely linked to being married, women are having fewer children, and cohabitation and repartnering have increased substantially. These patterns have led to both greater heterogeneity in U.S. families and a smaller proportion of one's life spent being married and/or caring for dependent children.

The mechanism underlying the deinstitutionalization of the life course is the cultural emphasis on individualism (Beck & Beck-Gernsheim, 2002). The cultural and normative ideal of individualism obviously requires a level of affluence and political, economic, and social infrastructures that makes individualism possible. It appears that these levels of infrastructure were achieved in developed societies by the last half of the 20th century. As a result, increased heterogeneity can be observed in virtually every domain of life (e.g., work, family life, and religion). This heterogeneity reflects the wide range of choices that societal members make in shaping their lives. Because of this increased heterogeneity of choices, the standard life course—with its broad stages of childhood, young adulthood, middle age, and late life—no longer neatly describes the majority of the population.

Thus, one must wonder whether, in the midst of a historical dynamic of deinstitutionalization, it makes sense to claim that a new life stage has emerged. One of the ways that the notion of the Third Age may be misleading is that, although it is asserted to be a new life stage, broader social and cultural conditions are informing us that human lives are shaped into heterogeneous paths by external conditions, the opportunities available in affluent nation states, and human agency.

Also at the macro-level, one can argue that what appears to be a new life stage is simply the result of structural lag (Riley, Kahn, & Foner, 1994). As Riley and others note, structural lag occurs when the behaviors of masses of individuals change such that preexisting structural arrangements no longer meet the needs of or are irrelevant to a large proportion of societal members. This seems to be precisely the case with the Third Age. Retirement policies and programs have lagged far behind the capacities of most adults to work until age 70 and later. Social Security, the retirement income program that covers more than 95% of the U.S. population, was never intended to support large numbers of healthy adults capable of working for decades. Yet the age requirements for receipt of full benefits from Social Security and other programs have increased only slightly despite rapid increases in both total life expectancy and disability-free life expectancy. If there is a large group of adults between the approximate ages of 50 and 75 who have retired from the labor force but remain healthy, I view this as evidence of the failure of social policies to adjust benefit levels and eligibility criteria in line with changing population demographics.

In short, I find little evidence that a new life stage has emerged in the midst of rapid deinstitutionalization of the life course. We have no idea how many adults meet the criteria of Third Age membership or how long they meet those criteria. We do know that large numbers of people in the approximate age range that encompasses the Third Age have significant health problems and/or remain in the labor force. Taken together, these patterns provide little, if any, support to the idea that the Third Age has emerged as a distinct life stage.

DOES IT MATTER WHETHER THERE IS EVIDENCE THAT THE THIRD AGE IS A NEW LIFE STAGE?

Once a concept catches on in public discourse, its validity ceases to matter very much. Therefore, unfortunately, I doubt that it will make much difference whether or not the Third Age is an empirically verifiable new life stage. It already has the attention of the educated public, people who aspire to be third-agers (and who would not eagerly embrace a time when paid labor is done and health remains good), and some politicians and policy makers. As W. I. Thomas remarked nearly a century ago, "If men define things as real, they are real in their consequences" (Thomas & Thomas, 1928, p. 572).

Accepting the Third Age as real has several negative consequences, all of which have been recognized by some of the chapter authors. I will briefly discuss four of them: the potential that unpaid productivity becomes normative (or even coercive) for adults in the age range labeled the Third Age, the potential for exploitation via commitments to unpaid labor, the likelihood that social programs needed by third-agers who are not healthy and affluent will erode, and the likelihood that ageism remains, but is simply postponed to the fourth age.

The Development of Third Age Norms

As noted elsewhere in this volume, a rather strong image of what the Third Age is and how it should be spent has developed. Specifically, the Third Age is a time when one is healthy, financially secure, and has shed (at least full-time) employment responsibilities. Nature abhors a vacuum, and so norms are developing for this presumed life stage. These norms emphasize unpaid labor (i.e., volunteerism) and the multiple ways that third-agers can "give back" to their communities. If these norms become institutionalized, a number of problems will emerge. First, and most important, an unknown, but large proportion of older adults in the approximate age range of the Third Age (i.e., ages 50–70) are working, are not financially secure, and/or are not healthy. Asking these third-agers to increase their unpaid labor may be unreasonable. But the stronger the norms that emphasize volunteering as a hallmark of the Third Age, the more that adults who are unable to do so will be marginalized. They will be seen by others as failing to meet social expectations and, to the extent that they internalize these norms, will view themselves as failures. Second, strong norms of any kind for the Third Age run counter to the cultural ideal of individualism. At the same time that age norms in other areas of society are eroding, it is asking a lot for adults facing the least constrained period of their adult lives to commit to unpaid productivity. Third, as Carr and Hendricks (Chapter 11) point out, strong norms can be experienced as coercive.

I am not opposed to adults of any age engaging in pro-social voluntary activities that assist those in need, or help meet societal goals—indeed,

I find it quite admirable. But I am opposed to expectations that are so strong that they virtually force voluntarism (note that "forced voluntarism" is, by definition, an oxymoron). I also believe that establishing such norms is a "hard sell" at an historical time when the cultural ideal of individualism is eroding other age norms.

The Potential for Exploitation

At its worst, commitment to Third Age norms of community service and other forms of unpaid productivity have the potential to result in exploitation. Urging third-agers to generously volunteer their time and energies to community service can imply that these tasks are discretionary and of limited value—otherwise, why would not people be paid to do them? In addition, I believe that there should be limits on the number of hours that third-agers would generally be allowed to engage in public unpaid productivity. Excessive contributions of unpaid labor constitute exploitation, regardless of whether or not the volunteer defines it that way.

Scott Bass (Chapter 9) describes the Silver Human Resource Center system in Japan in which corporations of adults retired from their main jobs contract and are paid for goods and services that they produce. The wages are apparently below those earned by nonretired workers and these corporations have a level of flexibility (e.g., for short-term projects) uncharacteristic of larger enterprises. Thus, there are strategies for making use of the skills of retirees without exploiting them. Similar programs could be of great value to third-agers in the United States. Not only would they avoid exploitation, they could provide a mechanism whereby those who are not financially secure could switch from their main jobs to different kinds of part-time work and sustain an adequate standard of living. These programs could exist alongside unpaid volunteer programs and provide third-agers with a broader choice of paid and unpaid productivity—including the choice to not participate at all.

Possible Harm to Social Programs

To the extent that politicians, policy makers, and the public believe that third-agers are healthy and financially secure without working, this is strong ammunition for further reducing social, economic, and health programs that serve third-agers. Indeed, as Holstein (Chapter 12) points out, both scientific and public discourse about the Third Age has been largely apolitical. In particular, the language of social justice is virtually absent. To the extent that third-agers are viewed as healthy, relatively affluent adults with the obligation to contribute to the society via voluntary unpaid labor, there is little reason to sustain or increase public policies that serve third-agers. As discourse about the Third Age neglects the heterogeneity among adults in that age group, it is easy—and arguably justifiable—to ignore or decrease programs for those who are needy. Failure to provide a social safety net for those who do not resemble the general image of third-agers as healthy and economically secure will be especially painful for women and people of color. Women comprise more than half of the population in the age range of the Third Age. The non-white population in that age range is also substantial and growing faster than the white population.

The cultural forces of individualism and political conservatism, along with the recent economic downturn both in the United States and globally, have already led to the demise and/or diluting of many social programs for Americans of all ages (e.g., Hacker, 2004). The challenges of financing current and future Social Security and Medicare benefits is a long-standing concern of lawmakers. Recent health-care reform legislation also carries a hefty price tag with no identifiable stream of revenue to pay for it. The image of third-agers as healthy and economically secure despite departure from the labor force provides an easy target for eliminating or reducing federal programs upon which that age group relies. It would be both ironic and tragic if gerontologists provide policy makers with the ammunition to destroy or seriously wound the programs upon which many of the "young-old" rely.

The Long Arm of Ageism

Perhaps the strongest reason that so many people—scientists, policy makers, the public at large—resonate to the concept of the Third Age is ageism. By claiming that "real" old age does not begin until the mid-70s or later, Americans are able to postpone their identification with negative stereotypes of old age. Everytime that I hear someone proclaim that "70 is the new 60" (or a similar comment), I interpret it as an attempt to avoid ageist stereotypes. The new 70 may be better, on average, than the 70 of the past, but it is 70 nonetheless. Why cannot we celebrate the gains in longevity, disability-free longevity, and quality of life without labeling them an avoidance of aging? The eagerness of many to proclaim the

Third Age strikes me as first and foremost a desire to avoid or postpone being labeled as old and suffering the negative social stereotypes that accompany that label. It has long been known that a majority of adults age 65 and older describe themselves as middle-aged rather than old (e.g., Uotinen, Rantanen, Suutama, & Ruoppila, 2006; Westerhof & Barrett, 2005). The image of the Third Age appears to reflect the same desire to view oneself and have others view one as not being old. It saddens me that mature adults remain highly motivated to avoid being identified with old age despite the tremendous gains in well-being achieved over the past half-century.

Arguably, postponing the threshold of old age will create even more severe and widespread ageism for Fourth Agers. Just as the image of a Third Age is socially desirable because it is not old age, the image of a Fourth Age is socially undesirable because it reinforces negative stereotypes of later life. Fourth Agers will be viewed as frail, dependent, lonely, sick, and as coping with impending death. In my view, one of the important tasks of gerontology is to fight ageism, not simply postpone it to a shorter segment of the life course.

IMPLICATIONS OF THE THIRD AGE FOR GERONTOLOGISTS: DÉJÀ VU ALL OVER AGAIN

For reasons that I do not claim to understand, gerontologists seem firmly committed to viewing later life as a largely homogeneous segment of the life course. This remains true despite the fact that each attempt to define "successful aging" or other adult "passages" has proven to be empirically indefensible.

The desire to characterize later life as a uniform experience with an identifiable pathway to success began in the 1960s, with the publication of two influential books: Erik Erikson's *Childhood and Society* (1963) and Elaine Cumming and William Henry's *Growing Old, the Process of Disengagement* (1961). Although Erikson was a psychologist and Cumming and Henry were sociologists, both books argued that there are psychosocial prerequisites for a satisfying late life.

Erikson first presented his "Eight Stages of Man" in *Childhood and Society.* Each stage was lined to approximate age ranges and the next stage could not be resolved until all previous stages had been completed. Each stage was characterized by a dominant psychosocial task. The eighth and last stage was titled "Integrity vs. Despair." Success at this task requires individuals to come to terms with the lives that they have led—integrating and accepting the good, the bad, and the ugly. When this process of integration results in individuals taking ownership for everything that their lives have and have not been, a sense of integrity is achieved. Failure to achieve this integration leaves individuals in despair. A successful last stage of life, then, requires embracing this sometimes painful, but ultimately liberating process.

Cumming and Henry's disengagement theory considered old age from the perspective of both the older adult and the society. They posited that the best old age is one in which older adults and societal institutions mutually withdraw from each other. Old age was described as most satisfying when older adults voluntarily forfeited their major role obligations, especially work roles, and spent their time in unstructured, generally passive activities. Society benefited from this pattern as well. Because older adults voluntarily vacate important social roles, social institutions can plan for their departures and smoothly transition other younger adults into those positions.

Neither Erikson's stage theory nor Cumming and Henry's disengagement theory received strong empirical support. Erikson's theory received less empirical attention because it was tautological, essentially rendering it untestable—older adults who expressed high levels of well-being were assumed to have successfully integrated their lives; those who expressed despair either had not completed the process or had failed to integrate their lives into an acceptable whole. Disengagement theory generated a large body of research indicating that older adults who lacked roles and led passive lifestyles were typically not as satisfied as those who remained active and socially engaged. In fact, this body of research generated two new theories that purported to identify the conditions under which late life was satisfying: activity theory (Maddox, 1963) and continuity theory (Atchley, 1989).

For the record, none of these theories is a valid depiction of the pathway for satisfaction and contentment in late life. Specifically, none is totally true and none is patently false. What all these theories ignored was the heterogeneity of the older population. Some older adults are happiest when they live a disengaged lifestyle—devoting most of their time to passive leisure. Some older adults are most satisfied with their lives when they continue activities that satisfied them earlier in life, which is compatible with continuity theory. Still others are most content when they develop new interests and hobbies that represent stark changes from their earlier lives—a pattern compatible with activity theory. And undoubtedly, some older adults pursue multiple pathways—for example, a period of continuity of activities, followed by a move to more passive leisure.

At the same time that these competing theories were generating heated exchange among social and behavioral scientists, the component of gerontology that focused on policy and advocacy for older adults also butted heads with the heterogeneity of the older population. During the 1960s and 1970s, the dominant image of old age generated by those (well-intentioned) gerontologists who sought to establish economic security and affordable health care for older adults was one of a neglected and needy population. Older adults were portrayed as poor (and they were more likely to be poor than any other age group at the time), lonely (and there were high rates of widowhood then, as now), and lacking health care (which was often true after retirement). This image of the needy older adult who had contributed to society for decades but was now left without the minimal resources needed for a safe and adequate life was tremendously successful in generating political support for Social Security and for establishing Medicare and Medicaid. This image also managed to neglect other important facts—for example, the majority of older adults had frequent contact with relatives and friends and older adults disproportionately controlled the country's wealth.

By the 1980s, a more balanced view of the older population emerged. Some politicians and pundits even went too far in the other direction, portraying the older population as "greedy geezers" who were taking luxurious trips and spending their days on the golf course while the younger population was taxed mercilessly to pay for these luxuries. Thankfully, the "greedy geezer" image did not become the dominant view of later life—due in part to science, in part to advocacy groups such as AARP, and in large part to the fact that the parents and grandparents of most young and middle-aged adults were not living lives of luxury.

The primary lesson to be learned from this history is that statements along the line of "Old people are . . . . . ." are inherently invalid. The older population has been and is at least as diverse and heterogeneous as its younger counterparts. There are always older adults struggling to make ends meet and older adults are always a large proportion of the wealthiest 10% of the population. There are 65-year-olds who are totally disabled and 90-year-olds who still go to work everyday. If there is one task that gerontologists are ideally equipped to do and should want to do, it is to provide an accurate description of the older population to the larger public, documenting its diversity and the lack of basis for positive or negative stereotypes.

Is that what gerontologists have done since then? Yes and no. I believe that there has been less movement to depict the older population in a general and consistent way. The emergence of the life-course perspective, which emphasizes heterogeneity in many dimensions (e.g., sequencing of events, multiple pathways to a given outcome, contingencies that generate turning points in life), has played an important role in portraying the diversity of late life. Nonetheless, some aging researchers apparently cannot resist descriptive generalities that often nearly become prescriptions for what one should be and do in later life. Rowe and Kahn's depiction of *Successful Aging* (1998) is a case in point. There are many things to like about this book—although written for a lay audience, it is well documented and based on research; it provides information that people can use immediately to confront a variety of age-related issues; and it covers a lot of territory (although mental health is clearly short changed). But in the categorical style that is apparently so attractive to gerontologists, the book rests on a comparison of two types of aging: successful and usual. Successful aging is defined by three criteria: good physical health (chronic diseases are possible, but must be adequately controlled and nondisabling), good cognitive function, and social engagement. Anything short of meeting these three criteria is usual aging, with the implication that it is really unsuccessful aging. As is true for third-agers, a sizeable number of older adults meet the criteria for successful aging. Many do not—and many of those who qualify as successful agers now will fail to do so at a later time. A major criticism of this definition of successful aging is that it marginalizes (and, at times comes perilously close to blaming the victim) the majority of older adults.

My major complaint with Rowe and Kahn's concept of successful aging is that it fails to take into account older adults' *personal* evaluations of their quality of life. *Successful Aging* ends up being one more in a long line of prescriptions for what one should strive for in life—with the corollary that if one fails to live up to the prescriptions one has failed at building a successful life. If one pays attention to older adults' own evaluations of their quality of life, very different conclusions emerge. As I have described in detail elsewhere (George, 2006), the vast majority of older adults with chronic illnesses, including disability report that their lives are satisfying and meaningful (e.g., Pennex et al., 1998; Yang, 2008). The same pattern is observed for mild cognitive impairment and for those with small social networks and low levels of social interaction. It is certainly true that good health is associated with better perceived life quality than poor health and that older adults with sizeable social networks with whom they interact frequently report higher levels of life satisfaction than those who are isolated. But that does not mean that the majority of older adults who do not meet Rowe and Kahn's formula for successful aging report compromised quality of life—indeed, the opposite is true. The reverse pattern also is observed. A significant minority of older adults who meet Rowe and Kahn's criteria for successful aging nonetheless report that they are dissatisfied with their lives (e.g., Covinsky et al., 1999).

Once again, a clear message emerges from efforts to categorize the older population as a whole or into broad categories that are assumed to be homogeneous. Such efforts are inevitably invalid and fail to do justice to the diversity and complexity of the older population.

The newest label on the block is the Third Age. It already is clear that this label has the same problems that rendered previous labels problematic: we do not know how many people fit the criteria for the label, but we know that many millions do not fit it; there is an apparent evolution from descriptive to normative; the label ends up saving one group from ageism while implying that a sizeable group of older adults meet the negative stereotypes on which ageism rests; and the courage of many older people who build satisfying and meaningful lives despite erosion of physical, economic, and social resources is ignored.

Data are data and facts are facts. At this point in history, there is undoubtedly a larger number and proportion of adults who retire while healthy than ever before. It is appropriate to describe that trend and explore the demographic, economic, and social conditions that led to the emergence of this group. It is appropriate to recognize the unpaid labor that many of these individuals contribute to society through either informal care of others or formal voluntarism. Although this takes us beyond science, it is also acceptable to provide opportunities for these healthy retirees to begin or increase their unpaid productivity. What I find unacceptable, at this point in history, is the interpretation that a new life stage has emerged and that it is our responsibility to define the roles to be played and the activities to pursue during this segment of the life course.

REFERENCES

Atchley, R. C. (1989). A continuity theory of normal aging. *The Gerontologist, 29*, 183–190.

Beck, U., & Beck-Gernsheim, E. (2002). *Individualization.* London: Sage Publications.

Carr, D. C. (2009). *Demography, ideology, and stratification: Exploring the emergence and consequences of the Third Age* [Doctoral Dissertation]. Networked Digital Library of Theses and Dissertations.

Covinsky, K. E., Wu, A. W., Landefeld, C. S., Connors, A. F. Jr., Phillips, R. S., Tsevat, J. et al. (1999). Health status versus quality of life in older patients: Does the distinction matter? *American Journal of Medicine, 106,* 435–440.

Cumming, E., & Henry, W. E. (1961). *Growing old: The process of disengagement.* New York, NY: Basic Books.

Erikson, E. (1963). *Childhood and society.* New York, NY: Norton.

Flippen, C., & Tienda, M. (2000). Pathways to retirement: Patterns of labor force participation and labor market exit among the pre-retirement population by race, Hispanic origin, and sex. *Journal of Gerontology: Social Sciences, 55B,* S14–S17.

Freedman, M. (1999). *Prime time: How baby boomers will revolutionize retirement and transform America.* New York, NY: Public Affairs.

George, L. K. (2006). Perceived quality of life. In R. H. Binstock & L. K. George (Eds.), *Handbook of aging and the social sciences* (6th ed.) (pp. 320–336). San Diego, CA: Academic Press.

Gilleard, C., Higgs, P., Hyde, M., Wiggins, R., & Blane, D. (2005). Class, cohort, and consumption: The British experience of the third age. *Journal of Gerontology: Social Sciences, 60B,* S305–S310.

Hacker, J. S. (2004). Privatizing risk without privatizing the welfare state: The hidden politics of social policy retrenchment in the United States. *American Political Science Review, 98,* 243–260.

Maddox, G. L. (1963). Activity and morale: A longitudinal study of selected elderly subjects. *Social Forces, 42,* 195–204.

Midwinter, E. (2005). How many people are there in the third age? *Ageing and Society, 25,* 9–18.

Pennex, B., Guralnik, J. M., Simonsick, E. M., Kasper, J. D., Ferrucci, L., & Fried, L. P. (1998). Emotional vitality among disabled older women: The Women's Health and Aging Study. *Journal of the American Geriatrics Society, 46,* 807–818.

Riley, M. W., Kahn, R. L., & Foner, E. (Eds.). (1994). *Age and structural lag: Society's failure to provide meaningful opportunities in work, family, and leisure.* New York, NY: Wiley.

Rowe, J. W., & Kahn, R. L. (1998). *Successful aging.* New York, NY: Pantheon Books.

Sinnot, J. D. (2009). Complex thought and construction of the self in the face of aging and death. *Journal of Adult Development, 16,* 155–165.

Thomas, I., & Thomas, D. S. (1928). *The child in America.* New York, NY: Knopf.

Uotinen, V., Rantanen, T., Suutama, T., & Ruoppila, I. (2006). Change in subjective age among older people over an eight-year follow-up: Getting older and feeling younger? *Experimental Aging Research, 32,* 381–393.

U.S. Census Bureau. (1997). Americans with disabilities: 1991–92. *Current Population Reports, Series P70-33.* Retrieved August 14, 2010, from www.census.gov/population/www/pop-profile/disabil.html.

Westerhof, G., & Barrett, A. (2005). Age identity and subjective well-being: A comparison of the United States and Germany. *Journal of Gerontology: Social Sciences, 60B*, S129–S136.

Yang, Y. (2008). Long and happy living: Trends and patterns of happy life expectancy in the U.S.: 1970–2000. *Social Science Research, 37*, 1235–1252.

Index

Active aging, 60, 128, 179
Active engagement, in old age, 98
Active life expectancy (ALE), 96–97,
99–100. *See also* Total life
expectancy (TLE)
demographic research, 102
disability and, 97
health and activity
measures, 98, 99
Activities of Daily Living (ADL), 98
in ALE research, 98, 115
Activity code, 133, 136–137
ADEA. *See* Age Discrimination and
Employment Act (ADEA)
ADL. *See* Activities of daily
living (ADL)
Adult development, 18
Age Discrimination and Employment
Act (ADEA), 171
Age stratification system, 16
Ageism, 252
persistence of, 234–235
in the Third Age, 233
Aging, 3, 47. *See also* Third Age
active, 60, 128, 179
circumstances of, 229–231

distinctions among groups, 68, 69
dualisms, 158
microcommunities, 238
paradigm shift, 3
population, 52, 61, 213
positive, 229. *See also* Productive
aging
postindustrial society, 178–179
postmodern, 226, 227
socio-structural factors, 232
successful, 128, 151, 227, 233,
256–257
types of, 256
Agrarian society, demographics
of, 90–91
ALE. *See* Active life expectancy (ALE)
Alternative living arrangements vs.
remarriage, 199
Americans for Generational Equity
(AGE), 228
Assets and Health Dynamics of the
Oldest Old (AHEAD), 114
AUSER, 57

Baby boomers, 3, 34
Biographical time, 15